Strategic Technology Management

Strategic Technology Management

Pierre Dussauge
HEC – School of Management

Stuart Hart
University of Michigan – School of Business

Bernard Ramanantsoa
HEC – School of Management

JOHN WILEY & SONS

Chichester · New York · Brisbane · Toronto · Singapore

Wiley Editorial Offices

John Wiley & Sons Ltd, Baffins Lane,
Chichester, West Sussex PO19 1UD, England
National   Chichester (0243) 779777
International   +44 243 779777

John Wiley & Sons, Inc., 605 Third Avenue,
New York, NY 10158–0012, USA

Jacaranda Wiley Ltd, 33 Park Road, Milton,
Queensland 4064, Australia

John Wiley & Sons (Canada) Ltd, 22 Worcester Road,
Rexdale, Ontario M9W 1L1, Canada

John Wiley & Sons (SEA) Pte Ltd, 37 Jalan Pemimpin #05-04,
Block B, Union Industrial Building, Singapore 2057

Library of Congress Cataloging-in-Publication Data

Dussauge, Pierre.
    [Technologie et stratégie d'entreprise.   English]
    Strategic technology management / Pierre Dussauge, Stuart Hart.
Bernard Ramanantsoa.
       p.   cm.
    Translation of: Technologie et stratégie d'entreprise.
    Includes bibliographical references and index.
    ISBN 0–471–93418–6 (cloth)
    1. Technology—Management.   2. Strategic planning.   I. Hart.
Stuart L.   II. Ramanantsoa, Bernard.   III. Title.
    T49.5.D8713   1992
    658.5'7—dc20   91–39732
                                                                      CIP

British Library Cataloguing in Publication Data

A catalogue record for this book is
available from the British Library

ISBN 0–471–93418–6

Typeset in 10/12 pt Palatino by Inforum Typesetting, Portsmouth
Printed and bound in Great Britain by Biddles Ltd, Guildford and King's Lynn

Contents

us frank and helpful criticism. Kate Banbury and James Parham aided the cause greatly by checking many of the tables and ensuring that the data in the book were up to date. Rob Kazanjian also gave us important encouragement and guidance in the early stages of this joint undertaking between Paris and Ann Arbor. Finally, Joan Walker deserves special mention for her patience and diligence in the preparation of this manuscript and its many figures and tables.

REFERENCES

1. See, for example: R. Christensen et al., *Business Policy: Text and Cases*, Homewood: Irwin, 1982.
2. For example, M. Porter, *Competitive Strategy*, New York: Free Press, 1980.
3. For example, C. Hofer and D. Schendel, *Strategy Formulation: Analytical Concepts*, St. Paul: West Publishing, 1978.
4. See, for example: P. Roussel, K. Saad, and T. Erickson, *Third Generation R&D: Managing the Link to Corporate Strategy*, Boston: Harvard Business School Press, 1991.
5. B. Twiss, *Managing Technological Innovation*, New York: Longman, 1980.
6. W. Souder, *Managing New Product Innovations*, Lexington: Lexington Books, 1987.
7. L. Steele, *Managing Technology: The Strategic View*, New York: McGraw-Hill, 1989.
8. R. Rothberg (Ed.), *Corporate Strategy and Product Innovation*, New York: Free Press, 1981; M. Tushman and W. Moore, *Readings in the Management of Innovation*, Cambridge: Ballinger, 1988; R. Burgelman and M. Maidique, *Strategic Management of Technology and Innovation*, Homewood: Irwin, 1988.

Chapter 1

On Technology

Dramatic technological changes in the 1970s almost wiped out the Swiss watchmaking industry. Yet technology was the key factor which made it possible for the few Swiss watch brands which survived to meet the challenge posed to them by their Japanese, Taiwanese and Hong Kong competitors. The development of electronic watches upset the well-established Swiss firms, making the bases of their technical excellence obsolete virtually overnight. Indeed, the precision of quartz watches could not be matched even by that of the best mechanical watches; furthermore, quartz watches were cheaper to manufacture than mechanical watches. Because they were unable to identify the threat they were faced with, many Swiss watchmaking companies were forced out of the market. However, ETA, a firm resulting from the merger of several ailing companies of this industry, managed to turn the threat into an opportunity and has experienced considerable growth since the beginning of the eighties.

Faced with this technological threat, ETA's response was to use technology as a competitive weapon: ETA created the "Swatch". Although the success of Swatch appeared to be mainly the result of efficient marketing and fashionable styling, it was actually based on technology. The design of the product was revolutionary and its manufacturing process had little in common with conventional watch assembly. The case served as the supporting structure, thus allowing the traditional two-phased assembly process in which the clockwork was first mounted on the frame, the latter then being inserted in the case, to be reduced to one single operation. The new assembly process involved only about 50 elementary parts compared with 100 to 150 for a conventional watch. Moreover, the final assembly accounted for only 10% of the total cost of a Swatch compared with the usual 50%. ETA was able to achieve all this by resorting to new technologies such as the micro-injection of plastic under pressure, the use of polymethylemetacrylate to obtain an extremely resistant glass, a new technique for welding the glass and the case together which makes the watch totally waterproof, etc. The result is a watch manufactured at a very competitive cost which also has remarkable qualities; the Swatch watch can resist shocks of up to 5000 times its own weight, temperatures ranging between 14°F and 302°F, humidity of up to 90%, and it can work for 30 years without significant wear or loss of precision. Using this technology-based strategy, ETA sold over 10 million Swatch watches throughout the world in 1986 and was able to face its Asian competitors successfully.

The above example highlights the fact that technological change can completely transform competition in a given industry. Further, it indicates that technology, used properly, can give some firms considerable competitive advantage. The competitive impact of technology seems to be greater today than it has ever been before and to be affecting an increasingly wide range of industries.

KEY ISSUES IN THE STRATEGIC MANAGEMENT OF TECHNOLOGY

"Compact Disk or Tape?"—that was the question headlined by many music-fan magazines in 1987, a question of choice for potential buyers but also a question of technological capabilities, strategy and competition for manufacturers. Indeed, the quality of the sound reproduction of the DAT (Digital Audio Tape) is comparable to that of the compact disk; however, the DAT allows one to erase and to record, and has a much greater capacity (two to three hours of recording instead of one). By marketing the DAT, Matsushita, Sony and Sharp may not only put an end to the market for compact disk players but also seriously threaten the record industry. Competitors have responded loudly to this threat; Philips, which invested heavily to introduce the compact disk and also controls musical production subsidiaries, has launched a crusade against the DAT. Such vocal reactions are due to the high strategic stakes involved. Technological innovation in this case—as in many other cases—affects not only the industry in which it takes place, but also, through a sort of "chain reaction," many other industries. As another example, the dramatic technological change that has occurred in the last thirty years in the semiconductor industry has fueled competition between the firms in this industry as testified by the struggle to increase memory capacity. However, such change has also affected industries as varied as office automation, telecommunications, consumer electronics, aerospace, automobiles, toys, and even the above-mentioned watchmaking industry.

Although technological changes affect primarily manufacturing firms, corporations in service industries may also experience the impact of technological evolution. To quote T. S. Johnson, president of the Chemical Bank: "The banking industry is changing because of deregulation, because of competition, and above all, because of the rapid evolution of information technologies." Indeed, the capability to master such technologies is becoming an increasingly crucial factor for success in certain areas of the banking industry. According to Salomon Brothers analysts, this trend is at once the cause and the result of the considerable investments made by American financial institutions in computing and communication technologies. The banking industry is the second largest investor—after the computer industry itself— in such technologies. For example, the Chemical Bank has spent more than one billion dollars over a three-year period (20% of its total operating costs over the same period) to develop its capabilities in the area of information technologies. However, its management is still unsure of whether the Bank's investment in information technologies is too high or too low.

As these examples indicate, technological innovation often modifies the bases of competition in a given industry and technology is, in many cases, one of the main sources of competitive advantage. For a long time, firms seem to have expanded mainly by taking advantage of every opportunity the market offered; some companies are now increasingly concerned with capitalizing on their technological capabilities. After the era of market-led strategies, some experts are announcing the coming of the era of technology-based strategies, even predicting that the latter are generally more successful than the former.

Indeed, technology is the driving force behind the growth and diversification of many firms. For example, the prime contractor for the boosters of the European launcher Ariane, the Société Européenne de Propulsion (SEP), has become, almost involuntarily, the main supplier of brake disks for formula-one racing. SEP developed Cabron/Carbon composite materials for the rockets and the missiles it manufactured and noticed that they had interesting physical qualities such as low density, very high temperature resistance, and a very high coefficient of friction. These were the qualities required from the materials to be used in brake disks. Initially introduced on Dassault's Mirage 2000 fighter aircraft and later on the Airbus jetliner, the disks designed by SEP were used in 1985 by the McLaren and Ligier racing teams. McLaren became formula-one world champion the same year and seven other teams switched to SEP's brake disks in 1986. In the same way, although it was less publicized, Electronique Serge Dassault, a French defense firm, applied technologies it had developed while designing missile guidance systems to the manufacturing of automatic tellers for banks. Corning Glass Works leveraged its expertise in glass technology and ceramics to enter a range of businessess including fiber-glass insulation, silicones, fiber optics, and optical electronics. Aérospatiale, the largest French aerospace company, is working on the design of an artificial heart which incorporates technologies it previously developed for its aerospace programs.

But while corporations increasingly base their growth on technological skills, the role of the state—industrial policy—has assumed increasing importance. Indeed, it is well-known that in virtually all the industrialized countries, including those which claim to abide by the rules of free-market economics, the State plays a crucial role in helping some companies to develop their technological skills. For example, military research and government funded civilian high-technology programs can provide firms with a considerable technological edge. The Strategic Defense Initiative (also known as Star Wars) launched by the Reagan Administration was even termed a "technology pump" for American industry. In Japan, MITI has the explicit mission of promoting and financing the development of technological capabilities in Japanese firms. Indeed, the creation of a solid technology base is often more the result of state intervention than of traditional competitive strategies; the technological skills that these firms acquire with the help of the state are nevertheless a decisive advantage that they can later use in competitive markets.

Strategic alliances between firms that are potential competitors are also examples of strategic moves—often based on technology—which extend beyond the boundaries of traditional competitive strategies. For example, by joining forces to design, manufacture and market jet engines, General Electric and SNECMA avoided competing against one another and were better able to face other rivals such as Pratt & Whitney, Rolls Royce and MTU. In the same way, the joint-venture between Honda and British Leyland (now the Rover Group) can be seen as the exchange of Japanese technology for access to the British, and even to the European automobile market as well as a way of ending—temporarily or on a long-term basis—competition between them. Collaboration between competitors in the commercial aircraft industry, many of which are still competing in other activities, resulted in the setting up of the Airbus consortium; the partners in Airbus decided to team up against their common rival Boeing because they were unable to meet the rapidly rising cost of technological innovation in this industry individually. Interestingly, the Airbus consortium has forced Boeing to collaborate with the Japanese in order to gain access to R&D resources and remain competitive. Although strategic alliances provide a means to forestall competition among partners, they are not necessarily everlasting and may eventually give way to renewed rivalry between the former partners. Thus, strategic alliances based on technology raise an interesting question: Do such alliances put an end to competition between the partners involved, or do they merely alter the forms of the competition between the latter?

In short, the importance of technology as a strategic factor is now widely recognized. However, in practice, the organizational structures and processes that corporations set up in order to create and maintain their technological skills can take many different forms. For example, at Saint-Gobain, R&D has been totally decentralized and is now being conducted at the division level, whereas in firms like Thomson in France or DuPont de Nemours and United Technologies in the US, 5–10% of R&D is carried out in their central laboratories. Similarly, companies are experimenting with many ways to become faster and more effective at new product development as technological change and the globalization of markets have made "speed" a key strategic capability. These differences indicate that the management of technology poses complex organizational problems and that there is no unanimously recognized doctrine concerning this issue. The complexity of such problems is even greater in the case of firms participating in strategic alliances, which must also coordinate their R&D efforts with those of their partners. *important*

Lastly, since technology strategies are based on the technical skills of the individuals working for the companies, their success or failure ultimately depends on the people and the corporate "culture" of the companies concerned. Thus, although it builds aircraft, helicopters, satellites and missiles, Aérospatiale, willing to utilize its means of production to full capacity, has proved unable to manufacture camp trailers and refrigerators efficiently. Such a failure can obviously not be attributed to a lack of technological capabilities; rather, it reflects the conscious or unconscious opposition of the firm's employees to the production of "low-tech" products that have little to do with aerospace. Similarly, almost all the diversification moves of Matra, another French aerospace corporation, out of high-technology industries and into consumer goods such as watches, automobiles and television sets have met with failure. Thus, beyond strictly technical and economic considerations, the strategic management of technology requires taking into account organizational, social, and cultural factors.

Before turning to a discussion of each of the above topics, we first provide a definition of "technology" and analyze the reasons why the strategic management of technology has, in recent years, been given increasing attention both by business practitioners and academics.

DEFINING TECHNOLOGY

For many terms, there is a broad consensus as to definition or meaning. However, some terms can be interpreted too broadly or given the wrong meaning; others become over-used and become "buzz words." In such cases, terms risk coming to mean everything and hence nothing. Such is the case with the term "technology." Indeed, it has been pointed out that "technology" is virtually always used where the term "technique" would be more appropriate. What does "technology" really mean?

The Origin of the Word Technology

Technology is literally the "study of techniques," like anthropology is the "study of man" or sociology is the "study of society." One dictionary's first definition of technology is "the science of the application of knowledge to practical purposes"[1], which is consistent with the etymological origin of the word. According to this definition, the work by B. Gille on the history of techniques[2] can be defined as technology. However, according to such a definition, companies such as IBM, Texas Instruments and even United Technologies use techniques rather than technologies.

Both "technique" and "technology" appeared as terms in the eighteenth century. Prior to that, techniques were known as "arts and crafts." Indeed, the century which saw the early stages of the industrial revolution was also the time when the need was felt to distinguish, in the area of productive processes, between arts and techniques. Arts stem from individual skills which cannot be easily systematized and reproduced. Techniques, in contrast, are the result of *formalized* and *transmissible* knowledge which is the basis for the development of all industrial activities. Thus, this evolution of language in the eighteenth century reflects a fundamental economic change. In the same way, the increasingly common use of the term technology instead of technique, which suggests a scientific understanding of technical evolution, may reflect the so-called "new industrial revolution"[3]. The technology label seems to be given primarily to the "techniques" which are the cornerstones of the new industrial revolution, such as electronics, computers, and biotechnologies.

Definitions of Technology

The term technology has been used extensively in the management literature, frequently to describe the "production process" or the "throughput" of an organization[4]. More recently, however, the term has taken on a slightly different meaning. Indeed, the literature dealing with technology in a strategic management perspective can be classified into three main categories according to the definition—explicit or implicit—given to technology.

"Allusive" Approaches

We have termed allusive the approaches which do not explicitly define the word "technology." In this context, technology is described as a key factor of success like, for example, market share, product quality and adequate distribution channels. As such, like any other factor, technology does not require a definition. Most strategy consulting firms wishing to integrate a "technological" dimension in their analytical methods use the word technology in this way. The Boston Consulting Group, for example, does not define technology when examining its impact on the evolution of what they call competitive systems[5]. Though they developed a specific model for analyzing technology life cycles and limits[6], McKinsey & Co. do not base their analysis on any precise definition of technology. R. Foster, one of the directors of McKinsey and the author of a best-selling book on the management of technology, gives a vague definition[6] of technology, stressing that a more explicit definition is not necessary:

> By technology I mean several things. In some cases it's a specific process that produces a specific product. In this case it's hard to distinguish the product from the technology. More broadly, technology can mean a manufacturing process. . . . We can think of technology even more broadly as the way a company does business or attempts a task. . . . The point is this: technology, even variously defined, has a limit—either the limit of a particular technology or a succession of limits of several technologies that together make up the larger technology or product or way of doing business.

Evidently, methods developed by consulting firms are not meant to provide "academic" insight into the concepts used in management; they are aimed at establishing a set of guidelines for the practice of management. Arthur D. Little on the other hand, designed a specific methodology for the strategic management of technology in which the word is defined. This definition falls into what we call the "extensive" category.

"Extensive" Definitions

We have termed "extensive" approaches those which define technology, but which extend the sense of the term to all the areas of expertise existing in the firm. L. Steele[7], for example, defines technology as "the capability that the enterprise needs to provide its customers with its goods and services both now and in the future." A. D. Little's definition of technology is formulated as follows: "When we speak of a 'technology,' we are referring either to a practical application of science to address a particular product or manufacturing need, or to an area of specialized expertise"[8]. The second part of the definition is extensive (i.e. technology = area of expertise). The first, however, contains an interesting notion for the definition of technology, which is seen as "the practical application of science." We shall later examine this notion which recurs in a number of other definitions.

All "extensive" definitions are based on a view of technology as the application of knowledge. J. J. Salomon,[9] in particular, uses this notion to include a social process in technology:

> Technology is the application of knowledge and rational practices—scientific knowledge and technical know-how—to satisfy economic needs through the creation, the distribution, the organization and the industrial management of goods and services. Technology is a social process which materializes through technical innovation.

Similarly, J. Morin,[10] in a book on technological excellence, gives a definition of technology which extends to all aspects of the management of the firm. As the above, this definition is extensive, including all functions and areas of the organization. In this view, technology is:

> . . . the art of implementing, in a local context and in order to attain specific goals, all the sciences, techniques and basic rules which are involved in the design of products as well as in the manufacturing processes, the management methods and the information systems of the firm.

In this perspective, technology is present in all economic processes and in all functions of the firm, whether these functions are industrial and related to manufacturing, or whether they are staff and support functions. The skills and capabilities of marketing or finance are, in this view, as technological as those of an R&D or production department. It should be noted that J . Morin distinguishes between technique and technology. Techniques are basic and easily available capabilities, whereas technologies are specific and advanced capabilities which can give a firm a competitive advantage: "In 1850, steam power was a formidable technology, today it is only a basic technique"[10].

Another way of distinguishing between technique and technology can be deduced from W. Randolph's definition of technology:[11]

> Technology is how a task is accomplished. It may involve machines, tools, paper and pen, computers, procedures, knowledge utilization and information transfer. Technology also refers to the rationale and knowledge underlying the utilization of these means.

This extensive definition complements the "know-how" that technique implies with the "thinking" about know-how that is involved in technology. Technique is simple and easy to learn and put into practice; technology, in contrast, is complex and comprises techniques enhanced with knowledge and rational reflection on these techniques. Randolph's definition of technology integrates the etymology of the word, that is to say "the study of techniques," which allows people to master technical progress and sometimes even to produce it.

In our view, "extensive" definitions are inadequate because they include any form of expertise or sophisticated know-how as "technology." Such definitions do, however, distinguish among science, technology and technique. They emphasize that what distinguishes technology from technique is the scientific knowledge implied in the latter's use. Thus, understanding the relationship between science and technology is essential; the definitions we have termed "specific" use this relationship as a starting point.

"Specific" Definitions

A. D. Little's definition which we mentioned above emphasized the direct relationship between science and technology. Two other A. D. Little consultants[12] also followed the same approach and described technology as the practical application of scientific or engineering knowledge. Similarly, Friar and Horwitch[13] defined technology as "the ability to create a reproducible way for generating new and improved products, processes, and services." In this context, technology can be seen as being situated between science on the one hand and the commercial products or processes derived from the application of scientific knowledge on the other. All products and processes are thus related to the various technologies they integrate, which in turn are linked to science. As industrial applications of scientific research, technologies differ from techniques which are self-existent and do not depend on science to evolve, remaining confined to the industry that uses them. Figure 1.1 is an example of the relationship between science, technology and products in the case of PVC.

Such a definition of technology, which is far more restrictive than the "extensive" approaches, makes it possible to link technological skills to competitive advantage and, therefore, to analyze the situation of corporations which owe their strong position to their capability of applying basic science. This, for example, is the case in the area of biotechnologies where companies must bring together scientists, engineers and managers in order to be successful. In such companies, products and processes are created and evolve primarily under the influence of scientific progress, not necessarily previously identified market needs. Furthermore, with the aim of scientific

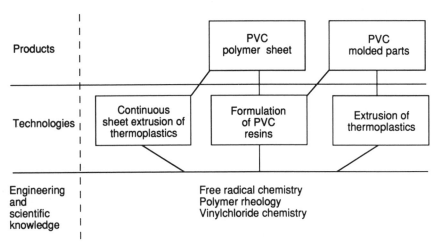

Figure 1.1 Relationship of technologies to scientific and engineering knowledge and to products and processes (Ketteringham and White 1984)

research being universal knowledge, some upstream technologies, closer to science than to its applications, can be defined as "generic" technologies. Several such technologies can be combined, thus leading to a wide range of applications in varied areas. Strategies based on the exploitation of generic technologies have been termed "technology-cluster strategies" and will be examined in detail in Chapter 6.

Because of their close relationship with science, technologies have two essential characteristics:

- **Technologies are not confined to a specific application, business or industry.** They are potentially applicable to several businesses or industries. The invention of the spool, for example, affected only the textile industry, whereas microelectronics is revolutionizing almost all economic activities.
- **Technologies can be combined.** While their development generally occurs within narrow specialty areas, the advantages they produce can only be gained by linking different technologies together into larger systems.

"Specific" definitions describe technology as the industrial application of science on the one hand, and as the scientific understanding of this process on the other. The conjunction of these two dimensions explains why the word technique is progressively being replaced by technology. This semantic change reflects the fact that science is increasingly involved in industrial activities. Furthermore, this change may signal the beginning of a new economic phase, which can be compared, as we mentioned previously, to the emergence of the word technique accompanying the industrial revolution.

Technology and the New "Technical System"

The notion of "technical systems" is one of the fundamental ideas developed by B. Gille in his research on the history of techniques[2]. In this work, the word technology seldom appears, and when it does it is almost always used in the etymological sense; however, the term technology is sometimes used in its common meaning when the author analyzes very recent technical developments.

According to Gille, a "technical system" is a coherent set of interrelated techniques which characterize a given historical period. This notion leads to a division of history into successive technical systems. In this perspective, the early nineteenth century can be seen as the advent of a technical system organized around steam power. This system has been represented as in Figure 1.2. The arrows in the figure represent interrelated technical dependency: "The production of iron and steel requires the use of the steam engine, which in turn can only be manufactured with metals capable of resisting very high temperatures and superheating." This entails a network of interdependencies which makes the technical system coherent and lasting.

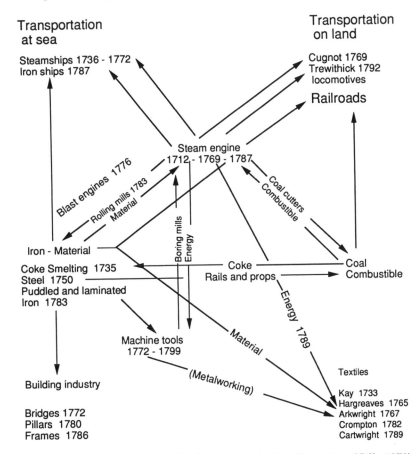

Figure 1.2 The "technical system" of the early nineteenth century (Gille 1978)

Gille views technical progress as the transition from one technical system to the next, when the former reaches a limit and begins to lose its internal coherence. As for the technical system of the twentieth century, it has certain characteristics that seem to validate the analysis we developed earlier:

- The current technical system reflects a closer relationship between science and technique, whereas previously, technical progress did not draw upon scientific discoveries or only did so to a small extent, in an unorganized fashion, and long after the latter were made and publicized. For example, advances made in the textile industry were due to new weaving techniques that emerged from experience, until the era of synthetic textiles which were developed as a result of advances in chemistry.
- Part of the research work tends to be carried out by firms through their R&D function, which comprises in-house laboratories. Thus, techniques

no longer evolve under the impulse of isolated inventors, but rather result from systematic research conducted by teams of specialists. Furthermore, this research is closely related to the "development" of products.

In other words, "invention" (a technical phenomenon involving the discovery of some new principle) and "innovation" (an economic phenomenon involving the commercial use of new products or processes) can no longer be easily distinguished. The length of time that separates invention from innovation, which before could be several years, now tends to be very short. Sometimes applied research is even ahead of fundamental research: industrial laboratories can draw up scientific results from empirical data gathered in the course of the development phase and thus contribute to the progress of science[14]. Since corporations do not want to depend on research they cannot control and direct, however, they tend to conduct fundamental research in their own laboratories[15].

It is significant to find in a work as far removed from our perspective as Gille's research on the history of techniques, the idea that the essential feature of the current technical system is the close relationship between science and technical progress. This relationship materializes in the existence of research and development facilities. Research and development is a meaninful denomination as it integrates a scientific approach (research) and a market-oriented process (development). Thus, for companies that build their competitive advantage on the industrial applications of science, the term technology is probably more appropriate than technique. The increasing use of the word technology and the widespread notion of research and development may simply be reflective of the current technical system.

Definition of Technology

In view of the above discussion:

Technology is not . . .

- individual know-how, craftsmanship or artistic skills, that cannot be formalized and which are improved in isolation, on the basis of experience and not as a result of a systematic research process. For example, there is no technology for fashion and haute couture.
- a basic technique, available to all, which can be improved through means other than scientific knowledge (e.g. milling, casting, welding, etc. are not technologies).
- skills or knowledge that do not lead directly to industrial applications, in other words, that do not materialize in manufacturing or product capabilities. Accounting, marketing and financial techniques are not technologies.

We can speak of technology . . .

- only in the context of a business situation; basic scientific research carried out without any clear economic goals is not technology.
- only when there is production of material objects (goods and services). The design and manufacture of satellites, automobiles, or aircraft draws upon a wide range of technologies, whereas marketing activities are not technology-based.
- only if an explicit or even implicit phase of research and development can be identified in the production process. Research and development is the function that defines technology by linking science, technique and production.

We suggest the following definition of technology:

A process which, through an explicit or implicit phase of research and development (the application of scientific knowledge), allows for commercial production of goods or services.

We do not claim that this definition is universal or even that it is superior to some of those we reviewed previously. However, we designed it according to the specific objectives pursued in this book and we believe that it is suited for examining the competitive impact of technology, and for improving the strategic management of technology. The above definition can be represented graphically as in Figure 1.3.

Table 1.1 contains a few illustrative examples of technologies and their linkages to problems, science, and technique.

It must be noted that though technology, as we have defined it, is

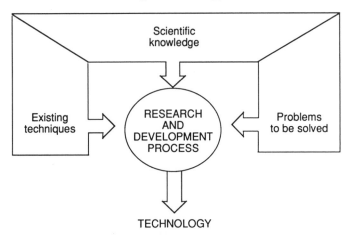

Figure 1.3 Towards a definition of technology

Table 1.1 Science, technology and industry: a few examples

Problems to be solved	Scientific fields	Existing techniques	Technology
To produce energy while reducing the dependence on imported oil	• Nuclear physics • Science of heat	• Transformation of thermal energy into electrical energy	Nuclear electricity
To balance the brake system according to the grip of a vehicle's wheels on the road	• Fluid mechanics • Strength of materials	• Conventional brake system technique • Microprocessor data analysis • Transmission of data through sensors	ABS brake system
To obtain a photographic print right after taking the photograph, without having the film processed by a laboratory	• Optics • Chemistry	• Miniaturization • Isolation of chemicals	Polaroid process

developed through an explicit or implicit research and development process, the latter does not necessarily need to be carried out within the firm that applies the technology. Technological competence can be bought or sold and, in order to create competitive advantage, a company can combine in-house technologies with other technologies purchased from an outside supplier. Thus, not all technologies have the same potential for impact on the firm or its competitors. There are clearly different types and levels of technological change and innovation. Understanding these different types and levels of technology is an important prerequisite to effective technology management.

Types of Technological Innovation

The distinction between "incremental" innovation (refining and improving existing products or processes) versus "radical" innovation (introducing totally new concepts) is a central notion in the literature on technology[16]. Radical and incremental innovations appear to have very different competitive consequences: incremental changes reinforce the positions of established firms while radical innovations force incumbents to develop new skills and capabilities[17].

R. Henderson and K. Clark[18], however, have suggested at least two other important types of technological innovation (see Figure 1.4). They distinguish between a product as a whole—the system—and a product in its parts—the components. Since most products are composed of a number of distinct "technologies" and components, it is crucial to consider changes in the components themselves as well as the linkages among the components. An automobile, for example, consists of dozens of component technologies combined together into a larger system. Innovations can occur both in the core concepts associated with individual components as well as in the way those components are combined into a larger system—the "architecture." Framed in this way, radical and incremental innovation are extreme points on these two dimensions. Radical innovations like transistors and instant photography established new system designs as well as new sets of core components. However, incremental innovations—for example, the next generation of Microsoft Word software—only served to refine and extend established designs and components. Modular innovations involve changes in core components without altering a product's overall architecture. The change from analog to digital telephones, for example, represents a modular technological change. Architectural innovations, however, deal with a product's configuration but have little impact on underlying components. Products such as the CT scanner or personal computer are examples of such innovations—they link together existing technologies and components in a new way. The innovation is at the system level.

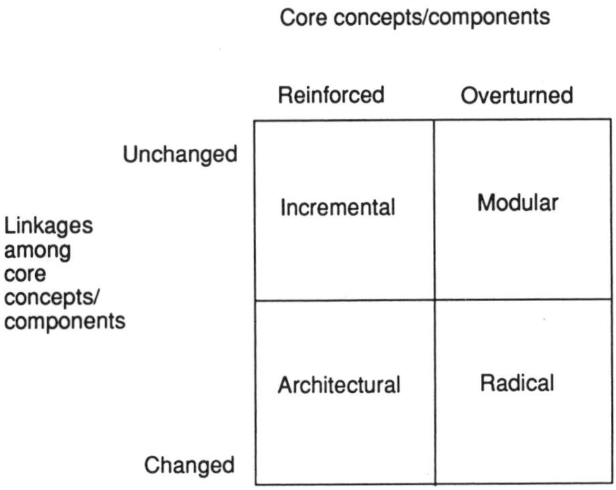

Core concepts/components

	Reinforced	Overturned
Unchanged	Incremental	Modular
Changed	Architectural	Radical

Linkages among core concepts/components

Figure 1.4 Types of new technological innovation (Reproduced by permission of *Administrative Science Quarterly* from Rebecca M. Henderson and Kim B. Clark, "Architectural Innovation: The Reconfiguration of Existing Product Technologies and the Failure of Established Firms", **35**, 1, p. 12. Copyright © *Administrative Science Quarterly*, 1990.)

Having defined technology, discussed levels of technological innovation, and highlighted the key issues in the strategic management of technology, we will now examine why it has been given so much consideration by academics and managers alike in recent years.

THE IMPORTANCE OF TECHNOLOGY TODAY

Rapid advances in science and technology, from supercomputers and super-conductors to biotechnology and new materials, have amplified the importance of R&D to long-term competitive success over the past two decades. This is reflected, in part, by trends in R&D investments made by firms. Indeed R&D investments by US, Japanese, and European corporations have been increasing faster since 1983 than during any other period in the last thirty years[19]. This growth in R&D spending is evident in Table 1.2. Clearly, Japanese corporations have increased their rate of R&D expenditure at a more rapid rate than either American or European firms. However, the overall pattern of growth is unmistakable.

For US corporations, an 8.5% growth in R&D investments can be compared with a 0.5% growth in capital spending in 1986[19]. According to the McGraw-Hill economics department, similar growth rates in R&D spending have not been seen since the 1953–63 period. From 1963 to 1978, the growth rate of R&D spending averaged only 0.8% in the USA. These figures indicate that American corporations have been increasingly aware of the fact that technology has become a vital factor to survival and growth in a world where competition is more intense and more global. This also implies that most of the literature on strategic management produced in the 1960s and 1970s did not have to deal with an emphasis on R&D and technology.

Recent trends, however, are somewhat mixed. R&D spending by US companies in 1989 totalled $65.2 billion, up 5.6% when adjusted for inflation. This compares with a 6.6% real increase in 1988, suggesting a downward drift in R&D investment[20]. In the late 1980s, companies were under intense cost pressures, engaging in mergers and acquisitions, restructuring,

Table 1.2 Percentage growth in industrial R&D expenditure (Source: OECD)

Time period	USA	Japan	EEC
1980–81	7.9	12.0	3.8
1981–82	5.3	9.2	2.8
1982–83	5.9	12.0	2.1
1983–84	8.7	11.3	6.3
1984–85	6.1	13.9	7.8
1981–85 (average)	6.5	11.6	4.8

laboratory closures, and consolidations. Joint R&D ventures also had an impact on the level of R&D spending by individual companies.

Industry, however, is not the only source of R&D funding. As can be seen in Table 1.3, total expenditure of R&D (public and private) has been increasing steadily since the middle 1970s. In 1985, R&D spending attained 2.3% of GDP among industrialized nations. Furthermore, R&D grew faster than GDP in almost all countries[21]. The USA, Japan, and Germany head the list in terms of R&D with 2.7%, 2.6%, and 2.6% of GDP, respectively. The picture looks quite different, however, if military R&D is excluded. The USA, France, and the United Kingdom devote a significant proportion of their R&D budgets to defense programs. If only civilian R&D is considered, only five countries exceed 2% of GDP—Switzerland, Japan, Germany, Sweden, and the Netherlands.

It is interesting to analyze and compare how R&D is funded on the one hand and conducted on the other. The role of government in financing R&D has declined over the past decade in almost every country except the United States where government funding still accounts for about 50% of the total R&D effort. In contrast, the average R&D contribution by government among other industrialized nations in 1987 was 43%, and in Japan the figure was 21% (see note 21).

In the face of declining government support, companies have become more active in both funding and conducting R&D. Table 1.4 looks back in time and compares spending levels by industry across a broad range of countries[22]. Clearly, the technological effort of corporations has been increasing significantly in all major industrialized countries. By the mid-1980s, industry funded 53% of all R&D and almost two-thirds of the actual R&D work was carried out by companies[21]. Moreover, the growth of corporate research and development in the different countries reflects quite accurately the competitive position of their national economies. The data we have cited

Table 1.3 Total R&D expenditures by nation as a percentage of GDP (OECD, 1989)

Country	1975	1979	1983
USA	2.3	2.4	2.7
Japan	1.7	2.0	2.6
Germany	2.1	2.3	2.6
Sweden	1.8	1.9	2.5
Switzerland	2.2	2.4	2.4
France	1.8	1.8	2.1
UK	2.1	2.2	2.2
Netherlands	1.9	1.9	2.0
Canada	1.0	1.1	1.4
Italy	0.9	0.8	1.1

Table 1.4 Percentage of national R&D funded by industry in five major countries (H. Fusfeld[22])

Country	1970	1985
USA	38	48
Japan	59	69
Germany	53	61
UK	42	47
France	37	42

show that the funding of technological research by industry is not only a major phenomenon of the twentieth century, but also one that is now increasing. We can suggest a few hypotheses concerning this trend.

Hypotheses on the Importance of Technology

The growth of R&D expenditures reflects an increase in the perceived importance of technology in two ways. First, it is a reaction of corporations faced with the quickening pace of competition; and second, because it produces innovation, R&D itself is the source of more rapid and technical progress. The growing importance of technology and the increase in R&D spending are thus linked in a chicken and egg relationship. This higher rate of technological change can be interpreted as either a radical change (or crisis) or as a more sustained trend which is currently at a peak.

The "Crisis" Hypothesis

If the economic crisis, which was set off by the rise in oil prices in the 1970s, corresponds to the end of the "petrochemical" technical system which operated during the thirty years of growth following the Second World War, we can interpret (in the manner of B. Gille) the current allocation of resources to technology as the sign of a profound regeneration of technique. Based on the idea of technology life cycles recently made popular by McKinsey[5,6], we can speculate on the existence of life cycles of entire technical systems. We would thus be at a turning point in history, passing from one technical system to another, the transition being reflected in a greater effort to promote the emergence of the technologies essential to the new technical system.

The "Sustained Progress" Hypothesis

Some authors have emphasized the fact that the length of time between the discovery of a fundamental process and its application has become progressively shorter[2,23]. For example, one hundred and twelve years

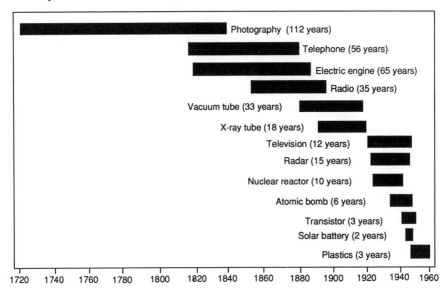

Figure 1.5 The pace of technological innovation (Center for Integrative Studies, *World Facts and Trends*, Binghamton, New York: School of Advanced Technology, State University of New York, 1969)

(1727–1829) passed between the discovery of the physical phenomenon applied in hotography, and photography itself. In contrast, it took only three years (1948–51) in the case of the transistor (see Figure 1.5).

Admittedly, Figure 1.5 is questionable since many current technologies are complex combinations of science and techniques, which makes the actual "source" of the first discovery difficult to trace. Moreover, one technology tends to lead to another through a snowball effect. This can be related to the fact that corporations conduct a growing fraction of total research, thus reducing the delay between invention and commercialization by internalizing the R&D process. In this context, some analysts have tried to formalize the relationship between R&D spending and technological innovation. N. Rescher[24] suggests a mathematical formula which is applied by H. Fusfeld[25] to the case of American industry: in order to maintain a constant rate of innovation, R&D expenditures must be increased exponentially over time.

The growing globalization of trade and competition forms the basis for a third hypothesis which may account for the increased importance of technology and the growth of R&D spending.

The "Global Competition" Hypothesis

Companies from developed nations are increasingly faced with challenges posed by firms originating from newly industrialized countries (NICs).

Thus, the Japanese steel and shipbuilding industries, the American and European textile industries, among others, are at a disadvantage when competing with Korean, Singaporean and Hong Kong firms.

K. Ohmae[26], comparing the Triad (USA, Europe, Japan) to other parts of the world, observed the following phenomena:

- The Triad countries have lost ground mainly in lower technology industries.
- High-technology industries have a greater profitability potential.
- Most high-technology sectors remain dominated by Triad countries.

The above observations imply that, faced with the competition from NICs, firms of the Triad are concentrating their activities in areas where they can benefit from their strong technological capabilities. This move has amplified the importance of technological factors for firms in developed countries which appear to be engaged in a "technology race."

CONCLUSION

In this chapter we have attempted to define the concept of technology by contrasting it to the notion of technique. The use of the term technology, as we define it, reflects the emergence of a significant link between scientific knowledge, technical capabilities and industrial production. We have also tried to explain why technology has come to be viewed in recent years as a crucial competitive factor. Techniques are used whereas technology is created and continuously improved. We will therefore next examine how corporations can manage technology in order to create competitive advantage.

NOTES AND REFERENCES

1. *Webster's Third New International Dictionary of the English Language, Unabridged*, Springfield, MA: Merriam-Webster Inc., 1986.
2. B. Gille, *Histoire des Techniques*, Paris: Gallimard, 1978.
3. See, for example, D. Bell, *The Coming of Post-Industrial Society*, New York: Basic Books, 1973.
4. J. Woodward, *Industrial Organization: Theory and Practice*, Oxford: Oxford University Press, 1965; J. Thompson, *Organizations in Action*, New York: McGraw-Hill, 1967; C. Perrow, *Organizational Analysis: A Sociological View*, London: Tavistock Publications, 1970.
5. R. Foster, "A Call for Vision in Managing Technology", *Business Week*, May 24, 1982.
6. R. Foster, *Innovation: The Attacker's Advantage*, New York, NY: Summit Books, 1986, pp. 32–33.

7. L. Steele, *Managing Technology*, New York: McGraw-Hill, 1989, p. 8.
8. Arthur D. Little, "The Strategic Management of Technology," material presented at the European Management Forum, Davos, 1981, p. 11.
9. J. J. Salomon, *Le Gaulois, le Cow Boy et le Samourai*, Paris: Economica, 1986, pp. 43–44.
10. J. Morin, *L'Excellence Technologique*, Paris: Jean Picollec-Publi-Union, 1985, p. 27.
11. W. Randolph, "Matching Technology and the Design of Organization Units", *California Management Review*, Summer 1981.
12. J. Ketteringham and J. White, "Making Technology Work for Business" in R. Lamb (Ed.), *Competitive Strategic Management*, Englewood Cliffs: Prentice-Hall, 1984, p. 502.
13. J. Friar and M. Horwitch, "The Emergence of Technology Strategy," *Technology in Society*, **7**, 1985, p. 144.
14. D. Sahal, *Patterns of Technological Innovation*, Reading: Addison-Wesley, 1981, Chapter 1.
15. B. Gille, *Histoire des Techniques*, Paris: Gallimard, 1978, p. 75.
16. See, for example, C. Freeman, *The Economics of Industrial Innovation*, Cambridge: MIT Press, 1982; M. Tushman and P. Anderson, "Technological Discontinuities and Organizational Environments," *Administrative Science Quarterly*, 31, 1986.
17. A. Cooper and D. Schendel, "Strategic Response to Technological Threats," *Business Horizons*, **19**, 1976.
18. R. Henderson and K. Clark, "Architectural Innovation: The Reconfiguration of Existing Product Technologies and the Failure of Established Firms", *Administrative Science Quarterly*, **35**, 1990.
19. "After 20 Years, R&D Breaks into a Run Again", *Business Week*, June 16, 1986, p. 17.
20. Business Week, *Innovation 1990*, special issue, p. 194.
21. OECD, *Science and Technology Indicators*, Paris: Organisation for Economic Cooperation and Development, 1989.
22. H. Fusfeld, *The Technical Enterprise, Present and Future Patterns*, Cambridge: Ballinger Publishing, 1986, p. 73.
23. P. Buigues, *Prospective et Competitivite*, Paris: McGraw-Hill, 1985, p. 14.
24. N. Rescher, *Scientific Progress: A Philosophical Essay on the Economics of Research in Natural Science*, Pittsburg: University of Pittsburg Press, 1978.
25. H. Fusfeld, *The Technical Enterprise, Present and Future Patterns*, Cambridge: Ballinger Publishing, 1986, pp. 102–103.
26. K. Ohmae, *Triad Power: The Coming Shape of Global Competition*, New York, NY: The Free Press, 1985.

Strategy and Technology

Chapter 2

Technology and Industry Structure

The first stage in the strategy-making process is the identification of the segments or "strategic business units" which will form the basis for the entire strategy process. This consists of categorizing the firm's overall activity into homogeneous units for which a specific strategy can be formulated and to which resources can be allocated independently. The strategic segmentation process is difficult to carry out in practice; its relevance, however, contributes greatly to the quality of the implemented strategy.

Even in the early stages of strategy formulation, it is essential that technology be taken into account. Indeed, as one of the fundamental components of a business, technology must be analyzed in the strategic segmentation process. Moreover, technological change can modify the firm's competitive environment, thus requiring a new division of its activity and a re-definition of its businesses.

The next stage of the strategy-making process, namely industry analysis, aims at identifying the specific characteristics of all the firm's businesses, evaluating the latter's growth potential, as well as defining the "rules of the game" for the firms competing in these businesses. This stage is linked to the previous one, with industry analysis confirming or disconfirming the relevance of the strategic segmentation, since it serves to check the utility or relevance of the defined segments. Thus, in practice, strategic segmentation and industry analysis iterate with the strategy-making process.

In this context, however, technological changes, whether occurring in the industry in which the firm operates or in other industries, can directly affect the current health and the long-term growth potential of the firm's businesses. Some technological changes are likely to boost the growth of particular businesses, while others can slow growth and induce acceler-ated obsolescence. Indeed, by altering the key factors for success, tech-nological change can radically transform the mechanisms of competition in a given industry. Technological changes can even spawn new businesses or contribute to the sudden disappearance of industries that have become obsolete.

TECHNOLOGY AND STRATEGIC SEGMENTATION

While the classic question "What business(es) should we be in?" has long been considered the starting point of the strategy process[1], finding the answer is a difficult task which cannot be easily formalized. There is a great variety of potentially useful ways to define business segments. Since there is no specific "technique," the segmentation process amounts to making in-formed choices from a wide range of possibilities. Many terms have been used to describe the entity which is the outcome of the segmentation process and the basis of strategic thinking. These include: strategic unit, strategy center, business, strategic business unit, and strategic segment. Some au-thors introduce nuances in the meaning of these different terms (e.g. dis-tinguishing strategic segment from industry). In the following chapters, we will use these terms interchangeably.

Behind the variety of terms used to describe this basic unit of strategic management, there is a variety of different, sometimes conflicting, defini-tions of strategic segmentation[1]. We will define a strategic segment or busi-ness unit as a *subset of the firm's overall activity having a specific combination of key factors for success*. Thus, in order to compete successfully in a given business, a firm must have the particular set of capabilities corresponding to the combination of key factors for success that characterize and define the strategic segment.

Given the above definition, it seems obvious that technology is one of the main components of strategic segmentation. Admittedly, in certain service industries, technology, as we have defined it in Chapter 1, has a low compet-itive impact and cannot therefore be considered as one of the key factors for success in the industry. In contrast, in most manufacturing industries—and not exclusively in high-technology industries—technology plays such an important part that it forms the basis for the definition of businesses.

In order to achieve, in practice, a division of overall activity into separate pertinent businesses, the typical firm starts by listing its product-markets; these are then gathered in groups according to homogeneous combinations of key factors for success. Technology often forms the dividing line between two groups of product-markets, thus creating two distinct strategic seg-ments. Another operational approach suggested by some authors[1,2] considers technology as one of the dimensions according to which strategic segmentation is carried out; in this case, the firm's overall activity is divided into basic businesses according to the three following dimensions:

- the needs they meet or the functions they fulfill
- the customer segments they address
- the technologies implemented.

This leads to a division which is more complex than that based only on product-markets. In this operational approach of strategic segmentation, technology is explicitly a focal point of the process. Figure 2.1 represents the three dimensions which must be taken into account and analyzed when carrying out a strategic segmentation operation.

Businesses A and C correspond to the same need, fulfill the same function and draw upon the same technology, but serve different customer segments; A and B satisfy the same need, fulfill the same function, but implement distinct technologies. This last situation where technology is the factor which differentiates the two segments can be illustrated by numerous examples. Thermal or nuclear power plants fulfill the same function (to produce electricity), address the same customers (companies that produce and supply electricity), but use entirely different power production technologies. In both businesses, technology is a key factor for success but the technical skills required are so different that one can speculate on the existence of distinct strategic segments; this is reflected in separate competitive environments, each with different competing firms. We can also cite the instance of conventional gas or electric ovens and microwave ovens, for which the existence of separate segments is testified to by the fact that the major

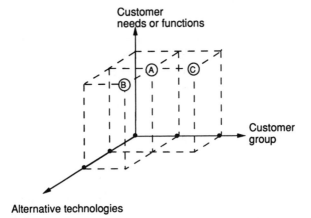

Figure 2.1 The role of technology in business definition (Adapted from Abell and Hammond 1979)

microwave oven manufacturing firms do not produce conventional ovens. This is also the case for domestic oil, gas or electric furnaces, and, to a greater extent, for the mechanical, electric or quartz watches.

It is important to note that strategic segmentation carried out according to implemented technologies is only justified when technological change implies mastering different key factors for success and requires new capabilities for the firm; if the technologies can easily be substituted one for another—for example if they are available on the market and do not require any specific know-how to be implemented—the different technological alternatives do not correspond to distinct strategic segments.

TECHNOLOGY AND THE DEFINITION OF INDUSTRY BOUNDARIES

The businesses, or strategic segments, of a firm are not immutable; on the contrary, they evolve together with the key factors for success according to which they were defined and, in particular, with technology. Technological change can indeed affect the division of the firm's overall activity into separate and homogeneous businesses and, consequently, the definition of the competitive environments in which it operates. Technological change can blur the limits between businesses which previously were different from one another, eventually leading to a new business. Alternatively, technological change can result in the further segmentation of a business into a set of businesses, clearly distinct from one another.

Technology and De-segmentation

By reinforcing the competitive impact of one or more technologies that are shared by distinct businesses and reducing the importance of the technologies specific to each, technological change can lead to the blending of these businesses—de-segmentation—resulting in a new enlarged industry. The key factors for success now shared in common, due in particular to the shared technologies, prevail over those specific to the pre-existing distinct businesses.

It appears that changes of this kind are occurring in businesses such as computers, telecommunications, and office automation. Indeed, it is significant that firms which previously operated only in one of these three industries, if not in subsegments of the latter, tend increasingly to compete simultaneously in two or three of these industries. IBM, the world's largest computer maker, has long been present in the office equipment industry (photocopiers, typewriters, etc.) and entered the telecommunications market by taking over Rolm in 1984. AT&T, the world's telecommunications leader, entered an alliance with Olivetti in 1983, acquiring 25% of the Italian firm's equity, to enhance its position in computing and office automation. More recently, in 1991, AT&T's hostile takeover of NCR was meant to further reinforce the firm's position in the various areas of what appears increasingly to be a single business. Even Digital Equipment Corporation (DEC), which presents itself as a specialist in minicomputers, has developed and marketed microcomputer systems and data networks because its managers think that this is indispensable if the company wants to improve its position within the business in which it mainly operates. This de-segmentation is perhaps seen most dramatically in NEC where the mission of the firm is structured around "C and C"—computers and communications.

The blurring of industry boundaries has resulted in the development of products and systems that are themselves difficult to classify in one particular category—such as, for example, word processors, fax machines, electronic directories, etc. The evolution we have just examined can be represented in a very simplified manner, as shown in Figure 2.2.

Additional cases of de-segmentation resulting from technological evolution are likely in the future. Indeed we already see this occurring in the aeronautic and space industries. With regard to the latter, the development of hypersonic aircraft capable of flying at a speed of over 15 000 miles per hour and at an altitude of nearly 20 miles would require a new type of engine whose development would draw upon both turbojet and ramjet engine technologies, as well as rocket propulsion technology. If such projects materialize, they will very likely broaden the competitive arena of engine manufacturers which will include both companies specialized in aircraft engines—such as Pratt & Whitney, General Electric, Rolls Royce and SNECMA—and companies specialized in rocket propellents—such as SEP, Martin-Marrietta and General Dynamics[3].

Another case in point is that of the machine tool industry which historically was characterized by a great number of small suppliers specialized in specific products (milling machines, lathes, etc.), each requiring particular skills and equipment, and forming a particular strategic segment. The development of numerically controlled machines, however, greatly affected the structure of the machine tool industry. Small specialized suppliers are now having more and more difficulty with major competitors which develop new technologies and apply them to a wide range of products. With the advent of robotics, and flexible manufacturing systems, these large competitors are capable of supplying their clients with integrated systems meeting all their needs[4]. Thus, the many segments associated with the old structure are blending to form a single "industrial technology" industry.

The de-segmentation of industries resulting from technological change is

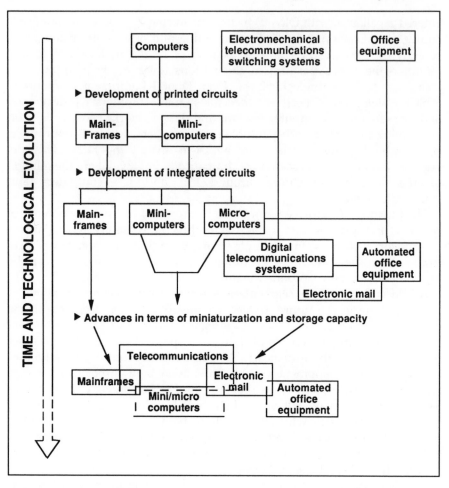

Figure 2.2 Technological evolution and business definition (computers–office automation–telecommunications)

often accompanied by a change in the cost structure in these industries. The proportion of research, design and development costs specific to each separate business tends to decrease, while the proportion of the costs incurred by the shared technologies tends to increase. In the above-mentioned example of the computer, the office automation, and the telecommunications industries, the proportion of the costs related to integrated circuits, microprocessors and software has significantly increased over the last few years in switching equipment and in office automation products, thereby contributing to the blending of these industries with the computer industry.

Technology and Globalization

When the impact of technology in a particular industry increases and, therefore, when the proportion of costs related to technology rises significantly, the market scope served by the industry must be expanded to accommodate the increased costs. As we have emphasized earlier in this chapter, the customer is one of the key criteria to be taken into account in the strategic segmentation process; the geographic distribution of customers is, therefore, an important element in this respect. When success in two geographic areas requires specific skills for the firm and when these skills correspond to key factors for success, it can be assumed that there are two distinct strategic segments. Thus, two separate markets can be identified for a given industry.

However, as the impact of technology increases, the significance of local and regional differences is diminished. Indeed, the cost of technology, which is often largely comprised of fixed costs, requires that the latter be compensated by a wider market scope. Thus, technological evolution and the growing importance of technology in many industries encourage globalization of markets[5]. Computers, automobiles, and semiconductors are examples of industries where advances in technology are so costly that global sales are necessary in order to remain competitive. This globalization of markets due to technology is one particular form of the blending of distinct strategic segments resulting from technological evolution which we examined in the previous subsection.

Technology and Re-segmentation

When technological change leads to an increase of the proportion of the costs specific to a strategic segment, and a reduction of the costs shared with other segments, the trend is towards a "re-segmentation" of the industry into smaller segments[6]. The performance and reliability level required for military equipment and, consequently, the specificity of the technologies involved has led, in several industrial sectors, to a clear segmentation between military and civilian activities; this segmentation tends to become further accentuated as a result of the different pace of technological evolution in military and civilian industries[7]. In France, for example, the production of commercial aircraft on the one hand, and fighters on the other, has been divided between two manufacturers, Dassault and Aérospatiale. In the arms industry itself, particularly in guided missile manufacturing, the different technologies used have produced a division in the production of air-to-air missiles, ground-to-air missiles and anti-tank missiles, each category being manufactured separately by specific firms (Matra, Thomson and Aérospatiale). Similarly, in the consumer electronics industry, technological evolution has resulted in increasing segmentation between appliances on the one hand, and video and hi-fi equipment on the other.

Technological change which requires standards to be adopted can produce segmentation within a particular industry until such change makes the different standards uniform, or until one of the competitors succeeds in imposing its own standard on the industry. Segmentation by standards was the case in the television industry where the PAL (developed in Germany), SECAM (developed in France) and NSTC (adopted in the USA and Japan) standards remained distinct. However, the latter occurred in the VCR industry with the VHS standard (adopted by Matsushita), Betamax standard (adopted by Sony) and the V2000 standard (adopted by Philips). Matsushita generally succeeded in imposing the VHS standard, with most of its competitors finally adopting it, but Betamax became the standard in certain markets, for example the Venezuelan market. Further technological innovation, notably the advances made in terms of miniaturization, should set a new single standard (8 mm) for the entire industry on which all competitors will agree.

Strategic segmentation, which is the first stage of the strategy-making process, is a complex and difficult process to carry out. However thoroughly done, it is only ephemeral insofar as the identified industries or businesses

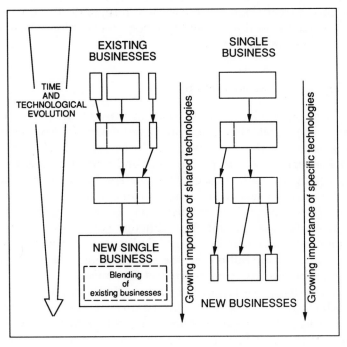

Figure 2.3 Changes in industry definition produced by technological evolution

change under the influence of many factors, among which technology plays a vital role. Overall, the impact of technological change on strategic segmentation can be represented as shown in Figure 2.3.

TECHNOLOGY AND INDUSTRY EVOLUTION

Knowledge of the growth rate (current and future) and the maturity of an industry are fundamental to strategic analysis. The well-known business portfolio planning models are all based on an evaluation of growth rate (in the case of the BCG model), industry maturity (in the case of the Arthur D. Little model) and the long-term growth potential (in the case of the McKinsey model) of a particular business[8]. Technological evolution can have a decisive impact on industry maturity and growth. Technological change can boost the growth rate of some industries, or, in other cases, slow growth. The emergence of new businesses is often the result of technological innovation. Furthermore, technological evolution can produce industry substitution phenomena by making existing industries obsolete and replacing them with new industries of emerging technologies.

The Emergence of New Industries

Technological innovation is undoubtedly the most frequent reason for the emergence of new industries[9]. Most industrial sectors, be it the steel industry, the chemical industry, the automotive industry, or the aeronautic industry to name only a few, originally emerged as a result of technological breakthroughs which were later transformed into economic activities. The history of industry is rich in epic biographies of famous inventors who succeeded in developing new techniques which themselves were the sources of new industries: for example, Watt and the steam engine, Alexander Graham Bell and the telephone, or Thomas Edison and the phonograph or the incandescent lamp. More recently, the emergence and the growth of the reprography (or photocopy) industry are due to Chester Carlson, one of the founders of the Xerox corporation, who invented the xerography method; the 1985 global sales of this industry exceeded ten billion dollars, even though the first photocopier was launched by Xerox only in 1959[10]. Many other industries, such as microcomputers, biotechnology, and video technology, which have emerged in the last decade originated in technological innovations.

Technological innovation can lead to the emergence of new industries only if the applications which result from it meet actual needs and lead to marketable products or services. Traditionally, a distinction is made between innovations that are pushed by technology and innovations that are pulled by the market[11]. In the first case, the technology is available before a market demand is even identified and applications likely to satisfy some needs must be found. In the second case, manufacturers are well aware of existing needs but the technologies that can satisfy such needs must be developed. The emergence of the reprographics industry mentioned above falls into the first category, while the development of commercial jet aircraft belongs to the second category of industries. This dichotomy of the ways in which new industries emerge and grow is interesting in terms of the strategies implemented by the firms responsible for the emergence of these industries. Indeed, it suggests that some firms base their strategies primarily on a set of technological capabilities, while others try to meet particular market needs, or even satisfy a specific customer base, by utilizing the most appropriate existing technologies. We will examine these approaches in greater detail in the following chapters.

When new industries resulting from technological change emerge, there is often an initial period of uncertainty concerning the size of the market and the real long-term growth potential. The use of market surveys and forecasting techniques does not, in such cases, reduce significantly the uncertainty, as evidenced by the gross forecasting errors made in the 1960s regarding the growth of the computer industry. Indeed, in the early 1970s, EMI invented the CT scanner and projected a market of five machines in the first year. This was later increased to 12 and finally 50. Ultimately, the company delivered 35 machines in the first year but had orders for 60 more. This increased dramatically in the second year to 450 machines delivered and 300 ordered. This level of market acceptance far outstripped even the most optimistic of initial forecasts and made it exceedingly difficult for a small company like EMI to keep up with demand. Ultimately, EMI was displaced by General Electric in this rapidly evolving new business. In the 1980s, all experts forecasted a dramatic growth in biotechnologies and bio-industries, but none of them attempted to give a quantitative estimate, nor to predict the time and the specific sectors in which the growth would occur[12].

Technology and Industry Dematurity

While technological innovation can lead to the emergence of new industries, it can also boost the growth of existing businesses and even revitalize declining industries[13]. Technological innovation can contribute to such industry "dematurity" in two different manners: it can improve the product performance and it can reduce cost.

The improvement of the product performance can serve to broaden the market to include new customer segments interested in the additional characteristics offered, but also has the effect of making generations of products become obsolete faster, thereby creating a more rapid replacement pace. For example, global sales of reflex 35 mm cameras which peaked at 7.7 million units in 1981, declined rapidly and totaled only 5.4 million units in 1984. At the same time, the introduction of autofocus cameras (first by Minolta followed by Nikon) led to an increase in industry sales which reached 6.1 million units by 1985[14].

The introduction of compact discs and laser CD players produced similar effects on the audio market. This industry reached maturity in the late 1970s and had a low growth rate until 1984 when sales increased by 15%—because of CD players—and rose by another 8% in 1985 and by 10% in 1986[15]. Another example can be found in the consumer electronics industry, where technological innovation (numerical processing of sound and image, laser reading, etc.) has minimized the difference between the technologies used in the audio industry (hi-fi, tape recorders, record players, walkmans, etc.) on the one hand, and in the video industry (television sets, VCRs, etc.) on the other.

While technological advances are a source of performance improvement, they can also reduce the cost of products. When demand is elastic, this reduction of cost, which is reflected in the price of products, leads to growth in the industry. Technological innovation in the aerospace industry has made it possible to build bigger, more reliable and less expensive aircraft; due to this trend, as well as to other factors, air fares have decreased steadily while traffic has increased (by 70% between 1975 and 1985), thus leading to an increase in the number of aircraft manufactured.

Technology and Substitution

Technological innovation can induce substitution phenomena where existing products are replaced by new products based upon new technologies, and occasionally, existing industries are displaced by new ones. Such substitution can occur in a more or less gradual manner; however, it is more often sudden, making an industry and the firms operating in it obsolete, or at least requiring them to undergo radical change in a very short period of time[16]. A well-known example of the substitution phenomenon is that of the slide-rule. In the 1970s they were replaced, in a matter of only two or three years, by electronic calculators developed from completely new technologies. The substitution of semiconductors for vacuum tubes is another well-known instance of rapid product substitution leading to the death of an existing industry and the emergence of a new one. And while the growth of the watchmaking industry was increased by technological change in the 1970s, it also resulted in substitution as indicated in Figure 2.4.

Sometimes the substitution process can be relatively long, especially when there are obstacles preventing the spread of the new products, such as

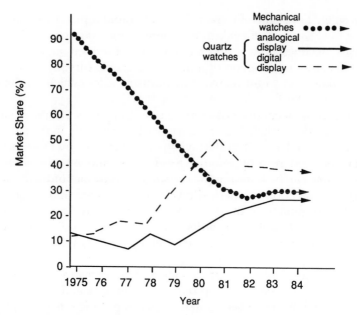

Figure 2.4 Technology substitution in the watchmaking industry: market distribution of sales of watches in France (*Sciences et Techniques* 1985[17])

compatibility problems and switching costs. Thus, despite considerably improved performance for price, the spread of CD players and the decline of LP players was slowed by the fact that consumers had to replace the rest of their equipment (amplifiers and speakers) in order to benefit fully from this new technology. Furthermore, they had to replace their entire record collection at a time when the number of available compact discs was relatively limited. Similarly, the spread of jet engine aircraft, especially medium-haul aircraft, was slowed in the beginning by the insufficient length of landing strips[18].

The classic indicator by which substitution threats can be evaluated is the comparison of the performance/price ratio of the competing products. Specifically, it is the change in the ratios rather than the simple comparison of these at a given time that is significant. As soon as there are concrete manifestations of the threat of substitution, most incumbents respond by lowering their prices in order to protect their endangered product base. This effort to maintain the industry can postpone the substitution process but also deprive the firms in the threatened industry of the resources necessary to develop capability in the new technology[16].

In contrast, technological innovation, whether leading to lower costs or to improved product performance, sometimes allows an industry to eliminate the threat of substitution. For example, while the French railways had lost a great deal of business to air transport in the sixties and seventies, the development of very fast trains on major, high-density traffic lines (e.g. Paris–Lyon) has completely reversed the substitution process in the eighties and nineties. These so-called TGV (Trains à Grande Vitesse) trains can reach maximum speeds of over 300 miles per hour. They are now challenging airlines on an increasing number of routes in Europe and a TGV line is soon to be constructed between Dallas and Houston, Texas.

Technology and Industry Decline

In some cases technological change leads to the opposite consequences: instead of boosting the growth of an industry, it hampers its long-term growth potential. This is relatively uncommon and generally involves technologies that increase the reliability and the life of products in industries with saturated markets. The problem is that improved performance does not create additional demand in such industries. For instance, the increased durability of rubber can reduce the need to replace products such as tires, thereby retarding the growth of the industry.

Even if technological change does not lead to the total substitution of one industry for another, it can result in partial substitution and decline in the initial industry. For example, while it did not entirely replace the movie industry, the spread of VCRs has reduced the audiences for movies shown in theaters. The opening of a very fast train service in France, which we mentioned earlier, did not stop air service between Paris and Lyon, but it did cut significantly into the airlines' customer base. The development of turbojet engines did not put an end to the manufacture of turbo propellers. It did, however, limit the applications of the latter to certain categories of aircraft (private aircraft, commuter aircraft, short takeoff and landing aircraft, etc.).

In addition to the effects on industry definition and segmentation, technology and technological change have a decisive impact on the growth, the life-cycle, and the attractiveness of industries. Figure 2.5 summarizes the different ways in which technology can affect the growth potential of an industry.

TECHNOLOGY AND COMPETITION

Even when it does not alter the definition and the limits of a particular business, nor directly affect its current growth, maturity, or its attractiveness, technological change can cause a dramatic transformation of the key factors for success specific to a business and, above all, modify the relative importance of these factors. Such a transformation amounts to changing the rules of competition in a given industry by curtailing the competitive

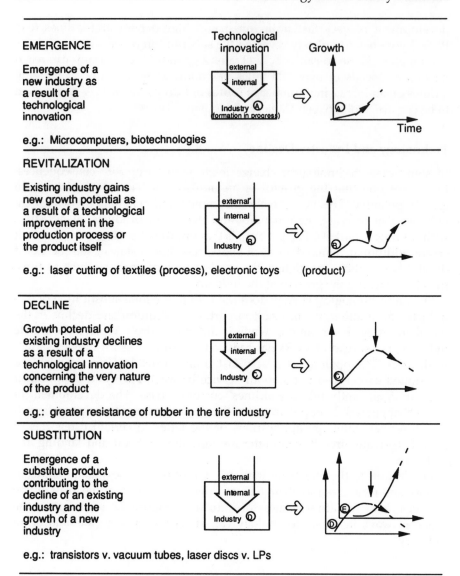

Figure 2.5 Technological evolution and industry growth potential

advantages enjoyed by certain rivals and reducing the handicaps associated with weaker competitors. Thus, in the end, the industry is restructured. It is important to note that the technological changes we are referring to are not innovations which one of the competitors introduces in order to strengthen its position. Rather, the change imposes itself on the industry as a whole and structurally modifies the nature of competition; each competitor has to adjust to it and benefit from it in its own way. Such technological changes generally originate from outside the industry, notably in upstream industries, such as equipment, component, and raw materials supply industries[16].

Technologies which have an impact on production systems can thus minimize or accentuate the importance of production volumes and the size of plants as key factors for success in a given industry. In the steel industry, the development of technologies allowing low-capacity production units (minimills) to operate at costs comparable to those of large mills considerably modified the rules of competition. The cost advantage of large units built in special locations (near mines, near ports etc.) was no longer so important compared with that of smaller units operating by downstream processing plants with much lower transportation costs. Similarly, in the aluminum industry, new casting techniques seem to have reduced significantly economies of scale and could cause this industry to evolve in the same way as the steel industry[19]. The spreading of numerically controlled machines in many manufacturing industries has tended to erode the distinction between large, standardized production runs and small, custom-made runs. This has led to the blending of businesses that until now were distinct and did not compete with one another.

Technological evolution can affect other factors for success such as the geographical location of production and the capability of getting raw materials or energy supplies on the best possible terms. In the above-mentioned example of the aluminum industry, the use of carbothermic reduction technologies that make it possible to transform bauxite directly into aluminum, without going through the alumina stage, reduces significantly the consumption of energy (which historically has been one of the major elements in the cost structure in the production of aluminum) and thus minimizes the competitive advantage of producers who pay less for energy because of their location near a dam or preferential rates granted by the government[19].

The structure of competition in a given industry can be analyzed by taking into account the five main competitive forces which affect the industry: the competition between incumbent firms, the threat of potential new entrants, the threat of substitute products, the pressure from suppliers, and the negotiating power of customers[20]. In this context, technology is likely to modify the structure of competition by changing the position of upstream or downstream industries or removing entry barriers, with new competitors thereby gaining access. Thus technological change, which greatly affected the watchmaking industry by causing a great number of firms manufacturing watches with mechanical clockworks to switch to electronic systems, also upset the structure of competition. The case of Texas Instruments—one of the world's major electronic component manufacturers—which entered and later abandoned the watchmaking industry can be analyzed in the light of these technological changes. The development of quartz watches and the importance of microprocessors in this product induced Texas Instruments to enter and enabled it to succeed in this venture for some time. The progressive standardization of the components used in the manufacture of watches and the growing importance of other complementary factors such as design, assembly, distribution and brand image, however, forced Texas Instruments out of the watchmaking industry[21].

The increasing standardization of microcomputers, the systematic subcontracting of components' manufacturing and the cloning of the most successful products have reinforced the importance of factors such as distribution and aftersales service in the microcomputer industry; this trend has favored firms such as Tandy, which has a very large distribution network, and IBM, whose reputation for excellent customer service and reliability is well-established. Since firms cannot differentiate themselves in terms of technology, there is renewed competition on price which was started by the clone manufacturers' seeking a means to offset the image and service quality handicap they had compared with IBM. In short, the rules of competition in this industry have been greatly influenced by technological factors.

CONCLUSION

Because it can be the source of major competitive advantage, technology must be given consideration by firms competing in a given industry. However, prior to examining how a company can use technology to its own advantage, it was necessary in the present chapter to specify how technology and technological evolution affect the definition of the industries and businesses in which firms operate. Also considered was the growth, maturity and attractiveness of such industries, and the forces driving competition in each of the businesses. The next chapter deals with the role of technology in the creation of a durable competitive advantage.

NOTES AND REFERENCES

1. D. Abell, *Defining the Business: the Starting Point of Strategic Planning*, Englewood Cliffs: Prentice-Hall, 1980.
2. D. Abell and J. Hammond, *Strategic Market Planning*, Englewood Cliffs: Prentice-Hall, 1979, Chapter 8.
3. "Suddenly the 'Spaceplane' is taking off," *Business Week*, February 24, 1986.
4. Committee on the Machine Tool Industry, *The U.S. Machine Tool Industry and the Defense Readiness Base*, Washington: National Academy Press, 1983; E. Ader and J. Lauriol, "La Segmentation, Fondement de l'Analyse Strategique," *Harvard-L'Expansion*, Spring 1986; M. Horowitch, "Les Nouvelles Strategies Technologiques des Enterprises," *Revue Francaise de Gestion*, March–April–May 1986.

5. M. Porter (Ed.), *Competition in Global Industries*, Boston: Harvard Business School Press, 1986.
6. C.K. Prahalad and Y. Doz, *The Multinational Mission*, New York: Free Press, 1987.
7. P. Dussauge, *L'Industrie Francaise de l'Arment: Intervention de l'Etat et Strategies des Enterprise dans un Secteur a Technologie de Pointe*, Paris: Economica, 1985, p. 122; S. Hart, "The Federal Photovoltaics Utilization Program: An Evaluation and Learning Framework," *Policy Sciences*, 1983, pp. 325–343.
8. A. Hax and N. Majluf, *Strategic Management: An Integrative Perspective*, Englewood Cliffs: Prentice-Hall, 1984.
9. J. Schumpeter, *The Theory of Economic Development*, London: Transaction Books, 1934.
10. G. Jacobson and J. Hillkirk, *Xerox: American Samourai*, New York, NY: Macmillan, 1986.
11. E. Von Hipple, *The Sources of Innovation*, New York: Oxford University Press, 1988.
12. "Biotech Comes of Age," *Business Week*, January 23, 1984.
13. W. Abernathy, K. Clark, and A. Kantrow, *Industrial Renaissance*, New York: Basic Books, 1983; W. Dowdy and J. Nikolchev, "Can Industries Demature? Applying New Technologies to Mature Industries," *Long Range Planning*, April 1986.
14. "Autofocus Cameras: Hot and About to Get Hotter," *Business Week*, March 3, 1986.
15. "High-tech Music Has the Audio Market Rocking," *Business Week*, June 2, 1986.
16. A. Cooper and D. Schendel, "Strategic Responses to Technological Threats," *Business Horizons*, February 1976.
17. "Rapport sur l'Etat des Techniques," *Sciences et Techniques*, special issue, March 1985, pp. 112–113.
18. G. White and M. Graham, "How to Spot a Technological Winner," *Harvard Business Review*, March–April 1978.
19. M. Porter, "Technology and Competitive Advantage," *The Journal of Business Strategy*, Winter 1985.
20. M. Porter, *Competitive Strategy*, New York: The Free Press, 1980.
21. D. Teece, "Profiting from Technological Innovation: Implications for Integration, Collaboration, Licensing and Public Policy," in D. Teece (Ed.), *The Competitive Challenge*, Cambridge: Ballinger Publishing, 1987.

Chapter 3

Technology and Competitive Advantage

While technological change can modify the relative importance of the various key factors for success in a given industry, thereby affecting the structure of competition in the industry, it is also a tool which firms can use to create competitive advantage. Indeed, technology appears to be one of the major elements which help define the two main generic strategies—"cost leadership" and "differentiation". Some companies even succeed in using technology to change the rules of competition to their advantage. By almost completely changing the key factors for success specific to an industry, such "new-game strategies" based on technology amount to a re-definition of the existing business.

The object of this chapter is first to provide an in-depth analysis of the ways in which companies can use technology to their advantage to implement either cost leadership or differentiation strategies. Then, we will examine how, by implementing new-game strategies, firms can use technology to place themselves in a favorable position by deliberately upsetting the competitive environment, forcing a re-definition of the existing business and a change in the rules of the game.

TECHNOLOGY AND COST LEADERSHIP

One of the most effective means to compete successfully and maintain or reinforce competitive position is to offer products whose cost is lower than those of competitors. The cost we refer to here comprises not only the production cost but also all other costs incurred, including R&D, marketing, distribution as well as overhead and depreciation. Since in free-market economies, price is largely determined through the market, cost leadership means larger margins and greater profitability for the most competitive firms. Cost leadership strategies require that the firm set itself a primary objective: to minimize its costs. Technology appears as one of the most appropriate means for achieving such a purpose.

Technology and the Experience Curve

Cost leadership strategies are sometimes termed *volume strategies*. The reason for this is the empirically observed relationship, in a large number of economic activities, between the cumulative production volume and the level of costs; in other words, the larger the cumulative production volume of a firm, the lower its unit costs. The identification of this relationship between costs and the cumulative production volume led to the concept of the "experience curve." According to the theory of the experience curve, each time a firm's cumulative volume of a given product is doubled, the total unit cost of such a product, exclusive of inflation, is reduced by a constant percentage, which is generally between 20% and 30%[1].

An experience curve is characteristic of a particular industry as a whole and not of any individual firm. As such, it is an important reference for all the firms competing in a given industry. The slope of the curve thus reflects the importance of the experience effect. The greater the slope, the greater its strategic consequences, and the firms with the most extensive experience (and consequently the greater production volume and market share) have a decisive cost advantage. It is important to note, however, that the experience effect is not automatic; i.e. an increase in the cumulative production volume does not necessarily entail a cost reduction. Firms can only benefit from experience through sustained effort, efficient management and constant monitoring of costs.

Although there are many factors contributing to the experience effect, they can be classified into three main categories: learning, economies of scale, and innovation. Learning is primarily organizational in nature and has few direct technological implications[2]. However, technology plays an important part in cost reductions resulting from economies of scale and from innovation and is thus a driving force behind the experience effect.

Economies of Scale

Research and development, the design of products or, more broadly, the maintenance of the firm's technological capability entail extensive overhead or fixed costs. The greater the importance of technology in a given industry and the more significant the investments required, the more the industry is likely to display the potential for economies of scale. That is, the firms having the greatest production and sales volumes can build a cost advantage[3]. In the commercial aircraft industry, for example, companies must maintain a considerable technological capability and the development cost of a new product or program can amount to billions of dollars. In this context, large volumes and long production runs are key factors for success. In such industries, competition takes the form of a bitter struggle to gain market share and thereby increase production volume. The greater the competitive impact of technology in an industry and the higher the fixed costs, the more the resulting experience effect is likely to be important. In such industries, the experience effect is due in part, if not primarily, to economies of scale, and size.

Improved products or production processes resulting from the firm's experience are another dimension of the experience effect. Indeed, the firm's technological skills and competence contribute significantly to its ability to implement innovations which will lower costs. The innovations that are likely to lower costs concern primarily the design of the product and/or the production process; they can also originate from outside the firm and are found in the components of the product or in the equipment used to manufacture the latter.[2,4] While the firm's capability of improving the design of products obviously requires technological skills, its ability to incorporate more efficient components in the products it manufactures or use more sophisticated equipment will also largely depend on its technological skills. The use of computer-aided design, which today is indispensable in the aerospace and automotive industries (and is increasingly used by a great number of other industries), has made it possible to lower some of the costs related to the design of products, but requires that firms develop new skills. Having become an integral part of the basic skills of firms, computer-aided design has contributed to the experience effect in these industries; firms which, regardless of their size, do not use computer-aided design because they lack the necessary resources, technical skills or experience, lag behind or are not able to survive at all.

More significantly, the advances made over the last twenty years in the semiconductor industry with respect to the cost of memory or of data processing, are due to the speed with which innovations were introduced rather than to long production runs[5]. Indeed, the increased number of integrated functions and connections introduced in a silicon chip has resulted in improved performance as well as lower costs and prices. However, these innovations were developed only by firms with the adequate technological skills and the necessary financial resources to invest in R&D and in the modernization of their production facilities; moreover, these firms held a market share that was large enough to make such investments profitable over a relatively short period of time while they continued to develop new technological advances.

Some authors[6] suggest that, in a given industry at a given time, the main force behind the experience effect can be identified (i.e. learning, scale, or innovation). They distinguish between three clearly distinct situations (see Figure 3.1). In the first situation, where the experience effect is primarily the result of learning, there are few direct technology considerations. Technology is extremely important, however, in both the other situations, as we have observed. When technology accounts for significant fixed costs, economies of scale, long production runs, and size largely determine costs and have a decisive competitive impact. When technological innovation is the main force leading to lower costs, the firm's ability to create a competitive advantage depends on its technological skills.

It is important to note that among the three different causes of the experience effect we have identified, the "main driving force" varies according to the industry and is generally transitional since it corresponds to a particular phase in the evolution of the industry. Furthermore, in such industries where technology requires substantial resources and leads to heavy fixed costs, economies of scale and size are significant and often create the potential for a definite cost advantage. On the other hand, in order to fully realize the experience effect, firms must be able to improve their products or production processes with innovations that further lower costs, especially variable costs. To accomplish this, firms need to invest in technological capability. Clearly, dominant firms should be able to take advantage of both forms of experience, investing more than their competitors in R&D without affecting unit costs; this superior technical competence should enable such firms to develop the innovations necessary to lower costs, reinforce position and continue to invest more heavily in R&D.

Nullifying Experience: Innovation

Small firms or even outsiders can, in certain circumstances, draw upon technology to compensate for their relative lack of market share, low production volumes and limited experience. Even without introducing product improvements—a case which we will examine later in this chapter—a process innovation made by such a company can bring the product's cost down considerably and nullify, or even surpass, the cost advantage that incumbents have because of their experience. For example, the use of the process known as "float glass" gave Pilkington such a cost advantage on flat glass products that, despite the firm's small size, most of its competitors were forced to buy the license for the process; this required them to pay high fees in order to remain competitive, while Pilkington succeeded in becoming one

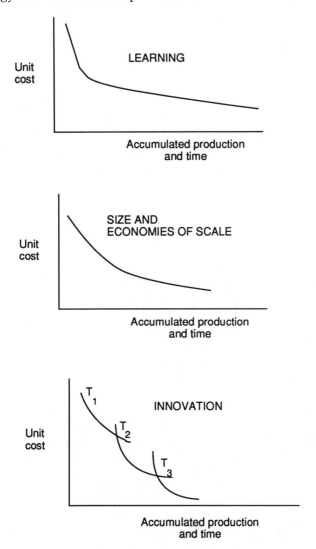

Figure 3.1 Main driving forces of the experience effect (Adapted from Martinet 1983)

of the leading corporations in the industry. Technological innovations often bring costs down—sometimes significantly—thus making the cost reduction solely attributable to economies of scale seem comparatively minor. The firms responsible for these innovations draw a significant competitive advantage from them in terms of cost, notably when they succeed in maintaining an exclusive right upon them for a long period.

At this stage of our analysis, it is important to distinguish clearly between the innovations which contribute to the experience effect, as we have examined them above, and those which, in contrast, nullify the competitive advantage resulting from size and accumulated experience. In the former case, the innovations are relatively minor, require small additional investments, and do not imply new equipment and facilities. Such innovations are primarily aimed at reducing costs while minimizing the modifications made both in the product and the production process. The logic of the experience effect, and consequently of the volume strategies based on the experience effect, dictates the pursuit of standardization and maximum stabilization of products and processes. Such a strategy leads to a certain inertia, especially in terms of technology. This is one of the factors that explains why dominant firms in a business often prove to be vulnerable to technological changes introduced by smaller firms which, despite far less experience, manage to compete successfully on cost[7].

A classic example of this paradox was Ford's loss of market leadership to General Motors in the 1920s. Despite larger production volumes and much greater experience, Ford failed to innovate, preferring instead to produce the same generic line of cars it had grown accustomed to making. Through innovative product definition, the much less experienced GM established market dominance that was to last nearly fifty years. Thus, technological innovation is a potential means for small, or even marginal, firms to overcome the cost handicap created by the accumulated experience of dominant competitors.

Technological changes that make it possible to overcome a cost handicap due to less experience are, however, quite different in nature. In most cases, they are fundamental innovations that affect the design of the product as well as the production process and lead to significantly lower costs. The utilization of more sophisticated equipment can temporarily have such an effect and match the advantage of dominant firms with older facilities, but this position of superiority is not sustainable since such equipment is usually available to all competitors[8]. For technology to translate into a sustainable cost advantage, the firm must maintain exclusive control over the innovation. Moreover, in order to compensate for the disadvantages caused by the firm's limited experience, it is necessary that the innovation fundamentally change the way dominant companies operate, thereby preventing them from "transferring" their experience to the new technology. Thus, the change of technology can be interpreted as the switch to a new experience curve on which all competitors are forced to start from scratch, the firm which developed the innovation having greater experience and therefore a cost advantage.

Not surprisingly, those innovations which contribute to the experience effect originate generally with incumbents, whereas those innovations which do not result from accumulated experience are usually developed by "outsider" firms. Indeed, it is in the interest of incumbent firms to increase the impact of experience and focus their R&D investments to enhance the benefits resulting from their size. Therefore, incumbents tend to introduce innovations only if these further reduce costs by drawing upon their cumulated experience. In contrast, it is in the interest of smaller firms to counter the impact of accumulated experience and promote more fundamental technological innovations in order to generate a new experience curve on which innovating firms will become leaders.

While technology plays a crucial role in the implementation of cost leadership strategies, paradoxically both as a driving force behind the experience effect and as a tool to overcome the advantage this effect can bring to a competitor, it has an even greater importance in differentiation strategies.

DIFFERENTIATION THROUGH TECHNOLOGY

The objective of cost leadership strategies, whether these are based on the experience effect or not, is, as we just saw, to provide firms with a competitive advantage created through costs that are lower than those of their competitors. Differentiation strategies on the other hand are aimed at giving firms a competitive advantage based on specific characteristics of their products which are recognized and valued by customers[9].

Specific characteristics of the firm's products or services include improved performance, higher quality, better reliability and durability, as well as any other feature considered as unique by customers. Differentiation also often takes the form of brand image or reputation. It is important to note however that in the context of a differentiation strategy, the specificity and the uniqueness of products or services only have meaning when the market as a whole, or at least significant segments of it, recognize value superior to that of traditional offerings. Thus, from a strategic perspective, the actual, objective specification of products and services is less important than the fact that it is perceived and valued by the market. In short, the customer defines quality[10].

Differentiation strategies make it possible for firms to soften the impact of price competition. Such strategies, however, do not imply that the market is totally indifferent to price, nor that firms enjoy great leeway in terms of costs. Indeed, a differentiation strategy is only viable if the demand for a product or service with specific attributes, at a given price and production cost level, is real and sufficient. Furthermore, for a firm to base its strategy on the specific nature of its product offering, it is essential that this specificity be sustainable over a period of time. If the product can be reproduced by competitors, a differentiation strategy is bound to fail, since the firm is forced to engage in price—and cost—competition, with offerings becoming similar and comparable. The sustainability of product differentiation can be achieved in two main ways:

- when the specificity of the product or service is due to a *proprietary capability*—protected by a patent or brand loyalty;
- when the firm is able to endow its offering with uniqueness and incur *costs that are significantly lower* than rivals would incur if they sought to produce a comparable offering with the same particular features.

These two basic characteristics of differentiation strategies are not mutually exclusive; they actually reinforce one another over time. The very nature of differentiation strategies suggests that they seek to create a niche within a broader industry. This niche, built upon the specific features with which a firm endows its offering, thus constitutes a "private game preserve" protected by entry barriers. In the niche, competition does not follow the same rules as those regulating competition in the industry as a whole. Successful differentiation can therefore be interpreted as the firm's voluntary creation of a new strategic segment characterized by special key factors for success.

The differentiated niche and the industry as a whole share many common features and differ only in a limited number of specific characteristics. There is, therefore, a high risk that the niche will be absorbed and become standardized; firms which implement differentiation strategies must thus constantly strive to maintain entry barriers to the differentiated niche, create specific key factors for success and develop distinctive skills that ensure them a competitive advantage based on the mastery of these specific key factors for success[11]. Differentiation strategies are often based on technology because it is a powerful means of endowing the firm's offering with features that are unique and defensible against rivals' imitation attempts.

Exclusive Technology

Differentiation strategies based on the exclusive mastery of a technology or a set of technologies are those which generally give the firm the greatest competitive advantage[12]. There are numerous examples of firms which have been extremely successful at exploiting an exclusive technology. For instance, it was the development of nylon by DuPont de Nemours that ensured it considerable prosperity for many years. This was made possible by its monopoly position preserved through patents. When the patents expired, however, nylon prices dropped dramatically within a few months owing to fierce competition. The importance of nylon in the history and growth of

DuPont de Nemours was so significant that its top managers still talk about the existence of a "nylon syndrome" among the research teams, whose dream is said to be to repeat the achievement of the inventors of nylon, to the detriment of the development of less innovative products or processes that the firm could exploit more rapidly.

Similarly, Michelin benefited considerably from the development of a product, the radial tire, which was perceived as unique and valued by customers because of its superior performance; the important characteristics of this product were based on technologies and processes developed and patented by Michelin. We can also cite the case of Xerox whose creation, in 1959, and remarkable growth are due to the exploitation of an exclusive technology[13], or that of Polaroid which, using processes developed during the Second World War by Agfa in Germany and Gevaert in Belgium, succeeded in developing as early as 1948 instant processing photographic film. More importantly, Polaroid maintained its exclusive use of the technologies on which these new processes were based. Owing to the technologies it owns and protects with patents, Polaroid dominates an entire segment of the photography market, having ousted Kodak after a lawsuit that lasted ten years. Kodak was forced to offer to take back sixteen million instant cameras it had sold between 1976 and 1986 and to liquidate substantial facilities and equipment[14].

Differentiation based on technology and the improved performance that it makes possible are the cornerstones of the strategies of some firms over very long periods of time. Hughes Tool Company, which was founded in the early 1900s by Howard Hughes Sr (the father of the famous multimillionaire Howard Hughes Jr, who built his industrial and financial empire with funds derived from Hughes Tool) soon became the leading manufacturer of rock bits used in oil exploration; Hughes Tool's success owes to a major technological breakthrough, and the many innovations that followed have enabled it to retain its dominant position. The initial innovation was an invention by Howard Hughes himself—the rock bit with rotating cones whose durability (a crucial factor for drill operators because it allows the rock bits to be replaced less often, thus reducing the idle time which is very costly) was significantly better than that of the other existing twist drills. Hughes Tool later developed tri-cone rock bits which further increased the durability of the tools and the drilling speed. Because its technological innovations were protected by patents until the late 1950s, the corporation managed to secure an 80% share of the world's rock bit market up to 1960. Slackening R&D, and a relaxed policy towards patent infringements, however, allowed Hughes Tool's market share to fall to less than 50%. However, through the development of a new generation of products and greater vigilance regarding its patents, Hughes Tool has been able to regain a market share of 70–80%[15]. The improvement of Hughes Tool's products,

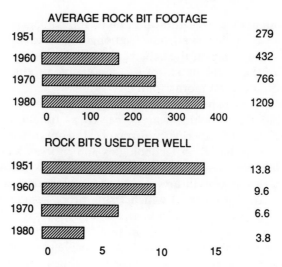

Figure 3.2 New technologies and performance improvement in oil drilling (Kistler and Galle 1982)

which was made possible by the use of more sophisticated technologies, is portrayed in Figure 3.2.

The strategy of Hughes Tool has been based for almost a century on technology, which has ensured its dominant position while allowing the firm to have a policy of high prices and large margins. Furthermore, Hughes Tool has always earmarked significant funds for technological research and development, and technology has played an equally important role in the firm's corporate culture, as we will analyze more extensively in Chapter 10.

Differentiation strategies based on technology as we define them here must be distinguished from "technology cluster strategies" which we will study in Chapter 6. Both types rely on the firm's technological skills; however, technology cluster strategies lead to diversification by using technology as the spearhead of entry into new businesses, whereas technology-based differentiation strategies aim at creating a sustainable competitive advantage in a given business by drawing upon technological superiority. In the case of Hughes Tool Company, although its dominant competitive position is the result of technological superiority, the corporation has not diversified extensively, but rather has leveraged its extensive knowledge of the oil business to maintain competitive advantage.

Key Factors for Differentiation

The logic of differentiation strategies based on technology is relatively easy to analyze; in practice, however, the implementation of such strategies poses some difficult questions and the decisions that need to be made are both critical and fraught with pitfalls. Two factors, in particular, which we have mentioned above are difficult to assess:

- *Imitability*—the true extent of the competitive advantage due to technology for the firm and the extent to which it is protected from imitation by other competitors.
- *Value*—the perception by customers of the product or service resulting from the utilization of the technology. This perception and the value associated with it governs both the price level that can be applied and the size of the potential market.

These two factors—the imitability of the advantage created by technology and the perceived value of the technology by customers—are two key factors governing the success of a differentiation strategy.

Imitability

For a viable differentiation strategy to be based on technology it is imperative that the competitive advantage created by the technology be sustainable. The specific nature of the product offering must thus be protected so that the firm is the only one to benefit from it[16]. When the key characteristics of the product or service result from technology, the firm must ensure its exclusive utilization of such technologies. There are two main ways of doing so: either the firm can maintain proprietary technological skills and know-how that no other competitor is capable of imitating, or it must seek the legal protection that patents confer.

The continuous improvement of *proprietary technological skills* is the 'natural' way for firms to create competitive advantage. The production of a technologically differentiated product requires many capabilities distributed among the different functions and organizational units composing the firm, with special emphasis upon the research staff or the research teams. These capabilities are often not formalized, resulting instead from the training and experience of key people and the organization as a whole. In many instances, the complex and tacit nature of these technological skills constitutes effective protection against imitation[11]. For example, the design and manufacture of the European Ariane launcher, which is one of the more sophisticated products of European high technology, involved very few patented technologies. The complexity of the system is such that it would be difficult for competitors to imitate it quickly.

In contrast, when differentiation is due to a technology or a set of technologies that are codified and formalized in a more precise way, imitation risks are greater and the issue of *legal protection* becomes more important[12]. In such cases, secrecy, provided it can be observed, can be an alternative to taking out a patent, and sometimes is the only possible option if the technology or know-how is not patentable. Secrecy, however, is not an effective means of protection when the technology can be understood and imitated by simply analyzing or "reverse-engineering" the product or service. This form of "competitor analysis" has been commonly used for a number of years in the automotive industry; Renault is said to have had its technicians dismantle several BMW and Mercedes models in order to learn things that would enable them to improve the reliability and quality of Renault automobiles. General Motors conducts similar analyses of all the Japanese cars sold on the American market. Even more methodically, Ford's R&D design teams went through a thorough examination of all existing car models on the market with the aim of introducing, at the design stage, the "best in class" technical characteristics found in the automobiles produced by competitors in its new Ford "Taurus" and Mercury "Sable" lines[17].

If a firm's technology is codified, readily understandable, and imitable by its competitors, then taking out a patent can be an effective way to afford protection. Such is the case with most formulas, recipes, and manufacturing processes. Generally, complex manufactured products consisting of many discrete parts and components are more difficult to protect with patents given the variety of ways that these can be assembled[18]. Additionally, the conditions for filing a patent are quite restrictive and further limit the cases where such legal means can be used as protection against imitation. To qualify for a patent, an invention must be new, constitute inventive activity, and have industrial applications[19]. A patent can be described as a contract signed between an inventor and society. The inventor agrees to reveal his invention, thereby improving the general level of science and technique, and, in exchange, society grants him the exclusive right to make use of his invention for a specific period of time (17 years in the United States). This legal monopoly granted to the inventor is justified by the need to compensate for the research effort that was made.

By granting a firm the exclusive right to make use of a technology, a patent is in total accord with the logic of differentiation strategies. Indeed, the aim is to create a monopoly situation in a given product niche. The patent institutionalizes this technological monopoly while at the same time setting a time limit. Some firms, however, manage to extend the differentiation strategy based on technology by planning the registration of patents in sequence such that one follows another, thus constantly conferring protection through the one patented subsequently.

The registration of patents by a firm allows it to grant other companies licenses; in other words, a patentee can grant, in exchange for a fee, other firms the right to make use of the invention or the technology it owns. In general, licenses involve restrictive conditions concerning the right to make use of the invention and where and in what fields it can be applied. The granting of licenses must be done with great care in the case of technologies which form the basis for differentiation, since competitors can often adapt the invention or apply it in new settings, thereby circumventing the patent and neutralizing the inventing firm's advantage.

While expensive and time consuming, patent infringement suits are an option where a technology has clearly been used illegally. When successful, such law suits often result in very stiff penalties. Since it lost a patent infringement suit against Polaroid, Kodak may have to pay its rival a penalty which, according to experts of the industry, could amount to over a billion dollars. Hughes Tool obtained, in 1985 and 1986, 135 million dollars from one competitor and 210 million dollars from another competitor which were both guilty of illegal use of technologies patented by Hughes; one of these competitors even went bankrupt because of the high penalties it had to pay Hughes.

Whatever the means a firm chooses to protect its technology, it must assess its effectiveness and strength critically. Indeed, its effectiveness will determine the viability of a differentiation strategy based on technology. The case of the British company, EMI, which invented the CT scanner, vividly exemplifies this: although it invented the scanner in the early 1970s, EMI was not able to create a sustainable strategic advantage. Major competitors, such as General Electric, which were better positioned in the USA, the main market for this kind of equipment, "leapfrogged" EMI by developing their own scanners; these were more successful than the EMI scanner which only dominated the market for a short period while it still had a monopoly. Ultimately, GE's superior sales and service organization combined with their ability to reverse engineer EMI's product and improve upon it proved too much for the initial technological advantage and patent position held by EMI[12].

It is clear from the above that a firm must not only find a reliable way to protect key technologies, but must also see to it that this protection is not bypassed. However, by using completely different technologies, some competitors may be able to give their products special attributes that are equivalent, or even more highly valued by customers. As we mentioned earlier, the very high level of technical sophistication of many Swiss watchmakers enabled them to manufacture the world's most reliable and precise watches for many years. However, the displacement of mechanical clockworks by electronic ones resulting in even greater precision, totally nullified—virtually overnight—the competitive advantage of the leading Swiss watchmaking firms which was based on technology.

While exclusive technological skill is indispensable to the successful execution of a technology-based differentiation strategy, it is also essential that the product features resulting from the technology be valued by customers.

Technology and Customer Value

Differentiation based on technology and the improved quality that it makes possible, can only be the cornerstone of a firm's strategy if the market, or a given segment of the market, perceives the quality and values it enough to pay a premium price. Thus, customer perception of value determines the size of the market and the price level at which the product or service will be attractive.

Customer perception and value are difficult to get a handle on in practice[20]. Indeed, many firms which thought their products were superior to those of their competitors have realized, often *a posteriori*, that customers did not see the difference and therefore were not willing to pay a higher price for characteristics they either were not aware of or did not value. For example, Texas Instruments, in the early 1980s, was engaged in heated competition with its rival Commodore in the emerging home computer market, but lost so much money that it eventually abandoned the market; yet Texas Instruments' microcomputers offered far greater performance in terms of capacity and speed of data processing than Commodore's machines and Texas Instruments thought it possessed a superior product. At the time, the home microcomputer market was still too new for average customers to perceive the value in TI's machine. Such performance differences were visible only to highly sophisticated customers. Since the differentiation attempt by Texas Instruments was neither perceived nor valued by most customers, competition could only focus on price. As a result, Texas Instruments' managers thought that a cost leadership and volume strategy would, in spite of everything, rescue the firm's position in the market; however, after severe price competition they realized that, owing to the initial attempt to differentiate their product, their costs were structurally higher than those of Commodore.

Concorde's commercial failure can, to a certain extent, also be interpreted as the result of differentiation based on technology which was not sufficiently valued by the market. The exceptional performance of the French–British supersonic aircraft carried such a high price that only a very limited fraction of the market was inclined to value it. The Concorde program has often been described as the most striking example of "technical drift" which appears to be a typical French failing, or at least, a common phenomenon in French high technology firms[21].

The tendency to use sophisticated technologies without taking the market's reaction into account is one of the pitfalls of the differentiation strategy based on technology. For the firm which initiates such innovation, the product's superiority is self-evident—the additional performance and service it provides are obvious and can only be highly valued by "intelligent" customers. This organizational egocentrism often leads firms to underestimate the difficulties customers have in perceiving the differentiation in new products. The commercial failure of Apple's "Lisa" microcomputer seems to be largely attributable to the firm's overestimation of how much the market would value the attributes of this new microcomputer.

Erroneous anticipation of customer perception and valuation of technology-based differentiation can have important consequences for the firm. In addition to higher variable costs, differentiation based on technology usually implies additional fixed costs, notably R&D costs; if a firm does not decide to write off these costs, it is forced to increase its prices in order to retrieve its investments on smaller production runs, thereby reducing the size of the market even further, starting a vicious circle of price increases and market shrinkage. Thus, while the value of a firm's product is based on many objective, quantifiable elements, it also contains a large subjective dimension that makes it difficult to assess. The value of a differentiated offering can be estimated using classical market survey techniques. This kind of estimate, however, must appraise both the market's perception of the offering as well as its valuation. As the products or services involved have attributes that are *a priori* unknown to the customers, carrying out market surveys can prove to be difficult and to pose specific methodological problems[22].

Provided that the quantitative data are available (often not the case), the value chain concept can be used to evaluate a differentiation strategy based on technology. Such a strategy is only appropriate if the differentiated aspects make it possible for the firm's offering to fit into the value chain of its customers. Technology can favorably affect this value chain in three ways:

- It can reduce the cost of the offering for the supplier and ultimately its price for the customer; in this case, the logic of the technology leads to the implementation of a cost leadership strategy.
- It can reduce the operating costs for the customer.
- It can increase the value of the offering, through higher performance.

These three factors are not necessarily mutually exclusive and can sometimes occur simultaneously. For instance, the use of composite materials in the manufacture of helicopter rotors, an innovation that was introduced by Aerospatiale and which was held exclusively by the corporation for several years, has made it possible both to increase the performance of such aircraft, in terms of reliability, and to reduce their operating and maintenance costs, thus providing users with greater value that compensates for higher prices.

In summary, differentiation based on technology is another type of competitive advantage that a firm can create using its technological skills and on which it can focus its strategy. Such a strategy, however, is not without risk since success requires that the advantage related to its technology be sustainable, so that the firm is not forced into price competition.

Furthermore, the differentiation resulting from the technology must be perceived and valued enough by customers to justify higher prices.

USING TECHNOLOGY TO DEFINE A "NEW GAME"

Cost leadership and differentiation strategies, which we have just examined, are strategies that fit within the framework of a given industry. Such strategies do not alter the definition of a business, nor the nature of the competitive environment. Rather, they aim at providing the firm with a competitive advantage in a business that is "stable" as far as its definition and the forces that shape competition within it. However, we showed in Chapter 2 that technological changes can, on the one hand, modify the limits of an industry and, on the other, alter the forces shaping competition within it. Often these technological changes, which affect the nature of competition in a given business, are not produced deliberately by one of the existing competitors— they affect all the firms of an industry in a similar way, even though some are better prepared to face them than others.

New-game strategies[23], in contrast, can be defined as deliberate attempts to modify the forces shaping competition and the definition of the business by particular competitors. The difference between spontaneous change in a firm's competitive environment and new-game strategies has less to do with the objective characteristics of the observed phenomena than with the attitude of the firm with respect to these phenomena. In the first case, changes are seen as external to the firm, requiring adaptation. In the second case, however, certain firms are responsible for the changes and have deliberately based their strategy on them. Such strategies alter the pace of the change, generally making it more rapid and direct the focus of change in ways that will best benefit the innovating firm(s).

Technology is one of the most important foundations for new-game strategies. Thus, by accelerating the pace of a given technology in an industry, a competitor with good capability in the technology reinforces its own competitive position. Such accelerated technological evolution increases the difficulty that other competitors have in adapting to it. By modifying the nature and the relative importance of the key factors for success in a given industry, the technological changes that are introduced by one or more of the firms can lead to favorable changes in the competitive environment. In an industry built upon high volume, new technologies that are introduced by some of the competitors that nullify or minimize the impact of scale can significantly alter the nature of the competitive environment by making size a drawback rather than an advantage. Thus, referring back to the examples of the advances achieved in small-scale steel production and new casting techniques for the production of aluminum that we developed in Chapter 2, these innovations were driven by the actions of a few relatively small competitors, the Italian iron and steel companies in the Brescia area (the so-called Bresciani companies). The changes that occurred in the competitive environment were thus the result of new-game strategies designed to change the rules of competition to their advantage: under the new rules, it was no longer a disadvantage to be a small producer.

As the above example suggests, new game-strategies are effective because they make it difficult for the dominant competitors to adapt quickly. By reducing the cost advantages of long production runs, the use of "just-in-time" management and flexible manufacturing technology can be, like other technological changes, the basis for a new-game strategy. This is particularly true in industries where long production runs have historically translated into lower costs[24]. The competitive impact of such strategies is especially strong when the other competitors cannot use the same type of equipment because it is not easily available, for lack of training, or for financial reasons.

TECHNOLOGY AND STRATEGIC ORIENTATION

The foregoing has shown us that firms can rely on technology to create a cost advantage. Firms can also use technology to produce a differentiated product which is less subject to price competition. However, beyond the two generic strategies we have discussed, technology can also foster a third type: the "new game" strategy.

Common to all three strategic orientations are several issues or concerns. Where do the technologies come from to fuel the firm's strategy? What is the nature of these technologies? What influence does a firm's current competitive position have upon the technologies used? What should the timing of adoption or entry be? Should the firm be a "leader" or a "follower"? Is it desirable to switch strategic orientations over time as the industry matures?

Sources of Technology

According to some experts[25] the source of the technologies implemented by firms impacts the size and nature of the competitive advantage they create. In the preceding chapter we discussed the two fundamental ways in which technology develops: technology push and market pull. Estimates based on empirical observations indicate that 20% of all innovations fall into the first category (they are the result of technology push) and 80% fall into the second category (they are pulled by the market); the same data indicate, however, that the commercial success of these two forms of innovation are quite different, with 80% of the successes resulting from technology push and 20% from market pull[25].

While these estimates—which are based on the judgments of experts rather than on thorough studies—must be considered with reservation, they do suggest that the competitive advantage derived from technology is much greater in the case of innovations resulting from technological break-throughs, than in the case of innovations that are implemented in response to identified market needs. This observation is not surprising since innovations resulting from fundamental technological change do not stem from capabilities shared by other firms in the industry and are therefore more difficult to imitate or acquire. Often, the most significant technological innovations are introduced by new competitors entering the industry.

The Nature of Technology

The nature of the firm's technologies also determines, to a large degree, the competitive strategy. Technologies which lower costs, without creating product differentiation, can only facilitate cost leadership strategies. The implementation of the float glass process, which we mentioned earlier, could only lead to a cost leadership strategy since it did not translate into any modification—except in terms of price—likely to differentiate the product in the eyes of the customer. In contrast, technologies which entail additional costs must endow the product or service with specific valued characteristics, and serve to promote differentiation strategies.

Some technologies can improve product performance while simultaneously lowering costs; such technologies often redefine industries, as was the case in the watchmaking industry, for example. Firms which manage to secure exclusive rights to such technologies have such a sizable advantage that it no longer makes sense to term the strategy cost leadership or differentiation, but rather *overall leadership*. Situations of this kind, which are more frequent than is commonly thought, can be found in very specialized industries where one firm has a worldwide monopoly.

Whether the firm is able to maintain exclusive rights to a technology is critical and, in a sense, determines the firm's strategy. When a firm can maintain its exclusive rights to a given technology, this can be the main competitive advantage upon which the firm bases its strategy, whether the technology minimizes costs or fosters differentiation. If, on the contrary, the competitive advantage created by the technology is not controllable, it must be used only to reinforce the firm's competitive position or to help it develop another source of advantage.

Technology and Competitive Position

The firm's competitive position partially determines the way in which technology is incorporated into the strategy-making process. Firms with a weak, or marginal, competitive position tend to use technology as a means of avoiding price and cost competition, and to create a sustainable niche. They can also, as we saw earlier, overcome the cost advantage enjoyed by the large incumbents in the industry by introducing technologies which make it possible to reduce costs without resorting to a volume strategy. Leading companies, in contrast, generally use technology as a means of reinforcing their position without changing the fundamental rules of the game. When technological change alters the key factors for success in an industry and nullifies the advantages of the leading competitors, it is not unusual to see dominant firms which, although they may have developed the new technology, attempt to prevent or slow the rate of the technology's diffusion. Thus, after having succeeded in imposing its VHS standard on the industry, Matsushita, the world's largest VCR manufacturer, strongly opposed the adoption of the new 8 mm standard, although it was more efficient and allowed for a significant reduction in the size of VCRs; it did so in order to maintain its dominant position and to recoup its investments over a longer period of time.

Because it may disrupt the nature of competition in a given industry, a new technology which modifies the key factors for success tends to be perceived as a strategic opportunity by marginal competitors, and as a threat by the leading competitors, even if they are the ones which developed the new technology.

Technological Leaders and Followers

Some analysts maintain[5,25] that the slow reaction of industry incumbents to the emergence of new technologies is a dangerous behavior which often contributes to their decline; indeed, the existence of technological limits (see Chapter 4) clearly indicates that the improvements to be expected from an existing technology are generally limited compared with that of a new technology. In such situations, a competitive advantage based on an older technology will rapidly decline when a newer, substitute technology is developed. However, the strategic shortsightedness of firms, including major corporations, with respect to these new technologies is often the cause of their demise.

Failing to sense the vast potential of electronic technology, NCR (National Cash Register), the leader in the electromechanical cash register market, was faced with difficulties created by new entrants such as Burroughs, which possessed electronic technologies. Most of the major firms in the vacuum tube industry in the 1950s, such as RCA, General Electric and Westinghouse, underestimated the importance of the transistor, and later the integrated circuit, and were rapidly obsoleted when these technologies became widespread, because they failed to internalize the new competence in time.

The main advantage of being the technological leader—the firm which is first to implement a new technology—is the ability to shape both the technical and the commercial environments in which the new technology develops[5]. The technological leader often sets the standards to which followers will have to conform, or try to circumvent; in addition, the leader creates a favorable corporate image for itself and, from the outset, occupies a dominant position on the experience curve that characterizes the new technology. When the leader also provides a product or service that is valued by the customer, it has achieved initial differentiation, which allows it to implement a high margin policy.

While the principle of "the attacker's advantage" has been proposed as a "rule" with regard to innovation[5], other authors[26] emphasize that, although a firm derives clear advantage from being a "pioneer," this strategy also entails significant risks. The technological leader must assume the substantial technical risks involved in major technological innovation (the cost, delay, and uncertainty associated with technological development) as well as the market risks (serving customers whose reaction is difficult to anticipate). Furthermore, technological leaders risk being caught on the wrong technological trajectory, committing specialized assets to products and processes that ultimately miss the mark. In contrast, technological followers can sometimes take advantage of the market created by the leader without having to bear the costs of the development of the technology and of the launch of the innovation. By delaying entry, incumbents with industry-specialized supporting assets (e.g. manufacturing, distribution) can also take advantage of the early mistakes made by pioneers, entering later with both superior product and organizational resources.

Despite the risks, some technological "pioneers" have indeed succeeded in their quest to establish a new business position. This was the case, for example, with Boeing and its decision to equip its B-707 aircraft with jet engines, thereby acquiring the dominant position which it still occupies. It was also the case of Minolta which, by launching the first autofocus reflex camera in 1985, stole the leading position from Canon, and saw its market share increase from less than 30% to more than 40% in less than two years; Canon, in contrast, which introduced the autofocus technology in its cameras only in 1987, saw its market share decrease from 40% to 22% within the same period[27].

However, many "pioneering" firms end up like their counterparts on the American prairie—face down with arrows in their backs! Indeed, many technological leaders have been overtaken by followers which now occupy more favorable competitive positions. For example, Philips, which invented the compact disc and was the pioneer of this product, is still the leader in the European market but has lost its dominant world position to Sony and Matsushita. Similarly, RCA, which launched the VCR, has remained in the business only as an importer and retailer of VCRs manufactured by Matsushita. Lastly, in the microcomputer industry, IBM, the world leader, entered the market several years after Apple and other competitors but now faces the threat of even more followers, the clone manufacturers.

These examples indicate that it is senseless to blindly advocate either a technological leader strategy or a technological follower strategy. As we will see in the next chapter, these policies should only be adopted in light of a number of factors—notably the firm's technological position, its market position, and the growth potential of the industry.

The "attacker's advantage" slogan makes sense provided it is interpreted as the firm's continuous technological evolution, which enables it to move from mature technologies to those earlier in the life cycle when strategic considerations require it. For example, Sony and Matsushita which have a dominant position in the compact disc player market will both shortly launch DAT players which could cannibalize compact disc sales. This clearly reveals their offensive behavior with respect to technology: to be a successful technological leader, a firm must make its own products obsolete *before* competitors do.

Competitive Dynamics

Although the firm's strategy depends on several factors, it is not etched in stone; rather, it will vary with the changes in the industry's key factors for success and the relative advantage that its technology represents. Two types of competitive behavior with respect to technology can be observed:

- switching from a differentiation strategy based on a technological advantage to a cost leadership strategy based on scale, accumulated experience and a dominant market position[28];
- constant effort to innovate and improve technology, thereby maintaining a dynamic competitive advantage[2].

Firms displaying the first type of strategic behavior are generally those which have been able to attain a dominant position because of exclusive technology. As their technology becomes diffused over time, however, they tend to resort to competitive advantage based upon their accumulated experience, good reputation and distribution network. For instance, when the production of nylon was no longer protected by patents and DuPont de Nemours ceased to have the exclusive right to produce this material, its accumulated experience, dominant market position, and reputation replaced the exclusive technology as a source of competitive advantage.

During the period when a firm controls an exclusive technology, it can easily recoup its investment through high prices; by the time this technology becomes more widely dispersed, such investments are a significant entry barrier, since prices tend to fall dramatically with the advent of new entrants. The end of DuPonts' nylon monopoly, for example, led to a significant drop in price. However, the firm still managed to retain its dominant position and a good level of profitability in the business, since it had recouped its initial investment many times over.

The second type of strategic behavior for firms confronted with the erosion of their technology-based competitive advantage is a sustained effort to improve or even "reinvent" their technology; rather than "milking" their initial technological advantage, such firms choose to create a new competitive advantage through technological innovation. The helicopter division of Aerospatiale thus successively introduced turbine engines and, once these had become a standard feature and were also used by the competition, rotor blades made of composite materials. Each of these technological breakthroughs enabled Aerospatiale to avoid facing direct price competition by offering more expensive but more sophisticated products. Rather than turning its initial technical advantage into a cost advantage, Aerospatiale, which holds a 20–25% share of the world helicopter market, directed its efforts at the constant improvements of its technology to maintain its competitive edge. Hughes Tool is another example of a firm with a dominant position in the drilling equipment industry (holding a 50–70% share of the world market) which has always followed a differentiation strategy through successive technology advances.

While the strategies of firms can thus change over time, a clear strategic direction is indispensable to success. In addition, the transition from one strategy to another is a very difficult and risky undertaking, since it requires a complete re-orientation of the firms' efforts and radically different patterns of resource allocation. As we have seen, technology is often a major factor behind both differentiation and cost leadership strategies. It is also a critical factor in "new-game" strategies.

CONCLUSION

Technology is one of the main sources of competitive advantage. It can lower costs through scale or experience. Technology can also contribute to the differentiation of the firm's products or services, becoming the foundation of a differentiation strategy enabling the firm to avoid direct price competition. Lastly, technological change plays a crucial role in new-game strategies where firms deliberately change the rules to their advantage by modifying the forces shaping competition in the industry. Technology plays a significant role in strategy-making, and the selection of technologies by the firm is a task which must be done with great care. The aim of the next chapter is to examine the analytical tools and techniques which can be used to assist the firm in the technology selection process, and to discuss the importance of a coherent technological strategy.

NOTES AND REFERENCES

1. B. Henderson, *Henderson on Corporate Strategy*, Cambridge: Abt Books, 1979; B. Hedley, "A Fundamental Approach to Strategy Development", *Long Range Planning*, December 1976; G. Hall and S. Howell, "The Experience Curve from the Economist's Perspective", *Strategic Management Journal*, **6**, 1985.
2. M. Imai, *Kaizen*, New York: Random House, 1986.
3. M. Porter, *Competitive Strategy*, New York: Free Press, 1980.
4. R. Hayes, S. Wheelwright, and K. Clark, *Dynamic Manufacturing: Creating the Learning Organization*, New York: Free Press, 1988.
5. G. Stalk and T. Hout, *Competing Against Time*, New York: Free Press, 1990.
6. A. Martinet, *Strategie*, Paris: Vuibert, 1983, pp. 98–99.
7. R. Foster, *Innovation: the Attacker's Advantage*, New York, NY: Summit Books, 1986.
8. M. Porter, "Technology and Competitive Advantage," *Journal of Business Strategy*, winter 1985; M. Keller, *Rude Awakening*, New York: Harper, 1989.
9. M. Porter, *Competitive Advantage*, New York: Free Press, 1985.
10. K. Ishikawa and D. Lu, *What is Total Quality Control?*, Englewood Cliffs: Prentice-Hall, 1985.
11. H. Itami, *Mobilizing Invisible Assets*, Cambridge: Harvard University Press, 1987.
12. D. Teece, "Profiting from Technological Innovation: Implications for Integration, Collaboration, Licensing and Public Policy," in D. Teece (Ed.), *The Competitive Challenge*, Cambridge: Ballinger Publishing, 1987.
13. G. Jacobson and J. Hillkirk, *Xerox: American Samourai*, New York, NY: Macmillan, 1986.
14. "Polaroid vs Kodak: the Decisive Round", *Business Week*, January 13, 1986; P. Taylor, T. Dodsworth and E. Williams, "Kodak Looks for a New Exposure," *Financial Times*, January 22, 1986.
15. W. Kistler and E. Galle, "Improved Rock Bit Technology Reduces Drilling Cost", Hughes Tool Company publication; R. Felsman, "Inventions, Patterns and Progress at Hughes," Hughes Tool Company publication, 1982.
16. E. Von Hipple, "Appropriability of Innovation Benefit as a Predictor of the Source of Innovation," *Research Policy*, **11**, 1982; R. Levin, W. Cohen, and D. Mowery, "R&D Appropriability, Opportunity, and Market Structure," *Issues in the Economics of R&D*, May 1985.
17. "How Ford Hit the Bull's Eye with Taurus," *Business Week*, June 30, 1986.
18. E. Von Hipple, *The Sources of Innovation*, New York: Oxford University Press, 1988.
19. See among others: R. Levin, "A New Look at the Patent System," *R&D, Innovation, and Public Policy*, May 1986.
20. S. Craig, "Seeking Strategic Advantage with Technology: Focus on Customer Value!," *Long Range Planning*, April 1986.
21. J. J. Salomon, *Le Gaulois, Le Cow-Boy et le Samourai*, Paris: Economica, 1986.
22. D. Ford and C. McKenna, "Market Positioning in High Technology," *California Management Review*, **3**, 1984; W. Shanklin and J. Ryans, *Marketing High Technology*, Lexington: Lexington Books, 1985.
23. R. Buaron, "New Game Strategies," *The McKinsey Quarterly*, spring 1981.
24. For an excellent discussion of this issue, see: J. Womack, D. Jones, and D. Roos, *The Machine that Changed the World*, New York: Rawson Associates, 1990.

25. R. Foster, *Innovation: The Attacker's Advantage*, New York: Summit Books, 1986; E. Von Hipple, "Lead Users: A Source of Novel Product Concepts," *Management Science*, July 1986.
26. W. Mitchell, "Whether and When? Probability and Timing of Incumbents' Entry into Emerging Technical Subfields," *Administrative Science Quarterly*, **34**, 1989; W. Mitchell, "Dual Clocks: Entry Order Influences on Incumbent and Newcomer Market Share and Survival when Specialized Assets Retain Their Value," *Strategic Management Journal*, **12**, 1991; M. Porter, *Competitive Strategy*, New York: Free Press, 1980, Chapter 5.
27. "Canon Finally Challenges Minolta's Mighty Maxxum," *Business Week*, March 2, 1987.
28. See, for example: W. Abernathy and J. Utterback, "Patterns of Industrial Innovation," *Technology Review*, June–July 1978.

Chapter 4

Technological Strategy: Analytical Tools

Technology is a factor which affects most aspects of the firm's strategy and its impact must therefore be taken into account in all the stages of the strategy-making process. Technology is indeed essential in the first of these stages, strategic segmentation, which aims at identifying the relevant business units on which strategy will be based. Moreover, technology directly affects the value of businesses as well as the forces that structure competition; as we saw in Chapter 3, technology is also one of the main sources of competitive advantage. In addition, technology can be an appropriate diversification lever where the firm enters new businesses because it has the technological skills they require.

This chapter discusses the principal tools and techniques developed to link the selection of technologies with the formulation of strategy. The first section of the chapter deals with the use of technological forecasting methods. The limits of forecasting are discussed and the use of "scenario" methods are then considered. The second section illustrates how a firm can conduct its own technology "audit"—the identification and evaluation of technological capabilities. The chapter closes with a discussion of how these techniques facilitate the strategic management of technology.

FORECASTING: THE ANALYSIS OF TECHNOLOGICAL TRENDS

A survey conducted in the early 1980s showed that, in most of the Fortune 1000 companies, top management was well aware of the increasing strategic importance of technology, and of the difficulty of preparing their firms to compete in an environment where technology is a prevailing factor[1]. This awareness, however, seems to have paradoxical consequences: the survey identified a strong discrepancy between the perceived importance of technology and the attention it was given by top managers. Except for a small minority, the surveyed firms were headed by managers who viewed technology as essential but difficult to manage, and spent most of their time dealing with marketing or financial issues. Technology decisions were delegated to lower level executives associated with the R&D or Engineering functions. Under such conditions, it is unlikely that technology can be managed strategically. Top managers are not involved in technology decisions, while technology specialists do not participate in the strategy-making process. This implies that technology is seen as an external factor over which the firm has little control. The management of technology is thus limited to the anticipation of technological changes and their impact on the firm's businesses, whether these changes are produced by the firm itself or originate in its external environment. Decision-makers are often only concerned with the question: How will a given technology evolve within a certain time span?

Methods designed to predict the future of a given technology have been designed to answer such a question. Some of them are based on the extrapolation of past trends, in which case they fall into the category of forecasting methods. Others, in contrast, envisage technological discontinuities and entail the use of scenarios. Traditionally, most firms have relied on such methods to manage technology, limiting themselves implicitly to the anticipation of technological change. It was not until recently that decisions regarding technology have been integrated in the overall strategy-making process, leading to the development of methods aimed at improving the strategic management of technology.

Principles of Forecasting

A forecast is a prediction of how a given variable will evolve within a certain time frame, associated with the probability of that prediction actually materializing. It is generally a quantified evaluation made on the basis of past trends and within the limits of particular conditions[2]. Technological forecasting is a quantitative method aimed at predicting some of the future characteristics of a technology, such as its levels of performance (speed, capacity, temperature, precision, etc.). Forecasting does not anticipate how this performance can be achieved. The forecaster's mission is not to invent or improve technologies, but rather to forecast how and when technological change will enhance performance—which is generally measured in physical terms. However, forecasting can provide insights into the impact of technologies which have not yet been developed, but without specifying the means by which the predicted performance will be achieved[3].

Forecasting methods are quite varied: mathematical extrapolation, econometric models, forecasting by analogy, expert opinions, etc. We do not intend to describe these methods since this is done in a much more complete way by the authors noted above; rather, we will examine why, however sophisticated and useful at times, they are not fully adequate tools for the strategic management of technology.

The Limits of Technological Forecasting

One significant limitation of the main forecasting methods is the overemphasis put on quantitative variables used to elaborate econometric models and the lack of consideration given to qualitative factors which are often essential in management situations. Forecasting methods are most useful where identifiable trends can be described with linear regression equations or time series analysis, for example. However, as far as technological evolution is concerned, it is usually not possible to identify such trends, discontinuities being the rule rather than the exception. Even in the semiconductor industry, where clear patterns have been observed over the past two decades—the capacity of memory chips was increased ten-fold while the cost of storing one unit of information was cut by a factor of three—the development of very large scale integration (VLSI) technology is improving performance at a pace which is difficult to predict.

Technological discontinuities destroy the very bases of forecasting by upsetting existing trends. They do not compromise the internal validity of forecasting models, but rather the interpretations made of the results produced by such models. In fact, forecasters should only make statements with the caveat "provided a given set of conditions are met, the outcome can be anticipated in the following terms." This almost always means: "provided past trends continue in the future." In practice, this restriction tends to be ignored, allowing the results of the forecast to acquire a validity they do not actually possess[4]. Decision-makers often consider only the quantified results of forecasting and tend to overlook the restrictive assumptions the models contain; they feel reassured by the highly mathematical appearance of the models. The very structure of forecasting models may, however, be totally altered by technological changes, if these call into question the basic assumptions on which the models are built.

Complementing mathematical forecasting methods with expert opinions does not eliminate the above-mentioned limitations. Indeed, it has been observed that experts tend to arrive at similar conclusions by extrapolating past or present trends, especially in the case of methods that induce them to agree on a common forecast, such as the Delphi method[5]. This method consists of consulting each expert several times on the same subject; from the second consultation onward, experts are given descriptions of the opinions expressed in the previous round, including the central tendency (median) and dispersion of the responses. The iterations are aimed at making the opinions of the experts converge, but the latter do not consult each other in this process. Rather, they are informed in each round on how the overall opinion of the group is evolving. Thus, if the committee of experts is asked to forecast when a particular level of technological performance will be achieved, the responses given are distributed around a median date, with the distribution getting narrower after each round (see Figure 4.1).

Sometimes, the opinions converge towards an erroneous answer, notably in cases where the future does not materialize as past trends would seem to indicate. Only phenomena that already exist, whether in an explicit or latent form, can be forecast. As a result, there is a long history of erroneous forecasts. It must be recalled, for example, that in the late 1970s forecasts predicted that in less than ten years teaching would be replaced by computer technology[6]. Ironically, a decade earlier, the French Planning Commission had forecast that by 1975 the country would be using only a few hundred computers, while in fact more than 30000 were being used by that time[7].

In short, the main limitation of technological forecasting is that it fails to

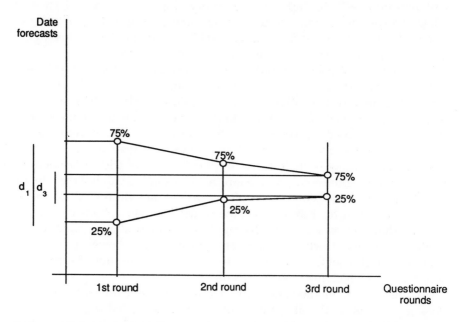

Figure 4.1 Convergence of expert opinions in the Delphi method; the percentages represent the proportion of experts who forecast an earlier date than the one on the ordinate axis (Adapted from Mahieux 1978)

consider discontinuities which alter past trends. Indeed, technological innovations do not result only from incremental improvements; rather, they are often produced by radical changes.

Anticipating Technological Discontinuities

Technological discontinuities, which are difficult to anticipate with forecasting methods, can be taken into account in two different ways. A firm can try to create a discontinuity by actively managing the innovation process internally, or it can prepare itself for discontinuities originating in its environment by generating contrasting scenarios of potential technological changes. These two approaches are compatible and can be used simultaneously. They depart from the deterministic style of forecasting methods, since they rely on creativity and innovation for the management of technology.

The Management of Innovation

Methods for the management of innovation consist of a set of more or less formalized techniques that fall into two broad categories: creativity enhancement and value analysis. Creativity methods (brainstorming, nominal group technique, synectics, etc.) aim at stimulating, in a systematic manner, the capacity to envision and articulate alternative futures. In fact, they consist more of group process techniques than of analytical tools and are oriented toward the generation of new ideas, deliberately ignoring the constraints existing in the firm's environment[8].

Value analysis techniques can be used to induce technological innovation. They are based on an in-depth analysis of all the component parts of an industrial product and their cost. Each part is examined in detail and its function as well as its physical characteristics and the way it is manufactured (materials, manufacturing methods, finishing, standardization, labor, supplies, etc.) are reviewed. These characteristics are then analyzed in order to find possibilities of improvement or cost reduction. Value analysis is primarily used in manufacturing, but it can also serve to focus R&D effort. It can therefore guide and rationalize technological innovation, rather than only stimulating invention as creativity techniques do. Indeed, "value" is analyzed on the basis of a function/cost ratio which makes it possible to assess a technical improvement. This method can help establish the criteria according to which potential technological innovations will be evaluated and screened.

Thus, creativity techniques facilitate the identification of radical technological changes, whereas value analysis promotes and helps evaluate more incremental improvements. These methods, however, only address the internal dimension of technological change. They do not take into account the firm's environment, its competitors, and potential external sources of technology. The scenario method, in contrast, focuses on the external factors which may produce technological changes.

The Scenario Method

The scenario method was developed to compensate for the limitations of forecasting methods. Instead of predicting in a purely deterministic way, it leads to the formulation of a set of alternative futures and the evaluation of their impact on the company[9]. The scenario method consists of envisaging all possible future trajectories, or scenarios, taking into account the trends of the past as well as the behavior of all participating actors. Each scenario—or set of coherent hypotheses—can be estimated quantitatively, in other words forecasted. Thus, the scenario method can be distinguished from forecasting insofar as it envisages several possible futures, instead of one single probabilistic trajectory[10] (see Figure 4.2).

The scenario method uses forecasting techniques to elaborate the various scenarios considered. Furthermore, these forecasts can be drawn up on the basis of expert opinions. In other words, the scenario method integrates forecasting methods which it uses to generate possible outcomes in a simulation process[10]. The consideration of contrasting and mutually exclusive scenarios makes it possible to imagine technological discontinuities and changes which are not identifiable from past and present trends. Some of the

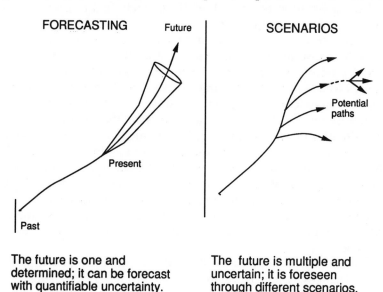

FORECASTING   Future | **SCENARIOS**

Potential
paths

Present

Past

The future is one and
determined; it can be forecast
with quantifiable uncertainty.

The future is multiple and
uncertain; it is foreseen
through different scenarios.

Figure 4.2   Forecasting versus scenarios (Adapted from Godet 1985)

Table 4.1 The limitations of forecasting and the contributions of the scenario method (Source: Godet 1983[11]. Reproduced by permission of *Economica*.)

	Limits of forecasting	Characteristics of the scenario method
Vision	Fragmented, "all other things being equal"	General, "no other things being equal"
Variables	Quantitative, objective and known	Qualitative, quantifiable or not, objective, known or unknown
Linkages	Statistical, constant structures	Dynamic, evolutionary structures
Explanation	The past explains the future	The future is the raison d'être of the present
Future	One and determined	Multiple and uncertain
Method	Deterministic and quantitative (econometric and mathematical models)	Intentional analysis, qualitative models (structural analysis), stochastic models (cross impact models)
Attitude with respect to the future	Passive or adaptive (future accepted)	Active and creative (desired future)

advantages of the scenario method compared with forecasting are listed in Table 4.1. The most significant advantage of the scenario method is that it allows for the elaboration of multiple possible futures, examining their respective consequences for the firm.

Thus, this method helps the firm prepare for the consequences of many potential futures and not only the scenario that seems most likely. Incremental scenarios are easy to forecast with traditional methods. This is not the case, however, with radical scenarios which, though they seem less likely, contemplate technological discontinuities. Such scenarios aid in understanding the futures that could have the greatest competitive impact. Indeed, what is important in anticipating technological changes is less identifying the paths that are probable than preparing for less predictable radical changes that may totally upset the bases of competition and create the most significant threats or opportunities for the firm.

THE TECHNOLOGY AUDIT

Managing technology strategically implies going beyond the anticipation of technological change and combining the external and reactive approach of forecasting and scenario methods with the internal and proactive perspective of management of innovation. The strategic management of technology is not so much the anticipation of technological change as it is the determination of how technology can be used to create competitive advantage. This requires taking into account both the firm's technological environment as well as its own technical capabilities, and integrating decisions regarding technology into the overall strategy formulation process.

Before selecting technologies to develop and formulating technological strategies, a firm must inventory the technologies it already possesses and assess the strengths and weaknesses these entail. This requires identifying all the technologies of the firm and evaluating relative technological capabilities; a competitive typology of technologies can then be drawn by critically analyzing such capabilities in a strategic perspective. Lastly, taking the life cycle of technologies into account puts the technological audit in a dynamic perspective, leading to the elaboration of the firm's technology portfolio.

Inventorying Technological Assets

Every product incorporates a number of distinct and identifiable technologies[13]. Thus, integrating technology into the strategy formulation process requires that all the technologies used in a given business be identified. Reviewing all technologies in the different businesses, as well as those it has but does not yet use, provides the firm with an inventory of its technological assets[14].

While doing the inventory of the firm's technological capabilities seems to be an obvious and common-sense step, it is surprising that a great number of firms are not aware of the technologies they possess or the extent of their capabilities. This lack of awareness contrasts with the accurate knowledge the same firms have of their tangible assets (real estate, facilities, equipment, etc.) and financial assets[15]. Thus, the CEO of a major corporation stated that "The firm's technological capabilities are not listed among the assets in its balance sheet, but they weigh significantly in its revenues"[16]. The ignorance concerning the firm's technological assets is partly due to the fact that they are integrated in the skills of the staff and employees, and blended into the human capital of the firm which is difficult to quantify. This situation is exemplified by the extreme case where the resignation of an engineer or the dismantling of a technical team suddenly deprives the firm of an important part of its technological skills.

Taking the inventory of the firm's technological assets is a difficult task because the technologies themselves are complex and because the degree of detail with which such a task can be carried out is extremely variable. We are faced with a problem similar to that of the strategic segmentation process: to determine the relevant degree of detail for dividing the firm's capability into "technologies." In this context, the identification and inventory of the firm's technologies can only be carried out with the active collaboration of the units which have developed or which implement such technologies.

Despite these difficulties, the inventory of the firm's technological assets is necessary for the subsequent steps of the analysis; it can also be useful in itself. Indeed, this inventory reveals some of the technologies that the businesses require but that the firm does not possess, perhaps drawing upon external sources instead. The technological inventory may also reveal potential applications of a firm's technologies. Lastly, the comparison of the technologies of the firm with those of its competitors can identify technological gaps, or enable the firm to identify some of its competitors' weaknesses. The technological inventory of the firm is not, however, an end in itself. It is of little use if it does not lead to an evaluation of the competitive impact of the different technologies.

Mapping Technology Types

The preceding chapter clearly showed that the different technologies implemented in a given business do not all have the same competitive impact. The mastery of some of them is a condition for success in the business, because of their implications for cost and differentiation, whereas the contribution of others is less important, either because their impact on differentiation or on the cost of the product is low, or because they are easily accessed by all the competitors in the industry. In short, the competitive impact of technologies is related to how much they affect the cost and the performance of the products in which they are integrated; it is also related to how easily all the firms in the industry can benefit from them, either by internalizing the technology, or by calling upon external suppliers. In the automotive industry, for example, the technologies used for model design, the automation of manufacturing, electronic control of functions, and new materials, have a higher competitive impact than the technologies of emission control or metallurgy.

Several classification systems for technologies (emphasizing the size of their competitive impact) have been developed. The consulting firm, Arthur D. Little, classifies technologies into three categories: base, key and pacing[13].

Base technologies are those which are extensively used in a given business. In many cases, skills in base technologies are what enabled firms to enter a business but today no longer provide a competitive advantage; they are readily available and all the competitors possess them. Thus, in the photography industry, the processing and use of silver bromide to produce sensitive surfaces, which initially enabled Kodak to develop photography, is now a common process used by all the firms in this industry. The mastery of base technologies is necessary for the firm to enter and remain in the business. However, this mastery is not a significant source of competitive advantage; it can at best help prevent firms which lack it from entering the business.

Key technologies are those which, for the time being, have the highest competitive impact. In other words, they are a driving force of competition and the strength of competitors in such technologies is reflected in their competitive position. The mastery of key technologies is therefore one of the distinctive and indispensable skills required for firms to succeed in a given business. The use of composite materials (fiberglass, carbon fiber, graphite, etc.), has become a key factor of success for tennis racket manufacturers; the corresponding technologies are thus key technologies in this business. In the 1980s, Donnay, one of the leading firms in this industry (which sponsored the world's number one player at the time, Bjorn Borg) went bankrupt because it was too slow in shifting from wood to composite materials, while its competitors had already made the transition. In 1988, Donnay was taken over by Bernard Tapie, a famous French entrepreneur, who tried to revitalize the firm by stressing the use of new technologies and sponsoring André Agassi.

Pacing technologies are those in the development stage which still do not have many applications and whose utilization in a given business is marginal. However, such technologies would seem to have important potential, and some of them are likely to become key technologies eventually. The implementation of pacing technologies involves risk because their reliability, their efficiency, and the way they affect costs and performance are still virtually unknown. The transition from laboratory testing or production in limited numbers to large-scale production is critical. The duration of the development phase as well as its impact on the cost of the technologies are particularly difficult to assess. Thus, in the electronics industry, there was much talk, between 1980 and 1985, about magnetic bubble memories, which proved to be much less successful than expected. Similarly, the substitution of gallium arsenide for silicon in semiconductors—as silicon itself had replaced germanium in the late sixties—which was seen as imminent by a large number of experts, is, for the time being, limited to certain specific applications, notably military equipment, because of costs that are too high for consumer goods applications. In 1989, supersonic propeller aircraft engines appeared as a pacing technology, the development of which will be a decisive element in the fierce competition between aircraft engine manufacturers (Pratt & Whitney, Rolls Royce, SNECMA, MTU and, particularly, General Electric, which seems to be one step ahead of the other competitors), and also between airframe manufacturers such as Boeing, McDonnell-Douglas and Airbus, whose designs must be adapted to accommodate new engines. The future of this type of engine and its diffusion in the aircraft industry is, however, far from assured. Besides technical considerations, success depends on such factors as the change in the price of fuel. Investments devoted to the engine's development or to the development of aircraft to be equipped with it are, therefore, very risky.

It is important to note that it is not so much the specific characteristics of a technology which make it possible to classify it in one of the above categories, but rather the competitive role it plays within a given business. A technology can thus be a base technology in one business, a key technology in another business, and a pacing technology in a third business; such is the case, for example, with computer-aided design and manufacture in the aerospace, the automotive, and the textile industries, respectively.

Other authors propose different technology classifications but generally emphasize the distinction between base technologies and the other technologies, termed "differentiation technologies." Although they are not always readily available, the former are required for the firm to enter and remain in the business, whereas the latter are those that define the difference between competitors[14].

The classifications of technologies which we have described provide only a static image of the firm's situation, of its competitive environment and technological capabilities; however, the competitive impact of technology

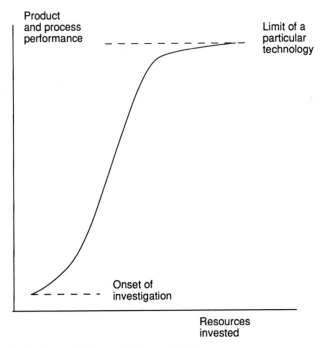

Figure 4.3   Technology of life cycle (Foster 1986)

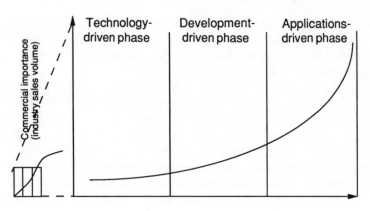

	Tool development	Product and process development	Application development
Effort on	Research	Development	Marketing
Key characteristics	Questions unknown	Questions clear answers unknown	Answers emerging
Key factors for success	Proximity to academia/ freedom to fail	Concentration of resources	Applications know-how

Figure 4.4 Strategic phases in the deployment of new technologies (Adapted from Hunsicker 1985)

can change over time. In order to take this phenomenon into account and analyze this issue in a more dynamic perspective, it is essential to examine the life cycle of technologies.

Technology Life Cycles

As we saw above, forecasts concerning the likely development of technologies can be a great aid to firms in the technology selection process. To a certain extent, scenario methods are designed to address this need. However, such methods remain far removed from the problems of strategic management. A tool which is useful as a guide to technology resource allocation is that of the technology life cycle, inspired from the concept of product life cycles, used in marketing, and business life cycles, used in strategic planning models. Indeed, the development of a technology seems to follow an "S-shaped" curve[17,18] where, instead of sales or revenues, the vertical axis represents the performance level of the technology (see Figure 4.3).

In the first phase of the development of a technology, the firm must invest heavily for some time before it can actually see any results. This initial phase is marked by trial-and-error experimentation and is characterized by the limited effectiveness of the applications resulting from the technology compared with the resources allocated for its development. This phase can be analyzed in a more detailed manner as shown in Figure 4.4[19].

In the second phase, the firm has gathered a certain amount of information, knowledge and know-how about the technology. Progress therefore accelerates rapidly and translates into an increase in the number and the effectiveness of the applications; additional investments thus produce greater performance improvements.

In the third and last phase of the development of a technology, improvements resulting from technological investments become progressively smaller. In other words, to achieve a given level of performance improvement, the firm must make increasingly heavy investments. This slowing down is due to the fact that the physical or chemical limits of the technology are being approached. Thus, the weight of an airframe is ultimately determined by the physical characteristics, notably the strength, of the materials used; similarly, the capacity of an electronic chip is limited by the molecular structure of the semiconductor material used (germanium, silicon, gallium arsenide, etc.).

The firm's ability to classify its technologies according to the stages of the life cycle has important strategic implications: it enables the firm to determine whether it should continue to invest in particular technologies or shift to others. Indeed, when a technology approaches its natural limits, even the smallest performance improvement will require significant investment which would probably produce greater payoff if allocated to the development of other technologies lower on the S-curve. This observation is important because it implies that firms should not systematically allocate R&D budgets to teams or units working on the improvement of existing technologies; zero-base budgeting should be the rule in terms of R&D resource allocation, which should be determined on the basis of each technology's remaining potential for improvement. It is possible to determine, more or less, the limits of most technologies by soliciting the opinions of fundamental research specialists in the specific areas. Moreover, within the firm, a number of signals suggest when the development process of a technology reaches its natural limits. These signals are[18]:

- a noticeable decline in the productivity of R&D departments;
- a trend towards missed deadlines on the part of such departments;

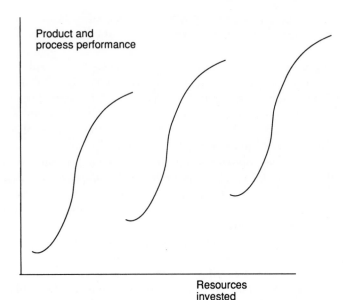

Figure 4.5   Managing technological evolution (A. D. Little 1981)

- a trend towards process rather than product improvement;
- the emergence of competitors which have chosen radically different technological alternatives;
- little difference in terms of performance between competitors, despite significant variations in technology expenditure.

One of the best examples, also developed by R. Foster[18], of firms overinvesting in a technology approaching its limits is that of the shipbuilding industry, which, at the beginning of the twentieth century, invested heavily to improve the performance of merchant sailing ships so as to combat the competitive threat from those which had converted to steamships. Steam propulsion offered greater performance potential than sail propulsion because of the natural limits of the underlying technologies. This potential had been almost exhausted in the case of sail propulsion, but it was still promising in the case of steam propulsion. In terms of the development phases of technologies we described above, sail propulsion was in the third phase of its development, while steam propulsion was only in the first phase, or at the beginning of the second phase.

Thus, technological change would be perfectly managed by the firm which followed a process which could be represented as in Figure 4.5[19]. The R&D investment priorities which make it possible for the firm to best manage this technological evolution and shift from one technology to another are represented in Figure 4.6[13]. Inventorying the firm's technological assets,

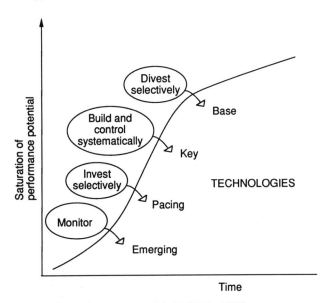

Figure 4.6 Technological investment (A. D. Little 1981)

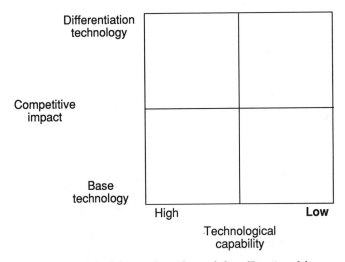

Figure 4.7 Technology portfolio: technical capability (Reprinted by permission of the publisher from "Strategic Management of Technology" by C. Pappas, *Journal of Product Innovation Management*, **1**, pp. 30–35. Copyright © 1984 by Elsevier Science Publishing Co., Inc.)

evaluating the competitive impact of its various technologies and assessing their place in the life cycle can lead to a fuller understanding of the firm's technology portfolio.

The Technology Portfolio

A direct offshoot of the methods used for developing the firm's business portfolio, the notion of the technology portfolio aims at providing an overall diagnosis of the firm's technological situation. Thus, the various technologies deployed by the firm are positioned in a matrix whose two

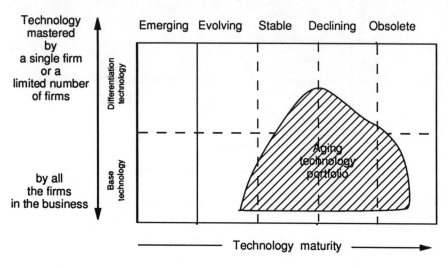

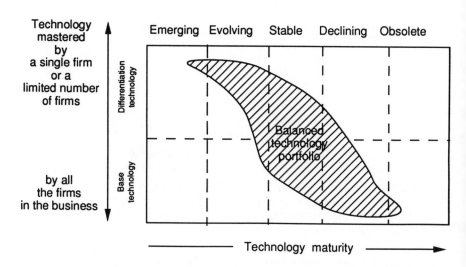

Figure 4.8 Technology portfolio: maturity (Morin 1985. Reproduced by permission of Publi Union.)

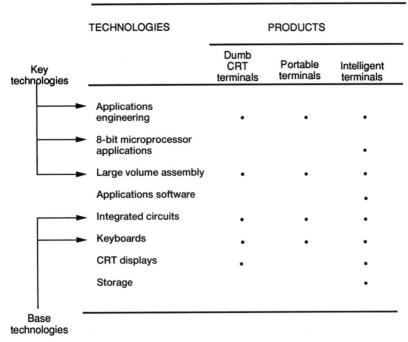

TECHNOLOGIES	PRODUCTS		
Key technologies	Dumb CRT terminals	Portable terminals	Intelligent terminals
Applications engineering	•	•	•
8-bit microprocessor applications			•
Large volume assembly	•	•	•
Applications software			•
Integrated circuits	•	•	•
Keyboards	•	•	•
CRT displays	•		•
Storage			•
Base technologies			

Figure 4.9 Technology portfolio: products (A. D. Little 1981)

dimensions reflect criteria that are considered essential for evaluating its technological assets in a strategic perspectie. C. Pappas[20] developed a model built on the following two dimensions:

- the competitive impact of each technology—whether a given technology has differentiation potential; and
- the firm's capacity or position in each technology.

Positioning the firm's technologies in this matrix (see Figure 4.7) makes it possible to evaluate its technological assets; moreover, comparing this technology portfolio to the firm's business portfolio provides interesting information about the long-term sustainability of its strategic position.

Other approaches emphasize the necessity for a balanced technology portfolio by considering simultaneously the competitive impact of the firm's technologies and their maturity[14]. Figure 4.8 represents, according to these two criteria, an aging technology portfolio and a balanced technology portfolio.

Lastly, the firm's technology portfolio can be analyzed by relating the firm's technologies to its businesses and products (see Figure 4.9). Through this simple technique, it is possible to visualize in which products or businesses the firm's technologies are used, and to identify shared technologies as well as those that are specific to a particular business or a limited set of products. Relating the firm's technologies to its businesses and products reveals in which of two broad directions the firm's strategy is moving:

- *a product/market-oriented strategy*, focusing on taking advantage of market synergies, new technologies being developed or acquired only when required by the expansion of the product line; or
- *a technology-based strategy*, with new products or businesses being developed to draw upon and exploit the firm's technological capabilities— this type of strategy is discussed in Chapter 6.

In summary, the technology audit enables the firm to manage strategically the development of its technological assets. This depends upon the selection, by the firm, of particular technologies in which competence is developed. Such a process must take into account not only the maintenance of existing technologies, but also the identification of new technological capabilities to be acquired.

CONCLUSION

Future technological changes can be anticipated in a deterministic way, through forecasting methods, in a creative manner with management of innovation techniques, or by examining multiple potential futures provided by the scenario method. Management of innovation techniques are based on internal procedures and focus on the firm; they do not take into account the external environment and the behavior of competitors. Forecasting and scenarios, in contrast, view technological changes as external phenomena over which the firm has very little control and to which it can merely react.

Taking technology into account when formulating the firm's overall strategy requires a preliminary step: the technology audit, or diagnosis of the firm's current technological state. This entails inventorying its technological assets, evaluating the competitive impact as well as the maturity of the various technologies, and analyzing the firm's technology portfolio. These analyses can prove invaluable when it comes to making key technological choices involving the selection, acquisition, and exploitation of technology.

NOTES AND REFERENCES

1. J. Harris, R. Shaw and W. Sommers, "The Strategic Management of Technology," in R. Lamb (Ed.), *Competitive Strategic Management*, Englewood Cliffs: Prentice-Hall, 1984, pp. 530–555.

2. S. Wheelwright and S. Makridakis, *Forecasting Methods for Management*, New York: Wiley, 1985.
3. J. Martino, *Technological Forecasting for Decision Making*, New York, NY: Elsevier Science Publishing Co., 1983, second edition, p. 2.
4. W. Ascher, *Forecasting: An Appraisal for Policy Makers and Planners*, Baltimore: Johns Hopkins University Press, 1978.
5. M. Turoff, "The Design of a Policy by Delphi," *Technological Forecasting and Social Change*, **2**, 1970; F. Mahieux, *Gestion de l'innovation: théorie et pratique*, Paris, Sirey, 1978.
6. CPE, "Les Futurs au Passe," *Futuribles*, June 1986.
7. J. Pelissolo, *La Biotechnologie Demain*, Paris: La Documentation Francaise, 1981.
8. See, for example, A. Delbecq, A. Van de Ven, and D. Gustafson, *Group Techniques for Program Planning*, Glenview: Scott, Foresman and Company; S. Wheelwright and S. Makridakis, "Qualitative Approaches to Forecasting," in S. Wheelwright and S. Makridakis, *Forecasting Methods for Management*, New York: Wiley, 1980.
9. S. Arnstein and A. Christakis, *Perspectives in Technology Assessment*, Jerusalem: Science and Technology Publishers, 1975.
10. M. Godet, *Prospective et Planification Stratégique*, Paris: Economica, 1985.
11. M. Godet, "Prospective, Prevision et Planification. Pluralisme et Complementarites," *Futuribles*, November 1983.
12. M. Godet, *Crise de la Prevision, Essor de la Prospective*, Paris: PUF, 1977; P. Buigues, *Prospective et Competitivite*, Paris: McGraw-Hill, 1985.
13. Arthur D. Little, "The Strategic Management of Technology," 1981.
14. J. Morin, *L'Excellence Technologique*, Paris: Jean Picollec-Publi Union, 1985.
15. H. Itami, *Mobilizing Invisible Assets*, Cambridge, MA: Harvard University Press, 1987.
16. J. Beffa, "Les Strategies Technologiques," *Politique Industrielle*, summer 1986.
17. R. Foster, *Innovation: The Attacker's Advantage*, New York: Summit Books, 1986.
18. R. Foster, "A Call for Vision in Managing Technology," *Business Week*, May 24, 1982.
19. J. Hunsicker, "Vision, Leadership and Europe's Business Future," *European Management Journal*, **3**, 1985, reprinted in *The McKinsey Quarterly*, spring 1986.
20. C. Pappas, "Strategic Management of Technology," *Journal of Product Innovation Management*, **1**, 1984.

Chapter 5

Technological Choice

Effective strategic management calls for the integration of technology into the generic strategies chosen for each business and the incorporation of technological concerns into the firm's overall corporate strategy. To achieve this end, every firm faces three fundamental technological choices:

- **How to select technology**—identifying and selecting new or additional technologies which the firm seeks to master. This decision largely determines how resources are allocated toward technological development.
- **How to acquire technology**—determining the specific means for acquiring a given technology. The means through which a technology is acquired determines its cost, the time required, the level of competence developed by the firm, as well as the latitude the firm enjoys when it uses the technology.
- **How to exploit technology**—selecting the ways of implementing or deploying the firm's technologies. The way in which the firm decides to exploit its technologies is one of the basic components of its strategy and directly influences its pattern of development.

This chapter aims at defining the criteria that can help firms select, acquire and exploit technologies. It analyzes these technological choices in light of the analyses—technological forecasts and audits—discussed in the previous chapter. These are then integrated in the last section of the chapter, which is devoted to the formulation of overall technological strategies.

SELECTING NEW TECHNOLOGIES

Determining the directions in which the firm intends to expand its technological capabilities is a major decision. Because it generally implies heavy investment and greatly affects the firm's competitive position, such a decision has a decisive impact on the firm's future.

In the automotive industry, for example, companies which supported the development of the rotary engine poured significant resources into this ultimately unsuccessful project, thereby jeopardizing their competitive position. Because of this, NSU, which was the only European firm to actually manufacture a car with a rotary engine, was taken over by VAG (Volkswagen and Audi)[1]. A positive example of the importance of technological choice is that of Boeing which owes its current competitive position in the commercial aircraft industry to having adopted jet engines in its aircraft designs as soon as these were available; today, the key decision is whether or not to develop an aircraft equipped with supersonic propeller (or UDF) engines in the 1990s. This is a crucial decision for the firm and will play an important role in its competitive struggle with Airbus Industrie which has chosen more conventional engines for its A320 aircraft.

The decision to add a particular technology to the firm's technological asset base is thus a critical strategic decision. While such a decision must be consistent with the overall strategic direction of the firm, it must also take into consideration other factors which are strictly technical and specific to each business or each scientific field.

Technological Scanning

Selecting new technologies and deciding to develop capability in a given technical field require extensive knowledge of the firm's pertinent technological environment. This means answering the following questions: What are the technologies used by our competitors? What are the innovations likely to have application in the businesses we operate in? What technologies used in other businesses could be transferred to our businesses? Such questions are often answered through a function termed "technological scanning." This function is difficult to perform because it requires broad scanning of potential sources of knowledge, many of which are far removed from the firm's immediate businesses.

Compared with their Japanese counterparts, European and American companies seem to largely underestimate the importance of technological scanning. According to some estimates, Japanese firms spend on average 1.5% of sales in technological scanning activities[2], and Japan specialists have noted that, in some firms, scientific and technical information expenditures account for 5–6% of sales, exceeding actual R&D expenditures. Such efforts by Japanese firms allow them not to lose time and money in re-inventing what is already available.

The main sources of information which can fuel the function of technological scanning are the following[2]:

- personal relationships with customers, suppliers and competitors;
- ties to research centers, university laboratories, etc.;
- scientific symposia, congresses and conferences;
- specialized journals and publications; and
- databases.

Depending on the nature of the industry, different sources of information can prove to be the most fruitful. For example, some industries depend on customers as the source of most ideas for new products and processes (e.g. medical equipment) while others depend much more heavily on suppliers for such ideas (e.g. chemicals)[3].

In addition to the role they play in protecting the firm's technology, patents are also essential for technological scanning. Since all registered patents are public information, it is possible to use them to identify trends in technological change, to uncover promising technologies that could be exploited through the acquisition of a license, as well as to follow the position and progress of competitors in terms of technology.

Tools for Technology Selection

A method for selecting technologies should combine the potential competitive impact of the various available technologies with the probability of technical and commercial success of their respective applications. This is illustrated in the matrix in Figure 5.1.

The matrix contains a few examples of electronic and computer science

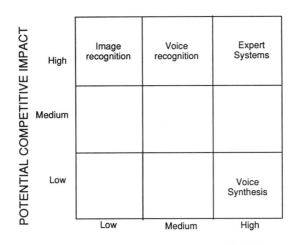

PROBABILITY OF SUCCESS

Figure 5.1 Evaluating technological options

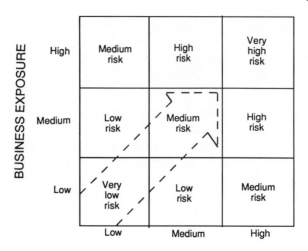

TECHNICAL UNCERTAINTY

Figure 5.2 Technological risk (A. D. Little 1981)

technologies as they were assessed by Texas Instruments R&D managers in 1986[4]. A complementary approach to this method is to distinguish technical uncertainty from business exposure when evaluating the overall risk involved in the various technologies analyzed[5]. Technical uncertainty measures the probability of meeting the performance objectives that have been set within the planned cost and time limits; business exposure is the extent to which the firm would be affected if performance objectives were not met. These two factors can be compared directly in a matrix combining the technical uncertainty and business exposure for each technology considered (Figure 5.2).

The two matrices in Figures 5.1 and 5.2 appear "objective," insofar as the evaluation of technologies only takes into account their intrinsic (commercial, technical, etc.) characteristics but does not consider the position of the firm with respect to these technologies. Yet the firm's technological position is a critical parameter, as important as the factors specific to the technologies themselves, in the selection of a given technology. From this perspective, a third approach combines the familiarity of a technology for the firm with the novelty or the familiarity of the markets it will serve if it uses the technology[6]. This can be represented in a "familiarity matrix" which evaluates the overall familiarity of the firm with the various technological options it is considering (Figure 5.3). This matrix defines regions of increasing risk associated with the new technologies. We will see later that this method can also be used as an effective tool in the selection of the most appropriate means for acquiring a given technology.

Finally, a fourth approach to the selection of new technologies by the firm

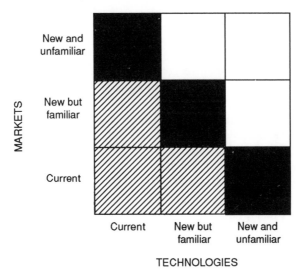

Figure 5.3 The familiarity matrix (Adapted from Roberts and Berry 1985; and from Parry 1986)

is based on an approach known as the "decision tree method." This method is used mainly to minimize risks involved in the allocation of resources for the internal development of technologies. It directs the selection process towards technological areas which offer the widest ranges of subsequent alternatives (Figure 5.4).

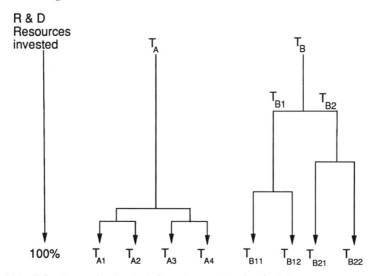

Figure 5.4 Selecting technological directions using the decision tree

The figure shows that, all other things being equal, it is preferable to develop technologies in the T_A area than in the T_B area because most of the resources invested will be profitable regardless of the final technical option chosen: T_{A1}, T_{A2}, T_{A3} or T_{A4}. In contrast, in the T_B area, critical decisions have to be made much earlier, and failing in T_{B1} or T_{B2} would imply more substantial resources invested at a loss. The T_{B1} option is preferable to option T_{B2} for the same reasons as in the selection between T_A and T_B.

All the approaches we have examined here tend to simplify to a great extent situations which, in reality, are extremely complex; however, they provide useful tools for aiding the technology selection process. In addition, because they entail different criteria, the methods provide complementary avenues for evaluating technology.

Once the firm has identified the new technological capabilities it needs to acquire, it is confronted with the issue of how it will achieve the mastery of such technologies.

MEANS OF ACQUIRING NEW TECHNOLOGIES

To implement effectively a technology-based strategy, a firm must have the necessary technological capability. There are many means of mastering new technology; we distinguish six main ways:

- *Internal development of the technology.* This approach requires a great deal of time and substantial resources. However, this is the solution which gives the firm the greatest freedom in the subsequent application of the technology and which enables it to best benefit from the competitive advantage such a technology may create. It is also the approach which involves the highest risk since it is difficult to anticipate the outcome of research projects or forecast the number of resulting applications. This approach proves most effective when the firm develops technologies which are closely linked to its existing technological assets by using the latter as a starting point.
- *Acquisition of a firm possessing the desired technology.* Although this approach may seem attractive, it can only be used when such a firm actually exists and is for sale. The cost of such an acquisition, however, is often prohibitive, varying according to the potential the desired technology appears to have. Moreover, this approach can entail subsequent difficulties: integrating the research teams of the newly acquired firms can be a critical step and, in cases where the technology resides with a few individuals, their resignation can seriously jeopardize the success of the acquisition.
- *Joint ventures or alliances.* Here, several firms join forces to develop new

technologies. Such approaches offer the advantages of sharing costs—although they commonly prove to be more expensive on the whole—and of reducing risks, but should only be considered by firms which totally agree on the resources required and the specific fields of research and development, and which are not likely to become competitors after the break-up of the joint venture or the alliance. Joint venturing centered on technology is a phenomenon which has become widespread in the past decade and which is expected to expand in the future. The economic and strategic implications of such a phenomenon are difficult to evaluate. The issue of technological alliances will be examined in further detail in Chapter 7.

- *External R&D contracts.* In this approach, the firm subcontracts with an outside party such as a laboratory, a research center, a university, etc., for the development of a particular technology. Such contracts allow the firm to call upon specialists or highly qualified research teams and still have the exclusive rights for the resulting innovations. However, they can make it difficult for the firm to subsequently improve the technologies it uses. This option proves most effective when it is accompanied by the development of internal capabilities.

- *Licenses.* This option gives access to technologies developed by firms in other industries or by competitors in the same business but operating in other geographic areas. Licenses significantly reduce the freedom of firms since they normally entail strict limits concerning the use of the technology. Fees are often directly linked to the profits the licences yield and firms may, in the long term, acquire greater freedom through sustained R&D efforts. The "NIH" (Not Invented Here) syndrome is often used to describe the reluctance of firms to draw upon innovations or inventions developed elsewhere, even though this can be an important source of enrichment for their technological assets. Indeed, the Japanese economic "miracle" has been based largely upon a significant number of acquired foreign licenses as well as on a considerable R&D effort which enabled the country to make up for its technological gap.

- *Private label.* Another means of acquiring a given technology is to buy finished goods or components to be assembled and sell them under the firm's own trade mark. However, this option only enables the firm to maintain its position in a specific market temporarily and may provide the technology supplier with the key market intelligence and knowledge needed to enter the business itself.

The various means of acquiring new technologies which we have examined above can be classified according to the technological "autonomy" they provide, with internal development providing the most. While the criterion of the strategic autonomy is important, it must be weighed against other equally important criteria such as the availability of the various alternatives, their cost, the time they require, and their risks. Figure 5.5 combines the strategic autonomy and time criteria so as to put the different means of acquiring and developing new technologies mentioned above into perspective.

Using the "familiarity matrix" presented earlier in this chapter, the "optimum" means of acquiring new technologies can be identified. These approaches, depicted in Figure 5.6, involve both the acquisition of new technologies and entry into new markets (i.e. diversification). Given our interest in technology, however, it is the two columns on the right, illustrating situations requiring the use of new technologies, which are most relevant.

This matrix includes three ways of acquiring or developing new technologies which we have not explicitly examined:

- *Intrapreneurship*, or internal venturing, is a way of developing internal technological capabilities based on specific organizational mechanisms which we will discuss in detail in Chapter 8. This process, which has been the subject of an abundant literature in the last few years[7], consists of setting up separate units within the existing corporate entity. These small units are entrusted with precise objectives, such as the development of new technologies or products, and are protected from the procedures and formal systems normally followed by the firm they are a part of—to preserve their dynamism, their creativity, their spirit of enterprise and their risk-taking behavior.

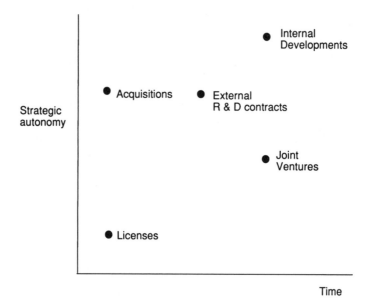

Figure 5.5   Means of acquiring new technologies: strategic autonomy and time

		Existing	Related	New
MARKET	New	Joint venture Internal venture	Venture capital Educational acquisition	Spin-off Sell
	Related	Internal development Acquisition	Internal development Licensing Acquisition	Venture capital Educational acquisition
	Existing	Internal development	Internal development Licensing Acquisition	Joint Venture Internal venture

TECHNOLOGY

Figure 5.6 Optimum means of acquiring new technologies (Adapted from Roberts and Berry 1985)

- *Venture capital* permits equity participation in new and expanding firms which were created to exploit a technological innovation. This approach, which differs from acquisition, nevertheless provides participating firms with knowledge about new technologies and some degree of control over their development. Firms can later choose to reinforce their positions, or even move to acquisition, if the technologies considered appear to be promising. Many large US corporations such as DuPont, General Electric and Exxon have followed the ventureicapital approach; in France, Elf-Aquitaine created its own venture capital subsidiary, Innovelf, to manage its holdings in such ventures, while Buli financially supported the creation of Trilogy, a small US company which was designed to develop and launch new-generation computers. It should be noted that this approach to new technology acquisition has become increasingly popular with Japanese firms; thus it is no longer a Western approach but a means that is becoming more and more common worldwide.
- *Educational acquisitions* provide firms with a "window" on technology. Through grants and affiliate programs, they give firms the opportunity to stay familiar with new technologies, without necessarily intending to use such technologies in the immediate future.

Thus, there are many means of acquiring new technologies. The choice of a specific approach depends, as we mentioned earlier, on its availability and on the firm's constraints in terms of cost, time and risk; the autonomy the firm will have in the use of the acquired technology also determines the firm's choice. Moreover, a firm can choose different approaches according to the technologies it wants to acquire and the businesses it seeks to enter. Kodak decided to enter pharmaceuticals by internally developing the required technologies; however, it chose to take over an existing company, Verbatim Corp., in order to acquire know-how in the manufacture of floppy disks and enter the computer industry, and it bought already assembled video cameras from Matsushita with an eye toward gaining rapid access to that business[8].

Whatever the means chosen, acquiring a new technology is a difficult and risky proposition which must be integrated as closely as possible with the strategy of the firm's businesses as well as with its overall corporate strategy.

EXPLOITING NEW TECHNOLOGICAL CAPABILITIES

Selecting the firm's technologies and determining the means of acquiring the ones it lacks are extremely important decisions. Defining the ways in which it will exploit its technological assets is also a critical decision which must be integrated with the firm's overall strategy[9].

The firm can exploit its technologies in two ways:

- *Internal exploitation*—using such technologies to design, develop, manufacture and sell products; or
- *External exploitation*—transferring its capabilities to other firms which implement them in their own businesses.

Exploiting its technologies internally amounts to the firm operating and competing in businesses where such technologies are used, some of which can be key factors for success in a particular business. We discussed in the preceding chapter the role of technology which, when exploited internally, was likely to serve as a source of competitive advantage; therefore, we will not re-examine this role here.

The external exploitation of technology, however, follows a totally different logic: the firm does not operate directly in such businesses, but allows other firms to use the technology instead. This implies a transfer of know-how, which often takes the form of licensing in the case of patented technologies. Technology transfer also usually includes training for the acquiring firm so that it can utilize the technology fully. It is important to keep in mind that the sale of technologies requires capabilities which differ widely from those required for internal development and exploitation. Even if firms are not really aware of it, technology transfer is a whole new business in itself. For example, the helicopter division of Aerospatiale, which has extensive experience with technology transfer, considers such transfers to be long-term propositions requiring significant effort and personnel from the selling firm to assist the licensee in implementing the technology successfully.

External exploitation of technology is the most appropriate option in the following circumstances:

- The firm's technology is easily protected via patents or copyrights.
- The firm wants to enter markets which it cannot directly penetrate because of trade barriers, local content, quasi-exclusive distribution networks, etc. Over the past three decades, for example, many US corporations have been required to license technology in exchange for entry into the Japanese market.
- The firm wants to impose the specific characteristics of its own technology as a standard. The predominance of the VHS standard in the video industry is largely due to Matsushita's aggressive strategy of granting licenses to firms which are well established in their markets.
- The firm lacks the resources or "complementary assets" to enter the market directly.
- The firm wants to exchange technologies with other firms. Double sourcing, whereby two companies market some of each other's products, is a common practice in the semiconductor industry.
- The firm desires to "control" potential competitors by restricting their freedom in the license agreement, by diverting them from research efforts which could lead them to develop their own technology, or even by favoring certain competitors, thereby structuring competition to the benefit of the firm[10]. We analyze this type of strategy in Chapter 7, which deals with strategic alliances.

Internal and external exploitation of technology are not mutually exclusive. Some firms choose not to implement their technologies themselves, thus acting as R&D centers. For psychological rather than strategic reasons, others are reluctant to sell—and thus share—their know-how. However, many firms are less clear-cut in their behavior and exploit some of their technologies themselves and license others; some deploy their technologies in certain markets and sell them to other firms which exploit them in other markets. A coherent policy must take strategic as well as purely technological criteria into account.

Figure 5.7 summarizes the technological choices to be made by the firm[11]. In formulating a technological strategy it is crucial for the firm to make the technological dimension explicit before integrating its technological choices into its overall strategy.

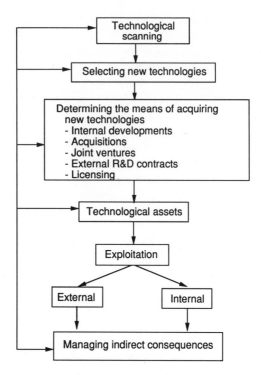

Figure 5.7 Technological choices (Adapted from Cremadez and Dumont 1985)

THE FORMULATION OF TECHNOLOGICAL STRATEGIES

Conventional strategy models, notably business portfolio models, do not explicitly take into account technological factors. At best, these factors are one of many considerations in the evaluation of the firm's competitive position and are thus lost among many other factors. Matrices which consider the technological dimension separately and then combine it with other conventional dimensions of strategic analysis—such as value, maturity, business attractiveness or the firm's competitive position—have been developed to fill this gap.

SRI International uses a matrix which combines the technology portfolio—which we discussed earlier—with the business portfolio. The latter reflects the firm's current business position. This analysis makes it possible to identify anomalies in the positioning of the firm's technologies and businesses, and to identify priority investments. Combination of the business and technology portfolios and identification of the competitive impact of the technologies in terms of cost and differentiation allows SRI to suggest "specific strategies" adapted to each particular situation[12].

Arthur D. Little has proposed one of the most thorough analyses of the relationship between strategy and technology. This analysis combines the maturity of the industry (distinguishing between two situations, embryonic/early-growth industries and late-growth/mature industries) with the competitive position and the technological position of the firm, and selects the technological strategies best suited to each combination (Figure 5.8). This approach, however, contains ambiguity concerning the interrelationships between the factors considered. Indeed, the firm's competitive position is linked to its technological position: a strong competitive position largely results from a strong technological position, and a strong technological position eventually leads to a strong competitive position.

Following the logic of the above approaches, it is useful to construct an analytical framework based on three dimensions:

- the growth potential, value and attractiveness of the business, which is a standard dimension of business portfolio models;
- the firm's market position, measured by its market share, its distribution networks, its image, etc—this dimension reflects the degree of control the firm has over its customers in each of its businesses;
- the firm's capabilities with respect to the key technologies in each of its businesses—this third dimension measures the extent to which the firm will be able to rely on its technology to gain a strong overall competitive position in the future.

This results in a three-dimensional space, represented by a cube (Figure 5.9), in which the various businesses of the firm can be positioned in order to determine the mix of the business portfolio, the necessary resources to be allocated to each business on the one hand and each technology on the other, the appropriate growth and diversification moves based on the strongest technological asset or the strongest market position, the most appropriate technological strategies, etc. If we simplify the approach and use a low/high or weak/strong evaluation of each dimension, we can classify the firm's businesses in eight categories, as follows.

(1) Businesses with a high growth potential, in which the firm has a strong market position and strong technological capabilities. Such businesses resemble the "star" businesses of conventional matrices. The firm must maintain its market position, reinforce its technological edge and grow with the business. [Figure 5.10(a)]

(2) Businesses with a low growth potential, in which the firm's technological capabilities as well as its market position are weak. Such businesses are

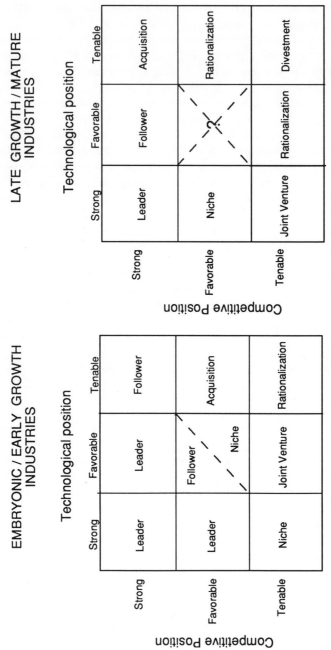

Figure 5.8 Technological strategies according to Arthur D. Little (A. D. Little 1981)

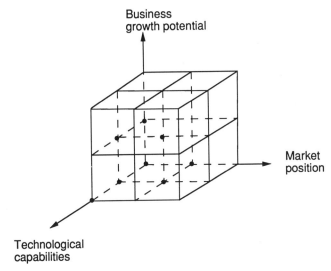

Figure 5.9   The firm's strategic three-dimensional space

"dogs" which the firm must abandon, except if they prove profitable without significant investments. [Figure 5.10(b)]

(3) Businesses with a low growth potential, in which the firm's technological capabilities are strong and its market position is very strong. Such businesses are "cash cows" which must provide the firm with the maximum cash with the lowest possible investments. In terms of technology, the firm must try to exploit its capabilities, either by deploying them in businesses with a higher growth potential, or by trying to license them. [Figure 5.10(c)]

(4) Businesses with a high growth potential, in which the firm's market position as well as its technological capabilities are weak. Such businesses are "question marks," in which the firm should either invest heavily to improve both its technological capabilities and its market position, or abandon. However, considering the two dimensions, "technological capabilities" and "market position," separately emphasizes the fact that these question marks involve many risks; they should only be developed if there is no other high-growth business for which the firm has at least one asset, either in terms of technology, or market knowledge. [Figure 5.10(d)]

The four situations examined above are those which most resemble situations analyzed in business portfolio models. Evaluations of the two dimensions, "technological capabilities" and "market position," converge, so that considering them separately does not provide any additional information. In the following situations the evaluations diverge, and considering the two dimensions separately improves our analysis.

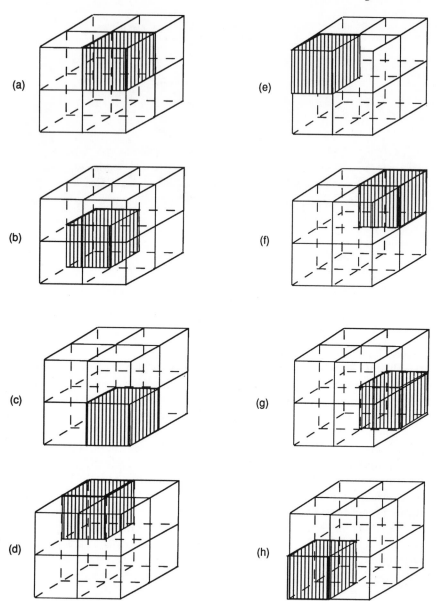

Figure 5.10 The eight positions in three-dimensional space

(5) Businesses with a high growth potential, in which the firm has strong technological capabilities but a weak market position. These are also, to some extent, "question marks"; however, because of the firm's stronger technological assets, the risk is lower. In such a situation, the firm could try

to enter a partnership with a firm having a strong market position but lacking the essential technologies. If the firm does not want to invest in this type of business, it should exploit its technological capabilities by selling its know-how. [Figure 5.10(e)]

(6) The opposite of the preceding, these are businesses with a high growth potential in which the firm has a strong market position but weak technological capabilities; they are also partially "question marks." In situations of this type, the firm must acquire the necessary technological skills as rapidly as possible, in order to maintain and later exploit the firm's advantage in terms of market position. In such cases, time is a decisive factor; the firm must try to acquire technologies from other firms, rather than develop skills internally which is a much longer process. According to the firm's opportunities and financial resources, the options to be considered are the purchase of licenses or the takeover of a company possessing the desired technologies. [Figure 5.10(f)]

In categories 5 and 6, considering the dimensions "market position" and "technological capabilities" separately allows the identification of the strategic complementarity between the firm and outside partners. Moreover, it urges the firm to take advantage of its strengths and to compensate for its weaknesses through alliances with other firms in its environment.

(7) Businesses with a low growth potential, in which the firm has a strong market position but weak technological capabilities. Firms in this type of situation must minimize investments in order to generate the largest possible cash flow. They should only acquire technologies if the latter are profitable immediately. [Figure 5.10(g)]

(8) Businesses with a low growth potential, in which the firm has a weak market position but strong technological capabilities. Firms in this type of situation must redeploy such capabilities. Their primary objective must be to abandon these businesses gradually, while generating cash flow if possible, and to exploit their technological skills, either by entering other businesses with a higher growth potential, or by transferring them to other firms which will deploy them in a more profitable manner. [Figure 5.10(h)]

The situations we have examined and the recommended strategies that can be deduced are clearly far too simplified, and should not be followed "mechanically." Our main intention is to show that taking technology into account explicitly in the strategy-making process leads to a better understanding of the situations the firm is confronted with. In addition, it makes it possible to suggest a broader set of strategic options than the somewhat monolithic recommendations that can be inferred from conventional business portfolio models.

CONCLUSION

The technology audit and other analyses help guide the firm on the new technologies it must select, the most appropriate means of acquiring such technologies and the best ways to exploit them. These diagnostic steps must also be integrated with the firm's overall strategy. Viewed in this way, technology is just one factor of many to be incorporated into the strategy-making process. It is possible, however, to place even greater importance on technology in strategy-making. Indeed, technology can prove to be the focal point of the strategy implemented by a firm, as opposed to a strategy based mainly on a product–market orientation. Some firms do employ technology-based strategies, their capability with a particular technology or a coherent set of technologies being their major distinctive skill.

In the strategic space we defined earlier, these firms occupy a "strong" or "very strong" position along the "technological capabilities" dimension, and the management of their various businesses in this space is based on technology. The predominance of technology is particularly clear in the firms' strategic moves such as diversification, which they often do by exploiting their technologies in other markets and industries. In these firms, technology is the focal point. Thus, in some situations, technology is the key factor for success and it is possible to say that the firm follows a technology-based strategy.

NOTES AND REFERENCES

1. *New York Times*, October 14, 1988.
2. J. Morin, *L'Excellence Technologique*, Paris: Jean Picollec-Publi-Union, 1985.
3. E. von Hipple, *The Sources of Innovation*, Oxford: Oxford University Press, 1988.
4. Source: interviews conducted by the authors.
5. Arthur D. Little, "Strategy and Technology," 1981.
6. E. Roberts and C. Berry, "Entering New Businesses: Selecting Strategies for Success," *Sloan Management Review*, spring 1985; C. Perry, "Choosing the Mechanisms to Help Your Innovation Thrive," *International Management*, March 1986.
7. C. Pinchot, *Intrapreneuring*, New York: Harper & Row, 1985; R. Burgelman and L. Sayles, *Inside Corporate Innovation*, New York: Free Press, 1986.
8. "Why Kodak is Starting to Click Again," *Business Week*, February 23, 1987.
9. E. Von Hipple, "Appropriability of Innovation Benefit as a Predictor of the Source of Innovation", *Research Policy*, 11, 1982; D. Teece, "Profiting from Technological Innovation: Implications for Integration, Collaboration, Licensing, and Public Policy," in D. Teece (Ed.), *The Competitive Challenge*, Cambridge: Ballinger Publishing, 1986.
10. M. Porter, *Competitive Advantage*, New York: Free Press, 1985.
11. M. Cremadez and A. Dumont, "Le Management Strategique de la Technologie," working paper, HEC, 1985.
12. J. Tassel, "La Methode SRI d'Analyse Strategique," *Futuribles*, 1983.

Chapter 6

Technology-based Strategies

The methods and models we have presented are tools which help us understand the actions and processes of firms whose technological capabilities play a crucial role in the strategies they implement. Yet, some recently developed approaches[1] go even further and consider technology as the primary foundation of strategy. Examples of this can be found among the most successful firms in the automotive, aerospace, computer, energy, new materials and biotechnology industries. Firms which implement strategies based on technology, termed "technology-cluster strategies," develop by applying a coherent set of technological capabilities in many different businesses which, in some cases, are far removed from their original or "base" businesses.

TECHNOLOGY-CLUSTER STRATEGIES

A technology cluster can be defined as a set of businesses sharing a common technological base (Figure 6.1). A technology cluster consists of a number of applications relating the core technology to products and markets[2]. Using "generic" technologies (which we describe below), some firms create a strong and consistent technological "potential" for which they find the widest possible range of applications in diversified products and markets. These technology-cluster strategies can be represented as in Figure 6.2.

Technology-cluster strategies have, in particular, been implemented by large Japanese corporations such as Honda, Canon and NEC; this explains their representation in the form of a tree—a bonsai—whose roots are the generic technologies, the trunk the technological potential developed by the firm, the branches the industries and businesses where the latter would be applied, and the fruits the products or product/markets[3].

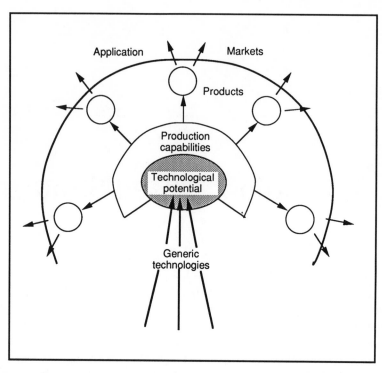

Figure 6.1 The technology cluster: a conceptual representation (GEST 1986. Reproduced with permission of McGraw-Hill France.)

Implementation of technology-cluster strategies requires that firms have the following three fundamental capabilities:

- a strong technological potential;
- the capacity to develop rapidly a wide range of applications, in the form of many different products to be sold in a large number of markets;
- the capacity to choose, from the large spectrum of available technologies, the ones that are not only intrinsically promising, but also consistent with the firm's technological and industrial potential.

Technological Potential

Technology clusters are based upon competency in several "generic technologies" which can be translated into applications. In Chapter 4 we noted a clear distinction between base technologies and key technologies. The notion of generic technology follows a totally different logic: a technology is described as generic if—through combinations with other technologies—it is likely to lead to numerous different applications in diverse businesses. Unlike

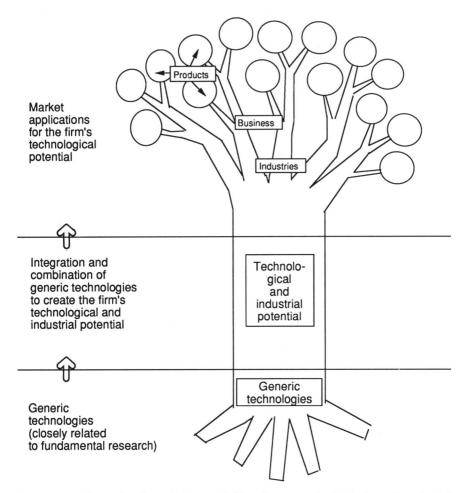

Figure 6.2 The technological "bonsai" (Sest-Euroconsult 1984. Reproduced with permission.)

key technologies, generic technologies are not defined with reference to a particular business; the generic nature of a technology is determined by its wide-ranging industrial and commercial application. For example, Honda's competence in engines and power trains has formed the basis for successful businesses in cars, motorcycles, lawn mowers, and generators. Similarly, Canon's competence in optics and imaging has provided the technological potential for it to enter product markets as diverse as cameras, copiers, and laser printers.

Generic technologies are often closely related to fundamental scientific knowledge, precisely because they must hold the potential for generating a broad spectrum of applications. The implementation of technology-cluster strategies requires strong scientific and technical capabilities allowing firms to integrate and combine these generic technologies so as to develop technological potential. In creating businesses as diverse as coated abrasives, photographic film, magnetic tape, and "Post-it" notes, for example, 3M has relied upon the creative coupling of competencies in adhesives, coatings, and materials. Indeed, the company has invested heavily to maintain its technological potential around these few generic technologies.

While in most cases generic technologies are not invented inside the firm, it is critical that the firm internalize them. However, technological potential can only be developed, maintained and enhanced by the firm itself, and it must also be controllable since it will constitute the firm's main competitive advantage in all the businesses where it is exploited. The technological potential of a firm implementing a technology-cluster strategy is constantly evolving. It evolves together with the generic technologies on which it is based, and with the businesses in which it finds applications; it is reinforced through the acquisition of new generic technologies.

Firms can only develop, maintain and reinforce their technological potential through frequent and close contacts between in-house scientific and technical teams and the outside scientific community (e.g. universities and research laboratories). Good communication between the R&D units and marketing departments responsible for finding commercial applications for this technological potential is also necessary. One of the main challenges the technology-cluster strategy poses is that of organizational structure—which structure permits the most rapid and efficient flow of information? We examine this question in Chapter 8.

Exploiting the Firm's Technological Potential

The very existence of the firm's technological potential and the significant resources invested for its development and reinforcement only make sense if the potential is exploited in a large number of applications and markets. In addition to developing technological potential, firms implementing technology-cluster strategies must systematically look for areas of application where, through their technology, they are likely to offer better performance, value, or quality than the existing products on the market. The expansion of the firm is thus the result of increasing the number of its markets.

The links the firm establishes with these various markets take on considerable importance in the implementation of technology-cluster strategies. The firm must be able to sense application opportunities in businesses which by definition are extremely varied; it must be able to assess the competitive advantage its technology could create, and evaluate whether this advantage offsets its lack of familiarity with a particular market (distribution networks, customer behavior, behavior of firms already in the market, etc.). The less familiar the firm is with the market, the higher must be the differential provided by technology[4]. This interrelation between the possibilities offered by the firm's technological potential, which is constantly evolving, and the application opportunities of different markets requires an organization which allows an efficient and rapid flow of information.

Technology-cluster strategies require that firms have great flexibility, allowing them to shift from one business to another and from one market to another. Indeed, firms implementing strategies of this type cannot aim at remaining in the same businesses forever because they would eventually have to compete in a more traditional way as their advantage due to technology eroded; on the contrary, they only stay in a given business as long as their technological potential provides them with a significant competitive advantage. Technological changes occurring in the application markets can affect the coherence of a firm's competence if such changes involve technologies far removed from the firm's technological potential. In such cases, it is important to abandons the businesses in which it can no longer rely sufficiently on its technological potential to compete; it must look instead for other applications of its technologies in new businesses. In essence, the technological potential of firms implementing technology-cluster strategies is what determines the choice of application markets; technological evolution in these markets is not what shapes the firms' technological potential. However, such firms must be conscious of technological change to ensure that their technological portfolio does not become overly mature.

Managing the Evolution of Technological Potential

The success of a technology-cluster strategy hinges on a firm's selective capacity. This capacity includes both choosing appropriate products and markets in which to exploit its technological potential, as well as selecting "exploitable" generic technologies which are likely to enhance its technological potential.

If we go back to the metaphor of the bonsai, we can say that selective capacity concerns not only the branches—the businesses and products in which the firm's technology is applied—but also the roots—the firm's generic technologies—which nourish the trunk, the firm's technological potential. This trunk represents the "core competence" of the firm—a technical as well as industrial capability[5]. In the diagram, the trunk represents a certain stability, whereas the roots consist of a set of ever-changing elements, some of which are growing while others shrink and are abandoned, the main objective being to combine elements in the best possible way in order to nourish a durable trunk.

Thus, the selection of appropriate technologies to be added to the firm's technological potential is extremely important. This role should be carried out by the firm's "technological decision center"[6], a unit which combines the technologies mastered by the firm in a systematic manner while at the same time being able to understand and call upon fundamental scientific knowledge to determine what other technologies should be developed or acquired by the firm. As firms have limited R&D resources, this unit must, on the one hand, assess and evaluate all the generic technologies the firm could conceivably develop or acquire, and, on the other hand, select only a few to focus on. In short, this capacity involves the active management of the firm's technological potential.

The implementation of a technology-cluster strategy makes this capacity crucial because it requires that certain technical skills be acquired before entering a new business. In this case, the definition of the product flows from the technological capabilities, whereas with a "classic" diversification strategy it is the products and markets which determine the technical skills to be acquired or to be used. Managing the selective evolution of technology combinations implies a prior step, technological scanning—a notion we presented in the preceding chapter and which, in this context, plays a fundamental role.

The concept of the technology cluster contributes to our elaboration and improvement of strategy models by emphasizing technology-related factors. It is now important to consider whether this approach confirms or invalidates the main aspects of business strategy as it has generally been viewed to date. Beyond terminology differences, there may be close relationships between the technological potential—and its applications—and the conventional bases of strategic analysis, namely businesses and industries. We will, therefore, try to point out the distinctive aspects of the technology-cluster concept.

THE CONTRIBUTION OF THE TECHNOLOGY-CLUSTER APPROACH

As we saw above, the technology cluster translates into a particular type of strategy in which the coherence of the diversified business portfolio is based on a common "trunk": the firm's technological potential.

The Irrelevance of Industry Boundaries

Japanese firms often use the metaphor of the bonsai to describe themselves and reinforce the logic of their strategy[7]. They note that the business they are in is defined by the firm's technological potential. Thus, they redefine what we termed a "business" in Chapter 2 along technological lines. The "technological potential" is thus analogous to the "business" of a firm for which the key factor for success is technology. The technology-cluster approach shows that there is a logic to the growth of some high-technology firms, whereas the more conventional approach based upon business units would interpret this growth as diversification moves.

If we revisit the concept of the "strategic segment" or "business" as we defined it in Chapter 2—"a subset of the firm's overall activity having a specific combination of key factors for success"—the notion of "technological potential" clearly inverts our perspective. The conventional strategic segmentation procedure starts with the definition of products or businesses and, *a posteriori*, identifies technology as a key factor for success. Technology clusters show that the opposite approach may be relevant, starting from the firm's technological potential and viewing its businesses as contingent "applications"; such an approach is also more general since it does not focus on the applications which a firm develops, but instead relates them to a common combination of generic technologies.

Starting from the firm's products and markets, strategic segmentation is implicitly based on the idea of "industry"; however, industry is only one way of categorizing the firm's products. This concept is totally irrelevant in the case of firms growing in the technology-cluster mode. Porter defines an industry as "a group of firms which manufacture substitutable products"[8]. According to this definition, the "industry" is where competition takes place. However, the industry is not a pertinent element in the analysis of technology clusters. Indeed, firms which grow as technology clusters do not compete in one specific industry, but in all the industries where their technological potential can provide them with an advantage. A competitor which achieves new combinations or which is faster to master and apply new generic technologies thus represents a threat, entry into a given industry being a possible consequence of such advantages. The technology-cluster concept produces a strategy which "changes the rules" of competition:

- Firms implementing technology-cluster strategies no longer compete on a product/market basis, but on the overall viability of the applications derived from their technological potential.
- Competition in a given industry is affected by the entry of new competitors having new competitive advantages and following a strategy which differs from that of firms well established in the industry.

The change in the rules of competition occurs because firms implementing technology-cluster strategies "ignore" the notion of industry in the way they define their economic role. A firm which develops one or several technology clusters does not define itself in terms of the industries in which the products it manufactures compete, or the markets it serves. Indeed, this definition would be far too transitory because of the flexibility with which the firm exploits its technological potential in the form of products; moreover, it would constitute a fragmented image of the firm whereas the technology-cluster concept provides a coherent strategy for developing an "entity"—namely its technological potential. A good example is that of Toray, the world's leading carbon fiber producer, which depicts its activities in a way consistent with this idea[9] (see Figure 6.3).

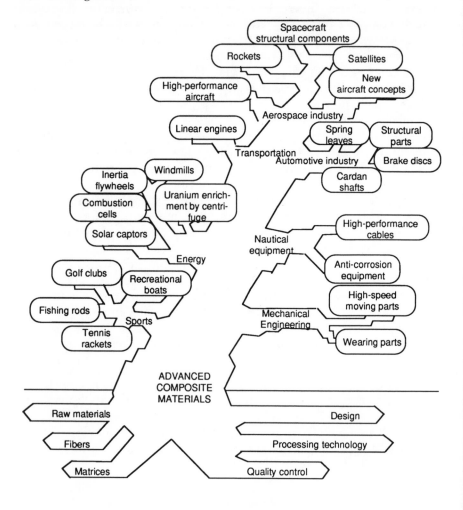

Figure 6.3 Diversity in the applications of materials, according to Toray (GEST 1986. Reproduced with permission.)

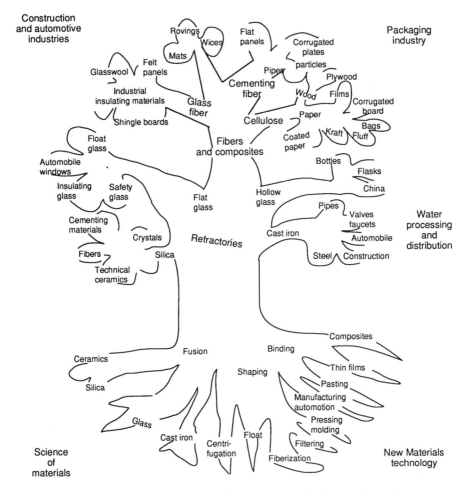

Figure 6.4 Saint-Gobain's technological tree (*La Tribune de l'Economie* 1986)

When it was privatized, Saint-Gobain also represented its activities as a tree[10] (and, perhaps because it is a French corporation, the tree looks like an oak or a plane tree rather than a bonsai . . .). We cannot help observing that the underlying technology of Saint-Gobain seems to be less convincing than in the case of Toray, since the same term is often used to designate both its generic technologies and their applications (see Figure 6.4).

"Technology Clusters" versus "Business Portfolios"

As a strategy, the technology-cluster approach questions the conventional model of strategic segmentation which uses the "industry" as a basic organizing principle. But strategic segmentation—which aims at answering the crucial question "What businesses are we in?"—is the first stage of the strategy-making process[10]. Business portfolio models[11] consider the firm's businesses as permanent entities; indeed it is on the basis of these entities, and according to their positions in the matrices, that decision-makers are supposed to make policy decisions. Yet, because technologies and their applications evolve, the definition of businesses may not be stable, but rather dynamic. This changing definition of businesses is not taken into account in business portfolio models.

Thus, the use of business portfolio models confines top managers to the role of "speculators operating in a stable environment"[12]. In other words, these models follow a financial logic in which the resources are distributed as if they were "investments," to develop a "portfolio" by selecting businesses which can be reduced to financial "assets." Thus the "business portfolio" approach gives an image of the firm which is antagonistic to the exploitation of its technological potential. Indeed, the implementation of a technology-cluster strategy requires inventorying the firm's technological capabilities and finding the widest possible range of applications; i.e. making strategic decisions in a dynamic perspective by taking all the possible options into account, instead of concentrating on the "static" management of its existing businesses. This implies shifting from a financial (allocating resources to businesses) and marketing (concentrating on market share, industry attractiveness, etc.) logic, to a capability logic (exploiting the firm's technological potential) based on research and development capabilities.

The technology-cluster strategy is exemplified by firms which have significant R&D resources and operate in many different businesses. The R&D function in such firms seems to be managed in a centralized way. A recent study noted that the importance of technology in such firms is reflected organizationally by elevating the position of the R&D manager[13]. In essence, this means that the R&D and technology activities must be given greater power than the financial and marketing functions. Indeed, R&D is where the definition of new businesses and products originates from, and thus the place where the firm's strategy is formulated.

In summary, the technology-cluster approach is based on a different paradigm in which the firm is viewed "horizontally" according to its technological potential rather than "vertically" as fragmented into static businesses and business units. This means that resource allocation decisions primarily concern the improvement of its technological potential and not its existing business portfolio. The difference between the two approaches can be represented as in Figure 6.5.

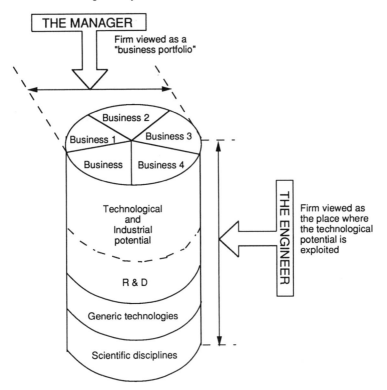

Figure 6.5 The "manager's strategy" versus the "engineer's strategy"

OTHER FORMS OF COMPETENCY CLUSTERS

We started our discussion of technology clusters by drawing a distinction between the notion of "business" and that of "technological potential." It is clear from the above discussion, however, that there are overlaps and similarities between these two concepts as well. A business is a concept which permits one to assess the firm's capabilities and determine how these capabilities provide it with a competitive advantage. Businesses have greater significance than the products and markets composing them; indeed, defining a firm according to its business(es) provides an integrated vision of its diverse capabilities and its specific know-how. When these capabilities are primarily technological in nature, the firm's business can be reduced to its technological potential.

However, in most cases, a business is not solely defined by technological capability; technology-cluster strategies imply that the firm operates in several businesses. Thus, a technology cluster is a combination of businesses which are linked by common technological capabilities. Such links have been termed "diversification pivots"[14] since technology-cluster strategies often appear on the surface to be simple diversification strategies (see Figure 6.6).

When the "pivot" is technological in nature, the firm develops a diversification strategy which closely resembles a technology-cluster strategy. Furthermore, recent studies[15] have defined pivots between businesses as "shared capabilities between the firm's initial business and the business it diversifies into" (see Figure 6.7). When the shared capabilities, or the intersection of businesses, is technological in nature, we again have a situation analogous to the technology-cluster notion.

Technology-cluster strategies can thus be viewed as a particular type of "related" diversification[16]. In this context, we can distinguish between Sommer–Allibert's technology-based diversification strategy and Salomon's market-based diversification strategy. Sommer–Allibert corporation grew in diversified industrial as well as household markets (sub-contracting in

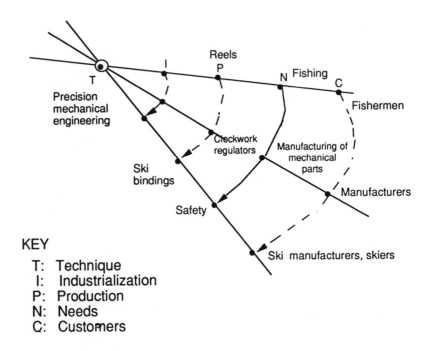

Figure 6.6 The "diversification pivot" (Translated from: Victor Berretta, *Politique et Strategie de l'Enterprise*, Paris: Éditions d'Organisation, 1975. Reproduced with permission.)

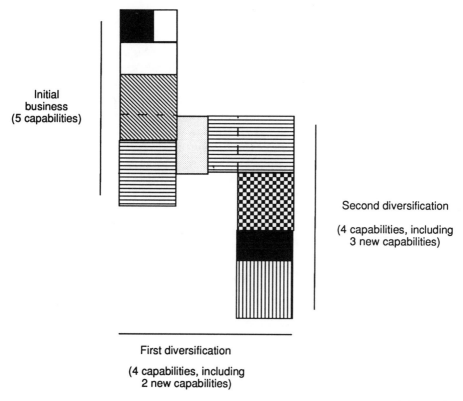

Initial
business
(5 capabilities)

Second diversification

(4 capabilities, including
3 new capabilities)

First diversification

(4 capabilities, including
2 new capabilities)

Figure 6.7 ''Pivots'' between businesses; each rectangle represents a capability and a line of capabilities represents a business (Détrie and Ramanantsoa 1983)

automotive accessories, furnishings, floor coverings, etc.) because it had technological capabilities in the processing of plastics, which it later applied to numerous areas. In contrast, Salomon grew by manufacturing all the different products intended for a specific group of customers (ski bindings and later ski boots followed by skis and other skiing equipment), and marketing them through the same distribution network, having acquired the necessary and widely differing technologies for each product. Thus, like technology clusters, other kinds of capability clusters can be developed, such as "distribution" clusters, "production" clusters, or even "brand image" clusters. When Philip Morris acquired Miller Beer, it was exploiting its core competency in and control of distribution channels; the diversification move had very little to do with technology or production. Christian Dior has leveraged its haute-couture brands to help sell ready-made clothes. Indeed, brand image is critical; visit a boutique, where you can find a wide range of luxury items bearing the firm's logo.

These strategies, aimed at exploiting particular capabilities, are all based on a coherent core of capabilities which provide the firm with a sustainable competitive advantage. This core competence has been described as the strategic "driving force"[17]. One such driving force is technology: in firms implementing strategies of this type, technology determines the scope of products offered and markets served; technology-driven organizations seek a variety of applications for their technology. Thus, growth occurs from the exploitation of the firm's technological potential.

Furthermore, we might suggest that, for some firms, technology-cluster strategies correspond to a stage in their development where their technological potential provides them with a competitive advantage in a wide and diversified range of activities. Firms like General Electric or Compagnie Générale d'Electricité evolved through a "technology-cluster" stage when they applied their core technology—electricity—to a number of different products. Later, they moved on to an unrelated diversification strategy, when electricity no longer was a key technology. However, the recent behavior of several companies, particularly Japanese corporations such as NEC, Honda, Canon, etc., would seem to suggest that the technology-cluster strategy may provide the basis for long-term competitive advantage. Thus, technology cluster strategies may be only a transitional phase for some firms, while providing the foundation for long-run growth and development for others.

CONCLUSION

The major advantage of the technology-cluster concept is the emphasis it places upon technology as a fundamental dimension in the strategy of some firms. While other strategy concepts, such as the strategic segment or the pivot of diversification, could encompass corporate strategies which are based on the firm's technological capabilities, they tend to focus on the products and markets to such an extent that the importance of technology is inevitably underestimated. Thus, it is less the novelty of the concept than the change in conventional thinking it requires concerning corporate strategy which makes the technology cluster approach important. It is a different mindset. In a time when technology seems to play an increasingly important role in competition, such an approach focuses, in a more direct way, on the behavior of firms which try to use their technological potential as their main source of competitive advantage.

Beyond these strictly strategic considerations, the concept of technology cluster also calls for a closer examination of the more psychological, cultural and social aspects of firms which appear to follow a development logic centered on technology. The major challenge in trying to implement technology-cluster strategies may not, after all, be strictly economic technological in nature; it may lie in the inability of individuals to accept that the firm follows a development logic which downplays the importance of businesses and industries. In western societies, at least, the concept of "the business" plays an important cultural and social role and is a difficult mindset to change.

NOTES AND REFERENCES

1. K. Ohmae, *The Mind of the Strategist*, New York: Penguin Books, 1982; GEST, *Grappes Technologiques: Les Nouvelles Stratégies d'Enterprise*, Paris: McGraw-Hill, 1986; C.K. Prahalad and G. Hamel, "The Core Competence of the Corporation," *Harvard Business Review*, May–June 1990; D. Ulrich and D. Lake, *Organizational Capability*, New York: Wiley, 1990.
2. GEST, *Grappes Technologiques: Les Nouvelles Stratégies d'Entreprise*, Paris: McGraw-Hill, 1986, p. 17.
3. M. Giget, "Les Bonzaïs de l'Industrie Japonaise," French Ministry of Industry and Research, CPE, publication 40, Paris: July 1984.
4. E. Roberts and C. Berry, "Entering New Businesses: Selecting Strategies for Success," *Sloan Management Review*, spring 1985.
5. C. K. Prahalad and G. Hamel, "The Core Competence of the Corporation," *Harvard Business Review*, May–June 1990.
6. GEST, *Grappes Technologiques: Les Nouvelles Sratégies d'Entreprise*, Paris: McGraw-Hill, 1986, p. 36.
7. Sest-Euroconsult, "La Valorisation des Technologies dans les Industries Japonaises Fournisseurs d'Equipements Aerospatiaux," France Ministry of Industry and Research, CPE, publication 47, Paris: December 1984.
8. M. Porter, *Competitive Strategy*, New York: Free Press, 1980, p. 5.
9. GEST, *Grappes Technologiques: Les Nouvelles Stratégies d'Entreprise*, Paris: McGraw-Hill, 1986, p. 168.
10. *La Tribune de l'Economie*, November 28, 1986, p. 12.
11. R. Wensley, "PIMS and BCG: New Horizons or False Dawn?", *Strategic Management Journal*, **3**, 1982.
12. GEST, *Grappes Technologiques: Les Nouvelles Stratégies d'Entreprise*, Paris: McGraw-Hill, 1986, p. 47.
13. GEST, *Grappes Technologiques: Les Nouvelles Stratégies d'Entreprise*, Paris: McGraw-Hill, 1986, p. 51.
14. V. Berretta, *Politique et Strategie de l'Entreprise*, Paris: Editions d'Organization, 1975, pp. 136–155.
15. J.P. Détrie and B Ramanantsoa, *Stratégie de l'Entreprise et Diversification*, Paris: Fernand Nathan, 1983, p. 87.
16. R. Rumelt, *Strategy, Structure, and Economic Performance*, Cambridge: Harvard Business School Press, 1974.
17. B. Tregoe and J. Zimmerman, *Top Management Strategy*, New York, NY: Simon and Schuster, 1980, pp. 47–48.

Chapter 7

Technological Partnerships and Strategic Alliances

In recent years, given the substantial financial resources necessary for the development of new technology, more and more firms seem to be engaging in activities which do not conform to traditional views on competition: many companies are entering strategic alliances, often with competitors, while others are turning to their governments to secure support for their technological strategies.

As we mentioned in the previous chapter, firms implementing technology-based strategies usually have established close links with external sources of technology, such as university research laboratories[1]. Relationships of this type facilitate the integration of "scientific" research with "technological" applied work, but they do not alter fundamentally the rules of competition. In other words, with industry–university collaboration, competition still takes place in the market (once products have been developed). Firms establishing a strong network of partnerships with R&D centers can thus improve their competitive position. This competitive position is evaluated in relation to that of the other competitors in the market which are clearly defined as rivals.

In contrast, when firms establish relationships with governments or with other firms which are competitors or potential rivals in order to improve their technological capabilities, they change the nature of competition[2]. Yet, thus far, we have only considered technology as a factor which bestows individual firms with competitive advantage. Some of the strategic moves made by firms in recent years, however, now force us to conceive of technology as a stake in a game between the firm and external partners; a game in which market forces and competition are relegated to a secondary position. Instead of having rivals compete in a free market environment, this new situation involves firms seeking support from their governments in order to compete more successfully and establishing collaborative relationships with other firms against whom they may later have to compete[3].

THE ROLE OF GOVERNMENT IN DEVELOPING TECHNOLOGY

As a cornerstone of both national security and economic development, technology is a priority concern for governments of all industrialized countries[4]. The importance conferred on technology is manifest in massive government intervention aimed at technology development. As the main sources of technology development, firms are usually the largest beneficiaries of state intervention.

Government intervention concerning technology takes different forms:

- *R&D financing*. By financing R&D conducted by firms, the government helps firms reinforce their technological potential. In addition, by conducting part of the R&D in government research centers, it develops technologies that firms can later use.
- *Steering technological development*. Through government contracts, the state provides a market for the technologies developed, and by favoring certain suppliers, it guides the technological specialization of firms.

Government intervention thus dramatically alters the rules of competition. To win government contracts, firms do not compete solely on traditional grounds such as performance and cost but, almost inevitably, are also submitted to political considerations. Later, in more open markets, firms benefit from technological advantages which they have developed as a result of governmental interaction.

Government Financing of Technology

In Chapter 1 we pointed out that the percentage of industry-funded R&D in large industrialized countries has tended to increase in recent years. This trend, however, does not change the fact that government plays a critical role in the development of the technological potential in a great number of firms. In 1987, for example, the average percentage of government-sponsored R&D among industrialized nations totalled 43%[5]; however, while R&D is heavily financed by the government in large industrialized countries, it is conducted primarily by industry. There is thus a significant transfer of government resources to firms for the purpose of technology development. In the aerospace industry, for example, it has been estimated that the development of the Boeing 707 aircraft was 80% financed by the US defense budget; the 747, which evolved from what was initially designed to be a military cargo aircraft, was also massively financed by the US government. In the field of aircraft engines, NASA granted $300 million for the development of Propfan engines (supersonic propeller engines) designed to equip future commercial aircraft[6]. Thus, the rivalry between Airbus—which gets substantial financial support from the European governments participating in the consortium—and Boeing diverges widely from the traditional model of perfect competition. Success depends as much on government funding as it does on their respective competitive strategies.

The nature of the financial support firms receive from government varies by country. While the importance of state intervention in France is widely acknowledged, the intervention of the American federal government is almost as important, even though it takes place in a more indirect way (e.g. tax policy). Thus, despite significant operating profits, Boeing paid no corporate taxes between 1970 and 1984. In fact, Boeing received a $285 million net tax refund during that period[6].

B. Bellon, an expert on the economic intervention of government, describes the US national R&D policy as follows: "The American federal state's fundings account for half of total US R&D expenditures, the other half being exempt from taxes"[5]. In Japan, MITI is the instrument of government industrial policy and matches the nation's economic objectives with the interests of the private sector. Our purpose here is not to compare the various systems of state intervention. Rather, we seek to deal with the government as an entity influencing the formulation of firms' strategies. We are thus interested in examining how the government affects competition rather than merely how it dictates or applies rules regarding competition.

The strategic role of the government is most evident in the defense sector. In all countries which have a defense industry, the bulk of the R&D conducted is financed by the government. For example, in 1984, government R&D sponsorship for defense totalled $28 billion in the United States[5] and almost 18 billion francs in France[7], accounting for close to 80% of total defense R&D expenditures. Indeed, firms active in defense-related industries owe a significant part of their technological capability to the financial aid they receive from the government. For example, between 1978 and 1982, the French government financed more than 80% of Aerospatiale's R&D investments; however, the corporation derived more than 50% of its revenues from civilian activities[7]. Similarly, approximately half of United Technologies' R&D expenditures are financed by the American federal government although the corporation has diversified into a broad range of civilian activities.

However, defense is not the only industry where government

intervention is significant. The technological development of the French telecommunications industry was also made possible by substantial financial support by the government. Digital switching technologies were initially developed by the CNET (Centre National d'Etudes des Télécommunications), a government research center, and later transferred to Alcatel which was the firm chosen by the government to manufacture the equipment used by the state-run telephone company. Alcatel, which acquired ITT's telecommunications business in 1986, is now one of the leading competitors in the industry worldwide but largely owes that strong position to support from the French government. Nuclear energy, electronics, and aerospace are other industries where mechanisms far removed from free market conditions operate.

The technologies firms in such industries possess and use to compete in global markets are thus largely due to government financial support. The competitive positions of such firms are, at least partly, the result of their relationships with the government. Indeed, the amount of government funding depends on the quality of the relationship; a firm having a sound relationship with the government can use the aid granted by the latter to develop and enhance its technological potential and thus be better prepared to cope with direct competition.

Government Steering of Technology Development

While the mechanisms of the free market are greatly altered by the intervention of the government, this clearly does not eliminate rivalry among firms. Indeed, there is fierce competition among firms over the distribution of the R&D resources granted by the government for technology development. This rivalry can be intense when the government seeks to determine which firms will be entrusted with the development of a new technology. In many industries, it would be too costly for governments to support technology development in several competing firms. In the case of France, the government would never finance simultaneously rival technology development programs. The awarding of important contracts to dominant firms in each industry tends to direct the efforts of firms towards the development of particular technologies and steers the industry toward increasing specialization. Thus, in a great number of industries in France, competition among rivals is being replaced by a situation where each industry has a single "national champion." In the defense industry, competition has almost disappeared; this is also the case in the nuclear and aerospace industries. In the United States, the same kind of evolution may also be taking place, although in a less pronounced and apparent manner. The rivalry that exists among the various suppliers to the Pentagon seems somewhat artificial; the dominant firms in each industry are awarded the prime contracts for large programs, often forcing other competitors to abandon the business or go bankrupt[8]. In the American commercial aircraft industry, as well, competition is decreasing and is now limited to a duel between Boeing and McDonnell–Douglas.

In the supercomputer industry, Cray Research has been able to take advantage of the fact that no real American competitors remain in the high end of the market. By spinning off the portion of the company developing the highest risk technology (gallium arsenide chips) to form a new entity—Cray Computer—the firm virtually guarantees itself on-going government research and procurement contracts. Such contracts are awarded only through a competitive bid process (requiring at least two bidders), but owing to national security implications would never be given to foreign competitors. Thus, for the moment at least, either Cray (Research) wins or Cray (Computer) wins.

The competition for government financial support to develop technology can also occur between firms in different industries which lobby to influence public officials in their decisions to allocate R&D funds to particular programs. In the defense industry in France, for example, although they are not direct competitors, Dassault (an aerospace company) and GIAT (a firm specializing in artillery equipment) compete for the allocation of defense funds to develop either a new type of battle tank or an advanced fighter aircraft. Indeed, the two corporations need the technologies that these programs would allow them to develop in order to compete successfully in global markets in their respective fields. This rivalry between firms for the allocation of government R&D funds does not take the form of market-based competitive strategy; rather, it takes the form of "relational strategy"[9].

In global markets, competition can also be affected by government intervention. Because technology is often a sensitive issue, for the acquiring country as well as for the selling country, the political dimension of competition is important. The relationship between the two countries and the pressures that the selling country may put on the acquiring one are factors which play a significant role, in some cases even more important than the respective competitive advantages of the firms concerned.

Thus, to a great extent, the debate about fair and unfair competition loses much of its relevance. In some industries, notably those where technology plays a decisive role and where, through government procurement contracts, the state is in a position to control the market, the success or failure of firms depends more on relations established with the government than on competitive strategy. While privileged relationships with the government often alter competition to a great extent in high technology industries, so do cooperative inter-firm agreements which are frequently based on technology.

TECHNOLOGY-BASED ALLIANCES

One of the most striking developments in the last decade regarding the evolution of industrial organization is the surge in the number of alliances between firms that operate in the same business. Indeed, it appears that firms trying to keep up with increasingly rapid and costly technological progress have produced not only a proliferation of upstream/downstream cooperative agreements, but also a growing number of partnerships between firms in the same business—cooperation among rivals. This latter phenomenon is more difficult to interpret than agreements between suppliers and buyers but is by no means a rare or marginal phenomenon. In fact, a recent study of alliances indicates that close to 85% of all alliances are set up between rival, or potentially rival, firms[10].

A Definition of Technology-based Alliances

Technological alliances can be defined as relationships where firms cooperate, on the basis of their technological capabilities, with their current or potential competitors. By engaging in such alliances, firms suppress (at least temporarily) the competition that exists between them or alter the way in which they compete in a given industry. This definition does not apply to relationships in which competition between the allied firms is not an issue. For example, the agreement signed between Thomson (the leading French electronics firm) and General Electric, in July 1987, which stipulated that Thomson would trade its medical equipment business for General Electric's consumer electronics division, does not constitute a cooperative agreement we would characterize as an alliance[11]. This agreement is basically an ownership transfer from Thomson to GE in medical equipment and from GE to Thomson in consumer electronics, resulting in greater industry concentration in both fields. In contrast, we consider most joint ventures to be alliances. For example, when a firm forms a joint venture to enter a new market with the help of a local partner (manufacturer or distributor) this poses the problem of potential future competition since the local partners may eventually acquire the entrant's technology and become an independent competitor. The entrant may also develop a local distribution network making it possible for it to bypass its local partner[12].

One of the oldest forms of alliance, which anti-trust laws were designed to prevent, are agreements among firms to regulate prices, reduce competition and share markets and businesses. Such agreements are necessarily kept secret. Some perfectly legal alliances may also be covert. Indeed, not all alliances result in the formation of specific legal entities nor in the modification of the existing structures of the participating firms. Examples of "structureless" alliances have been observed in the semiconductor industry in the form of mutual agreements between manufacturers. Large customer businesses often require second sourcing arrangements so as to prevent shortages if their main supplier fails to meet deadlines. Most manufacturers therefore enter into informal arrangements with competitors to produce each other's devices, the same products being listed in their respective catalogues. The existence of such mutual agreements over long periods of time leads to an alliance which does not translate into noticeable organizational change. In contrast, when technological alliances lead to the creation of new structures, or when they are based on international cooperative programs (such as Airbus, Concorde, etc.), they become highly visible[13].

With respect to technology, political–technological strategies and strategic alliances are not mutually exclusive. On the contrary, they can be combined in complex cooperative arrangements involving many partners. While it is obvious in Europe that the alliance phenomenon is associated with state intervention, the United States also acknowledges this link, even in the Silicon Valley where free enterprise reigns supreme. Indeed, the US semiconductor industry has received substantial federal military funds over the years. Furthermore, a consortium involving semiconductor manufacturers and user firms (Sematech) has been formed which includes substantial aid from the government to improve technology and thus better compete against the Japanese. The manufacturing firms involved include Texas Instruments, Motorola, National Semiconductor, Intel and AMD, while the user firms are IBM, DEC and Hewlett-Packard. Formed with the aim of reducing risk and uncertainty, such alliances would violate anti-trust laws if the US Congress had not adopted the National Research and Development Act in 1984 authorizing, under certain conditions, firms which compete in the same industry to conduct joint research and development. While such practices have long been in existence in Japan, this would have been inconceivable only ten years ago in the United States.

Types of Technology-based Alliances

Alliances are usually created by firms to pool resources and capabilities. Not all alliances are technology-based but in a majority of cases, technology is a key element. In a recent study of almost 200 alliances formed by rival firms in manufacturing industries, it was found that 16% were R&D agreements, while another 51% involved substantial R&D work and technology development[14]. Thus, about two-thirds of all strategic alliances can be considered as technology-based. The alliances we are examining here are those where technology is the key resource. Technology can play a role in alliances in two different ways:

- as a resource that is transferred from one partner firm to another within the framework of the collaborative agreement;
- as an end or partial objective of the alliance, the partner firms jointly developing technologies or new products.

Technology Transfer in Alliances

In this case, technology is exchanged in return for complementary technology. For instance, IBM focuses upon computers while NTT develops telephone switching equipment; the two corporations have established cross-licensing agreements as their respective technologies tend to be combined in their new businesses. The alliance between AT&T, Olivetti and Philips has the same aim. Their respective technologies led to different products which must now be combined.

This category of alliance also includes technology transfers in return for access to a larger market. One such example is the Rover–Honda alliance in which Rover (formerly British Leyland: BL) manufactures and sells cars designed and developed by Honda. Rover thus gets access to leading-edge automobile designs and technology while Honda gets access to the attractive European automobile market without having to face the current very restrictive quotas on Japanese imports. Manufacturing licenses and OEM agreements also fall into this category of alliance, which has existed for quite some time[15]. The US–Japan–Europe Triad is the scene of an exploding number of collaborative agreements of this type. According to K. Ohmae[16], with the cost of R&D increasing steadily and technologies spreading faster, innovations must be exploited rapidly and in large markets in order to be profitable. Only a very few corporations like IBM, Xerox and Kodak have distribution networks which enable them to gain sufficient market share on a global basis to recover technology development investments. Other firms must engage in cross-licensing or cross-distribution agreements with foreign competitors originating from other Triad countries in order to ensure their entry in foreign markets in exchange for technology. Thus, in the case of VCRs, for example, Matsushita succeeded in imposing the VHS standard worldwide because it implemented an aggressive licensing policy; the Betamax standard was left behind because Sony did not have the same success in ensuring allied distribution networks.

In this kind of exchange, the technologies that are transferred are developed by the partners before the alliance is set up. The alliance is thus formed to organize the exchange of complementary technologies that ultimately lead to the development of new products. Such alliances can also be set up to achieve better commercial exploitation of a given technology by organizing the transfer of technology in return for access to particular markets.

Technology: The Purpose of the Alliance

Some technology-based alliances are formed specifically to facilitate technology development; the firms involved thus join their R&D capabilities to work on projects termed "pre-competitive"[17]; that is, projects in the research stage and sometimes in the development stage of new products. Examples of such alliances are the Council for Chemical Research (1980, in the chemical industry), Eugenics (1981, in the field of biotechnology) and the Microelectronics and Computer Corporation—MCC (1983, in the electronics industry). In alliances of this type, R&D costs are shared by partner firms; such accords may even lead to the establishment of separate organizational units, or joint ventures, which conduct collaborative research and development providing benefits to each of the partners. Generally, such alliances remain confined to joint R&D.

Other technology-based alliances have broader purposes and include joint manufacture; this is the case with some European alliances in the aerospace and defense industries. The underlying strategic rationale for such alliances is simple: to develop technology, without contributing to the further concentration of European industry; indeed, such concentration would not be congruent with the national autonomy policy of the participating countries. Indeed, Aérospatiale's president Henri Martre presents European aeronautic alliances as an alternative to concentration: "The use of increasingly advanced and costly technologies in the aerospace industry as in other manufacturing industries, has resulted in an increase in the optimum size of firms in this market. However, in the aerospace industry, the resulting concentration was constrained within national boundaries: there are no cross-national aeronautic firms"[18]. This is primarily due to the policy of the different countries to remain autonomous in terms of defense. Such alliances thus address the two following issues:

- Unlike their US counterparts, European firms are too small because of the limited size of each national market.
- The policy of all European nations to maintain their own aeronautic industries results in excess productive capacity in Europe.

The solutions alliances provide are:

- The sharing of the fixed costs related to the development of programs which are too high to be incurred by one of the partners alone.
- The extension of markets: the "domestic" market includes all European nations instead of being limited to one single country; moreover, the competitive market is extended worldwide insofar as the products developed become competitive on a global basis.

This is the strategy underlying the Airbus Industrie alliance which was formed in 1970 by Aérospatiale and MBB, later joined by Fokker (in 1970), Casa (in 1972), British Aerospace (in 1978) and Belairbus (in 1979). However, Airbus Industrie is not a strictly European alliance competing against its giant US rivals. Indeed, the alliance was supplemented with accords signed between European and US firms in the field of aircraft engines: SNECMA and General Electric formed the CFM-International joint venture, while Rolls Royce and Pratt & Whitney created IAE (International Aero Engine) which also includes MTU (a German firm), FIAT (the Italian conglomerate) and a Japanese consortium[19].

In the aeronautics industry, a new pattern of industrial organization is beginning to emerge. This consists of a network of alliances which differs from the traditional set-up of individual manufacturers competing with one another. The case of the space industry is equally significant; the European space firm Arianespace is the prime contractor for the European Ariane launchers and awards development contracts to seven major industrial firms: Aérospatiale, SEP (Société Européenne de Propulsion), MBB/Erno, Matra, Contraves, Air Liquide and Santa/BDP. These firms sub-contract important parts of their manufacturing operations to companies originating from the eleven participating countries: West Germany, Belgium, Denmark, Spain, France, the Netherlands, Italy, Britain, Sweden, Switzerland and Ireland. The principle of multiple prime contractors implies that each of the firms is responsible for a specific sub-segment of the launcher, thereby specializing them in a particular activity and, consequently, minimizing future competition among them. This new pattern is even more obvious in the case of Airbus Industrie: the aircraft is divided into a number of elements, each partner firm being entrusted with the manufacture of each of the elements. Thus, while some of these firms were originally competitors, they now focus on the wings (British Aerospace), the cockpit and final assembly (Aérospatiale) and the fuselage (MBB). Alliances of this type encourage the technological specialization of the participating firms as well as a re-definition of their businesses through the sharing not only of R&D but also of manufacturing.

Figure 7.1 summarizes the different types of technology-based alliances we have outlined. This typology of technology-based alliances highlights the diversity of the strategic objectives pursued by firms that engage in the different alliances. These strategic objectives are in keeping with three major developments:

- *The globalization of markets.* It is in response to such globalization that a great number of firms engage in alliances in order to find large enough markets for their products and recover R&D and production capacity investments, as well as to monitor all the emerging technologies that are either rival or complementary to their own.

Technology-based alliances		
Technology transfer is the purpose of the alliance	Technology development is the purpose of the alliance	
	The alliance is constrained to joint R&D	The alliance also includes product development and manufacture
1	2	3
COMPLEMENTARITY ALLIANCE Example: distribution accords or cross-licensing agreements	PRE-COMPETITIVE ALLIANCE Example: Shared R&D facilities	JOINT PRODUCTION AGREEMENTS Example: European aerospace programs

Figure 7.1 Major types of technology-based alliances

- *Technological change.* Given the significant investments required to keep abreast of such change, firms are forced to pool their resources so as to master key technologies.
- *The emergence of new businesses.* Technologies which historically were distinct and developed in separate businesses are now increasingly combined in new, emerging businesses. Firms must thus develop complementary capabilities to remain competitive.

Strategic alliances can thus result in the emergence of networks linking multiple partners, often on an international basis. Figure 7.2 and Table 7.1 illustrate this development; the table describes Philips' network of alliances in 1985[20], while the figure represents the relationships established between firms of the computer and the telecommunications industries in the mid-1980s[21].

TECHNOLOGY-BASED ALLIANCES: COMPETITION OR COOPERATION?

In an environment marked by the growing importance of technology, more and more firms are developing relational strategies, and engaging in strategic alliances. These new behavior patterns affect, almost by definition, the rivalry between partner firms and competition within the industries concerned; indeed, they suppress head-to-head competition between allied firms since they no longer rely solely on their own resources to compete in a market governed by free trade.

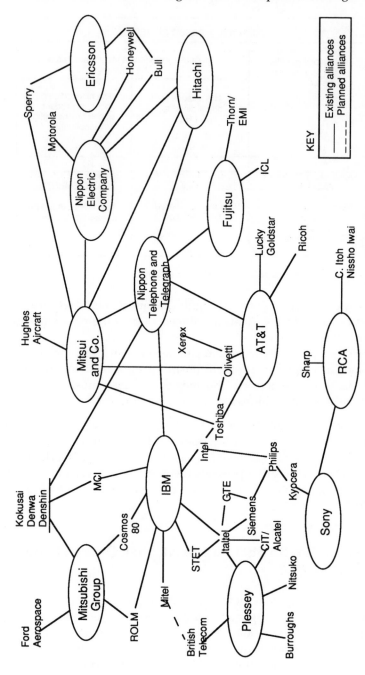

Figure 7.2 Alliances in the computer and telecommunications industries in 1985 (SRI International 1985–86)

Table 7.1 The alliance network of Philips in 1985 (H. Perlmutter and D. Heenan 1986)

Business	Partners	Country
Advanced telecommunications systems	AT&T	United States
Compact disc	Sony	Japan
Credit cards	Bull	France
Software	Bull	France
	ICL	Britain
	Siemens	West Germany
	Nixdorf-Computer	West Germany
	Olivetti	Italy
VCRs	Grundig	West Germany
	JVC	Japan
Electronic mail	Enidata	Italy
Electronic components	Matsushita	Japan
	Electronic Devices	Hong Kong
Semiconductors	Intel	United States
	Siemens	West Germany
	Asmi	The Netherlands

For firms engaging in such strategies to understand the behaviors of their partners and the new rules of competition, they must first comprehend the new "competitive" situation resulting from the alliance. While the way in which the government alters the rules of competition is obvious, the interpretation of the "competitive" situation created by alliances remains ambiguous. Are alliances durable alternatives to classical head-to-head competition? Are they formed by firms as a means of calling a provisional truce to rebuild their strengths or are they used rather to attack another competitor? Are they a means of digesting and incorporating a rival's capabilities where one of the partners progressively takes over the other in a sort of treacherous embrace[12]?

The nature and extent of the firm's involvement in alliances will differ according to how these questions are answered and how the phenomenon is interpreted. In some cases the firm will use all its strengths to pursue the objectives defined in the alliance while, in other cases, it will seek to enhance its capabilities to the detriment of its partners; in still other cases, it will be a loyal partner in the alliance while preparing for the time when the relationship will be terminated.

An Economic Interpretation

It is no longer possible to assert that economic activities are regulated by the "invisible hand." Indeed, it is obvious that other mechanisms, such as government intervention, protectionism and cooperation between competitors exist along side head-to-head competition. From an economic standpoint, alliances are only formed when each of the partners expects to derive benefits from cooperation. In this context, strategic alliances can be seen as a means of attaining mutually profitable ends for the firms involved, in a market which is no longer free, but "domesticated," to use the term of J. Arndt[22]. In Arndt's approach, the incentives that induce firms to engage in alliances with rivals are synergy obtained from combining complementary operations, lower uncertainty, and lower transaction costs.

The examples of alliances stressing complementary capabilities mentioned earlier illustrate the first incentive. The remaining two can be clarified using O. Williamson's transaction cost model[23]. While this theory was developed to analyze vertical integration strategies rather than strategic alliances, it is still useful for making an economic interpretation of the latter. The production and trade of goods can be organized in various ways ranging from transactions in a free market, in which each player is a single entity, to transactions within an organization or firm. The problem facing the manager is to determine which transactions should be made in the market and which should be controlled within the firm. According to Williamson, choosing between markets and hierarchies implies evaluating the transaction cost of each possible option; for example, the risk associated with depending on a powerful supplier can be seen as having a cost which is higher than that of vertical integration. As a transaction can be defined as that which takes place every time a good or service is transferred between two separate production units (whether these units are part of the same firm or not), transaction costs related to market mechanisms can be compared to those related to internal transactions (the notion of cost being used here in the broad sense of the term: price, risk, uncertainty, learning, etc.). In this context, there is no point in engaging in an alliance to make a transaction which is risk-free and does not require specific assets (as, for example, a particular piece of equipment or highly specialized skill). In contrast, an alliance should be formed when the transactions involved are characterized by their frequency, uncertainty or specificity:

- *Frequency.* The more frequent the transaction, the more it is in the interest of the players to organize it to save the costs of repeated negotiation.
- *Uncertainty.* When the terms of the transaction are not predictable and there is a high risk that the market will not meet the firm's specific need (for example, finding a distribution channel for a pioneering product), the risks associated with such uncertainty can be minimized by internalizing the transaction.
- *Specificity.* If the parties involved must make long-term and specific

investments, either in terms of equipment or in terms of personnel, it is in their interest to avoid short-term contracts and instead organize a system of stable collaboration.

This analytical framework has been used to study alliances in the European aerospace industry, where the notions of frequency, uncertainty and specificity of assets, related to transaction costs, are particularly relevant and explain the high degree of stability associated with such accords[24]. Similarly, "pre-competitive" alliances (which are based on transactions that *a priori* are extremely uncertain and require the sharing of specific capabilities and valuable expertise) can be analyzed from an economic standpoint using the same approach.

Firms engage in alliances only when they find that such relationships provide them with advantages. Therefore, it is not surprising to observe that collaborative agreements generally only cover part of the activities of firms: two firms can cooperate in the development of a particular technology, but compete against each other on other technologies, and even compete head-to-head in certain markets. For example, Chrysler and Mitsubishi collaborate in the US market, but compete in the Korean market. Furthermore, alliances can be terminated at any time. The partners involved usually have the option to choose between remaining in the alliance or withdrawing from it and relying on market mechanisms to carry out the transactions the alliance previously internalized. Firms are thus constantly choosing between classic competitive strategies and strategic alliances.

A Strategic Interpretation

While the economic interpretation of alliances and partnerships provides an analytical framework for assessing situations which are favorable or unfavorable to such collaborative behavior, it is limited in scope. Indeed, it does not take the firms' strategy into account. To gain a fuller picture of such relationships, it is crucial to analyze the strategic orientations of the participating firms, which all have specific resources, capabilities and objectives. There are two different schools of thought: in the first, firms engaging in alliances avoid having to confront one another in uncertain and mutually detrimental competition. As in the case of strategies based on government intervention, firms sign collaborative agreements to limit the risks they face and increase the stability of their environments thereby limiting the competitive pressures to which they are submitted[25]. In this interpretation, alliances are clearly a form of collusion. With the second school, firms engage in alliances to compete with one another in a different way. Alliances are viewed as a competitive weapon or a lure designed to attract their partners into a trap deliberately set to assimilate them. The latter interpretation of alliances postulates imbalance regarding the participants' resources and strategic intentions[12].

Some alliances do seem to result in relationships in which one of the partners becomes progressively weaker. If we go back to an example we mentioned earlier, the complementary collaboration between Honda and Rover (British Leyland) appears to have produced a rather unbalanced relationship, with Honda clearly taking the upper hand. As one British executive put it: "This is a perfectly balanced relationship; proof of this is that Honda recently acquired 25% of British Leyland's equity while BL holds 25% of Honda-UK's equity." Indeed, we can question whether, as time passes, Rover will retain comprehensive auto design skills or whether it will merely be a European subsidiary of Honda.

The alliance between General Electric and SNECMA to develop the CFM-56 aircraft engine also appears to be unbalanced. Despite the sharing of responsibility, GE builds the high-pressure core, having the strategic technological capabilities. SNECMA is largely dependent on the relationship with GE, whereas the converse is less true. In this situation, there are two possible outcomes for the alliance: either a reinforcement of SNECMA's position through the acquisition of key technologies, or an increased dependency of SNECMA upon its partner.

In contrast, other alliances can be viewed as stable and balanced relationships between the participants, with none of the partners reinforcing its position to the detriment of the others. This is often the case when the relationship leads to specialization of the partners and increases the complementarity of their technological capabilities. The Airbus cooperative program falls into this category of alliance. The general stability of alliances of this type results from the fact that each of the partners loses part of its capability (the part which relates to the operations carried out by other participants). This loss of capability can pose a strategic problem to all the partners if the alliance breaks up. Aérospatiale thus decided to cooperate, outside the Airbus consortium, with the Italian firm Aeritalia to develop the ATR42 commuter aircraft and took responsibility specifically for the operations it does not perform within the Airbus program, thereby retaining the overall capability to develop and manufacture a complete aircraft.

Thus, it appears that technology transfer alliances tend to be more competitive and less cooperative than alliances in which technology or new products are developed in common. Indeed, while in the latter kind of agreements the partner firms work together to develop new technology and therefore end up having similar capabilities, in technology transfer alliances, the very complementarity which led to the formation of the alliance motivates the partners to acquire the capabilities they lack. The extent to which this is possible will depend on[26]:

- the *appropriability* of the capabilities concerned—all capabilities are not equally easy to acquire, in particular, formalized, explicit technology may often be more easily captured than tacit know-how, managerial skills or access to specialized assets;
- the *transparency* of the technology-providing firm—some competitors seem to be more efficient than others at making access to their particular skills difficult. This can result from specific procedures set up to control the flow of information to outsiders, from the secretive nature of a firm's corporate culture or even from the nationality or language of the firm: for instance, it is more difficult for an American firm to learn from a Japanese or Korean partner—because all documents and conversations are in a foreign language—than from a British or Canadian partner.
- the *absorptive capacity*, or organizational learning capability of the firm which seeks to gain access to technology provided by the partner. Some firms appear to be a lot more receptive to information and knowledge acquired from external sources than other firms which suffer from the NIH (not invented here) syndrome.

In summary, entering an alliance can be seen as an attractive strategy in which each participants' weaknesses are offset by the contributions of its partners' strengths; however, the initial balance can prove unstable if one of the participant's capabilities are crucial and cannot be easily transferred. In particular, a distinctive technological capability which is difficult to transfer, because it is costly, or because it is tacit and based on expertise, can become a stranglehold in the relationship established by the alliance[27]. Similarly, in the case of alliances involving management methods and organizational competence, firms must make sure that what they are seeking to acquire is transferable before engaging in the partnership. Some Western firms (e.g. General Motors) which have signed collaborative agreements with Japanese companies have run into difficulties attempting to transfer Japanese management procedures: technology is easier to transfer than management methods. Thus, alliances can prove to be booby traps. There is a risk that the weaker partner will only become more dependent upon the other participant over time. Even if it is aware of the fact that by remaining in the alliance it will only get weaker, such a partner often has no other alternative.

CONCLUSION

Government intervention alters the rules of competition by increasing the technological capabilities of some firms and creating protected markets. Strategic alliances, in contrast, can be utilized in different ways. The extent to which an alliance is "cooperative" or "competitive" in nature is determined by the strategic intentions of each participant. However, the motives of the partners are less stable than the economic context of the alliance and can change rapidly, turning an alliance which was non-competitive into an unbalanced situation that fuels renewed rivalry between the former collaborators.

NOTES AND REFERENCES

1. "Business and Universities: A New Partnership," *Business Week*, December 20, 1982; D. Gray, T. Solomon, and W. Hetzner, *Technological Innovation: Strategies for a New Partnership*, New York: North-Holland, 1986; W. Evan and P. Olk, "R&D Consortia: A New U.S. Organizational Form," *Sloan Management Review*, spring 1990.
2. "Corporate Odd Couples," *Business Week*, July 21, 1986; H. Perlmutter and D. Heenan, "Cooperate to Compete Globally," *Harvard Business Review*, March–April 1986.
3. R. Reich and E. Mankin, "Joint Ventures With Japan Give Away Our Future," *Harvard Business Review*, March–April 1986; G. Hamel, Y. Doz, and C. K. Prahalad, "Collaborate With Your Competitors—and Win," *Harvard Business Review*, January–February 1989.
4. S. Ramo, "National Security and Our Technology Edge," *Harvard Business Review*, November–December 1989; R. Reich, "The Quiet Path to Technological Preeminence," *Scientific American*, October 1989; R. Reich, "Who is Us?" *Harvard Business Review*, January–February 1989; M. Porter, *The Competitive Advantage of Nations*, New York: Free Press, 1990.
5. B. Bellon, *La Politique Industrielle de l'Etat Federal aux Etat-Unis*, Paris: Economica, 1986.
6. A. Faujas, "La Rivalite Aerienne Americano-Europeenne," *Le Monde*, March 31, 1987.
7. P. Dussauge, *L'Industrie Francaise de l'Armement*, Paris: Economica, 1986.
8. J. Gansler, *The Defense Industry*, Cambridge, Mass: MIT Press, 1980.
9. J. Anastassopoulos and P. Dussauge, "French Savoir-Faire in Selling Arms: A New Way of Doing Business," *Long Range Planning*, October 1985; J. Anastassopoulos, G. Blanc, J. Nioche and B. Ramanantsoa, *Pour Une Nouvelle Politique d'Entreprise*, Paris: PUF, 1985, pp. 49–67.
10. M. Hergert and D. Morris, "Trends in International Collaborative Agreements," *Columbia Journal of World Business*, summer 1987.
11. "Un Accord avec General Electric: Thomson cede l'Equipement Medical mais s'etend dans l'Audio-visuel," *Le Monde*, July 24, 1987.
12. G. Hamel, Y. Doz, and C. K. Prahalad, "Collaborate with Your Competitors – and Win," *Harvard Business Review*, January–February 1989.
13. K. Harrigan, *Strategies for Joint Ventures*, Lexington: Lexington Books, 1985; K. Harrigan, *Managing for Joint Venture Success*, Lexington: Lexington Books, 1986; M. Hochmuth, *Organizing the Transnational*, Leyde: A. W. Sijthoff, 1974.
14. P. Dussauge and B. Garrette, "Patterns of Strategic Alliances Between Rival Firms," HEC working paper, 1991.
15. B. James, "Alliance: The New Strategic Focus," *Long Range Planning*, June 1985.
16. K. Ohmae, *Triad Power*, New York: The Free Press, 1985.

17. H. Fusfeld and C. Haklisch, "Cooperative R&D for Competitors," *Harvard Business Review*, November–December 1985.
18. H. Martre, "L'Aeronautique entre la Cooperation et la Competition," *Politique Industrielle*, summer 1986.
19. F. Germain, "Cooperer en Europe, l'Exemple d'Airbus," *Economie et Politique*, January 1985.
20. H. Perlmutter and D. Heenan, "Cooperate to Compete Globally," *Harvard Business Review*, March–April 1986.
21. M. Gorbis and K. Yorke, "Strategic Partnerships: A New Corporate Response," report 730, *SRI International*, winter 1985–86.
22. J. Arndt, "Toward a Concept of Domesticated Markets," *Journal of Marketing*, **43**, fall 1979.
23. O. Williamson, *Markets and Hierarchies. Analysis and Antitrust Implications*, New York: The Free Press, 1975; O. Williamson, "The Modern Corporation: Origins, Evolution, Attributes," *Journal of Economic Literature*, December 1981.
24. C. Koenig and R. Thietart, "Managers, Engineers and Politicians: The Emergence of the Mutual Organization in the European Aerospace Industry," Asociacion Espanola de macroingenieria, conference proceedings, Barcelona, December 1986.
25. K. Ohmae, "The Global Logic of Strategic Alliances," *Harvard Business Review*, March–April, 1989.
26. G. Hamel, "Competition for Competence and Inter-partner Learning within International Strategic Alliances", *Strategic Management Journal*, summer 1991.
27. R. Reich and E. Mankin, "Joint Ventures With Japan Give Away Our Future," *Harvard Business Review*, March–April 1986.

Technology and Organization

_____ Chapter 8

Technology and Structure

This book focuses on the firm for which technology is a key factor of success. Defining the issue of technology management in such terms often leads to an emphasis on the analytical dimensions of strategy, passing over the organizational and cultural dimensions. Yet, the issues of organizational structure, management processes, and corporate culture are as important as strategic analysis if the firm is to gain competitive advantage from its technology.

We started by examining the analytical side because it is consistent with previous treatments of strategy which have separated strategy "formulation" from strategy "implementation." However intellectually satisfying, such a sequenced model of the strategy process does not reflect the reality and complexity of the way in which firms develop their policies. Indeed, very rarely, if ever, are structures set up, processes designed and corporate cultures created in order to implement previously formulated strategies; instead, the strategy process is carried out within firms which already have a structure, processes and a corporate culture, all of which impact strategy. Clearly, a technology-based strategy requires an appropriate organization. In this last section of the book, we examine explicitly the role of organizational structure (this chapter), management processes (Chapter 9), and the importance of corporate culture (Chapter 10) in technological strategy.

The structure of an organization can be defined as the functions and relationships which formally determine the tasks that each of the units composing the organization must carry out, and the liaisons established between such units. Structure thus defines the specific roles for each unit as well as the hierarchical relationships and coordination mechanisms which ensure the coherence of the organization as a whole. The first problem technology-based strategies pose in terms of structure concerns the management of the

R&D function; i.e. the function which develops technology. This issue is closely related to that of the position of the R&D function in the organization and entails a fundamental paradox: the efficiency of the R&D function depends on its degree of specialization, while the overall success of the firm depends on the coordination between R&D and the other functions. After discussing the management of the R&D function, we will examine the needs for coordination between it and the other functions in the organization. This will enable us to analyze the case of diversified firms where the problem of coordination among functions is further complicated by the need for coordination across divisions. We will then see that the success of firms implementing technology-based strategies or engaging in strategic alliances depends on the quality of the coordination between centralized research departments and the marketing departments in the case of the former, and on the leveraging of technological capabilities that the firms possess in the case of the latter. The chapter then closes with a discussion of the larger problem of designing organizational structures to foster innovation in technology-based firms.

THE R&D PARADOX

Although the belief that great discoveries are made by geniuses in old, dusty laboratories is now increasingly seen as a myth, expectations concerning R&D are still both high and ambiguous; high because the future of many firms depends on the R&D function, and ambiguous because the real purpose of R&D—whether to innovate or to improve existing products or processes—is often unclear. The contribution of the R&D department to the strategy and growth of the firm is extremely difficult to assess. What are the pertinent criteria to be used in the evaluation of the "productivity" of a firm's R&D and in the allocation of R&D funds? Some firms measure R&D by counting the number of patents they have registered, the publications they have made in specialized journals, the number of projects they have initiated or the number of new products they have actually developed and marketed. Such criteria, while serving as useful indicators, are too quantitative; indeed, all patents and new products are not equally important. Moreover, when a product has proved profitable, it is difficult to attribute its success to either R&D, marketing, production or the sales force. For lack of reliable criteria, a great number of firms base their promotion system in R&D on seniority and analyze the function in terms of the resources used rather than in terms of the results obtained.

Thus, R&D strategy often amounts, in practice, to renewing or extending past plans and budgets. There are substantial risks inherent in such an approach:

- over-investment in well established "base" technologies which no longer have strategic importance;
- under-investment in new technologies—i.e. "key" and "emerging" technologies—on which firms will compete in the future;
- sudden cuts in R&D expenditures, when the firm faces financial problems, which jeopardize the long-run capability of the firm.

Added to the problems described above is the issue of where to locate R&D within the organization. Should it be centralized, in one location, or should it be dispersed by product or division, so as to achieve better coordination with production and marketing needs?

The Need for Differentiation and Integration

The paradoxical need to specialize the R&D function on the one hand and to coordinate it with the firm's other functions on the other, can be analyzed using the work of P. Lawrence and J. Lorsch[1], which stresses the concepts of "differentiation" and "integration."

Differentiating Technology

Differentiation in organizations is reflected in the distinctive cognitive and emotional orientations among members of different units and the variations in formal structure among units. Differentiation by function is necessary since each organizational unit deals with a particular aspect of the firm's environment. Functional specialization reflects the varying ways in which members of different units view the organization's environment; it also reflects the differences in the people they interact with and in the tasks that are carried out. Thus, sales managers conceive of the environment as consisting mainly of the following dominant issues: meeting customer needs, anticipating competitors' actions, negotiating prices, technology being only one of the elements embodied in the products they offer. R&D managers, however, deal with a part of the environment that is dominated by scientific and technological change, viewing the sale of the products they develop as the natural outcome of innovation. Thus, while top management may consider the environment as a general source of opportunities and threats, functional managers each view a different facet of it. Lawrence and Lorsch conceptualize the external environment of the organization as divided into three sectors: a market sector with which the marketing unit deals, a techno-economic sector with which the manufacturing unit deals, and a technological and scientific sector with which the R&D or design unit deals.

In businesses where technology is of secondary importance, the sectors of the environment are viewed by the different functions of the organization in a homogeneous way. In contrast, businesses where technology plays a crucial role are characterized by greater heterogeneity of perception among the three sectors: the environment of the manufacturing function is relatively certain, whereas that of the marketing and R&D functions are uncertain and dissimilar. For organizations operating in businesses of this type, the heterogeneity is reflected in a high degree of differentiation, which can be measured along four dimensions:

- *formality* of functional structure, which is much lower in the case of R&D units than for marketing or manufacturing units;
- *interpersonal orientation* of the unit members, where getting the job done is central in manufacturing units while getting along with others is key in marketing units;
- *time horizon* of the functions, long-term for R&D and short and middle-term for marketing and manufacturing;
- *goal orientation* of each unit, concern with market goals in the case of the marketing unit, concern with cost, quality and efficiency in the case of the manufacturing unit, and concern with scientific goals in the case of the R&D unit.

Integrating Technology

For technology-based firms, the specificity of each unit's goals complicates the issue of functional integration and the quality of collaboration among organization units[1]. Whatever the firm's chosen strategy, it must effectively move its technology to the market. In particular, an organization whose strategy is "pushed by technology" must achieve integration around the R&D function. Conversely, a strategy which is "pulled by the market" implies an integration of the organization around the marketing unit and gives priority consideration to the market environment

The concepts of differentiation and integration prove useful when applied to organizations with high technological potential, as shown by numerous publications on the R&D–manufacturing–marketing interface[2]. The findings outlined in these publications suggest that, for existing products and mature technologies, the manufacturing and marketing functions play the central role in achieving integration for the organization (the "output" end of the value chain). However, for new products and technologies, this role is best assumed by the R&D function (the "input" side). Moreover, in businesses where the development/research costs ratio is high, effective organizations seem to achieve integration of the research and marketing functions through an engineering or "development" function[3]. The fact that R&D must be differentiated from the other functions implies both the need for and the difficulties of integration. Thus, it was the competitive pressure from its rival Fuji that led Kodak to respond by stimulating innovation, seeking greater integration of its research units with the corporation's strategy and structure. This effort followed a decade of complete isolation of the research laboratory which was focused primarily on emulsions for photographic films; Kodak managers still talk about "the silver curtain" which separated this laboratory from other organization units[4].

Differentiation is essential to fundamental innovation since marketing organizations often have difficulty sensing opportunities in the scientific and technological environment. At Texas Instruments, for example, artificial intelligence was developed by the central R&D unit, but the various product divisions showed little interest in the innovation initially because they were unable to assess its strategic implications. Had the R&D unit been insufficiently differentiated from the product divisions, Texas Instruments would not have developed competence in this field. However, this differentiation had a negative effect when the innovation was proposed to the business unit managers. The latter dismissed the idea, arguing that it would be of no use since there was no market for artificial intelligence. Greater integration had to be achieved in order for the corporation to enter this new business with the commitment of the entire organization. Indeed, it was not until some time later that all the functions finally approved the technological innovation.

In organizations where technology is a key factor for success, poor integration has two potential negative consequences. First, the results of research may not reach the market and only "incremental" innovations (resulting from technological evolution rather than from breakthroughs) get past the R&D–marketing interface. Thomson, for example, pioneered research on the videodisc process, but none of the firm's marketing divisions believed that there would ever be a market for such a product. In fact, none of these divisions could have been entrusted with such a product because the markets they served did not include potential customers.

Second, at the other extreme, the marketing function may be dominated by R&D to such an extent that integration translates into sheer subordination. This contributes to the likelihood of producing a technological "chimera" which fails miserably once it confronts the reality of the market. The Concorde aircraft and the "aerotrain", a train system floating on an air cusion, are well-known examples of such failures. Similarly, the first VCR, developed by RCA, was not successful for lack of adequate market understanding; RCA's management believed that this failure was related to the nature of the product and that the latter had no future. However, by taking over JVC, a subsidiary of RCA in Japan, Matsushita inherited the project and launched a product which proved extremely successful.

MANAGING R&D IN DIVERSIFIED FIRMS

The difficulties of achieving differentiation and integration outlined above deal only with the complexities faced by single-business or dominant-business firms. In firms that are diversified into several related lines of business, these problems are combined with the need for technical coordination among the various businesses. This raises several additional questions: Should R&D be centralized or decentralized in diversified firms? How can R&D be managed without fragmenting the function into myriad divisions specialized by product or by market? How can technological synergy among the different businesses be exploited without affecting their autonomy? How can depth of technical competence (the firm's technological "potential") be maintained in the face of product and market diversity?

The Challenge of Diversity

When firms diversify, and particularly when they engage in related diversification, they tend to adopt a multidivisional structure[5,6]. In an effort to divide their resources among different businesses, each division becomes a nearly self-contained unit. The problem of integration is much more complex in this type of structure. Indeed, the volume of information which the organization must absorb and act upon no longer depends solely on the heterogeneity of the environment (as was the case with non-diversified firms), but is also contingent upon the number of products or businesses on the one hand, and the degree of interdependence among these activities on the other.

When businesses are interdependent, it is necessary that each division or unit communicate with the others which could be affected by their decisions. This analysis, which is based on the work of J. Galbraith[7], has direct relevance for the location of the R&D function in the organization: distributing R&D units in the various divisions allows these units to deal directly with the problems related to each division, but also results in a dispersion of the organization's technological potential. Furthermore, if the firm fails to take the interdependence of the activities into account, it runs the risk of duplicating research projects, of being unable to combine complementary technologies, even of acquiring, at great cost, technologies which it already possesses. This risk, and the cost it represents, often induces organizations to centralize R&D. But centralizing R&D makes it much more difficult to achieve integration of R&D with the other functions. The centralization or decentralization of R&D activities is a dilemma which must be resolved for each individual organization. There is no single best solution.

Centralization or Decentralization?

The choice between centralization or decentralization of R&D depends essentially on the nature of the R&D conducted by the firm. This can be illustrated through a case example. At Renault, in the 1960s, the R&D function focused on development. This focus enabled good coordination and integration with other units since development activities are more closely related to products than are research activities. Therefore, the laboratories were scattered across the various operational units with which they interacted. At the time, the automotive industry was entering a period of commercial expansion. The main concerns were adapting the product to the market and achieving lower costs. However, in order to prevent technological innovation from being stifled by the weight of marketing and manufacturing activities, a new task force called "Advanced Research" was created and staffed with members from various R&D specialties.

The oil shock in 1973 resulted in the need for fundamental changes in the design of automobiles. In 1975, the Direction des Affaires Scientifiques et Techniques (DAST) was created to cope with this situation. Positioned at the corporate level, its task was to conduct research relevant to all the divisions and to exploit the synergies between the different businesses. The consequences of the energy crisis required that a research unit with a long-term orientation be created; this research unit did not deal with existing or near-term products. Thus, changing environmental circumstances forced a more differentiated approach to R&D. Indeed, increasing competition later led to a broadening of the mission and financial resources of the DAST, and to the creation of the corporation's research plan (Plan Recherche) which was implemented in 1981.

While the development of products and processes was still carried out in the different units, at the corporate level, the DAST provided the resources and support necessary for conducting long-term strategic research. In fact, through the newly established research plan, the DAST controlled the entire research budget for the corporation. This search for a balance between centralized R&D and research units under the authority of the divisions, leads multidivisional organizations to take quite different courses of action: those that wish to avoid capability duplication or lost synergies set up centralized departments, whereas those that conclude that centralized R&D makes integration too difficult, try to decentralize the R&D function.

Coordination Between Central and Divisional R&D

The balance between centralization and divisionalization in terms of technology depends on the distribution of responsibility between the central R&D department and divisional R&D units. For example, Hughes Tool

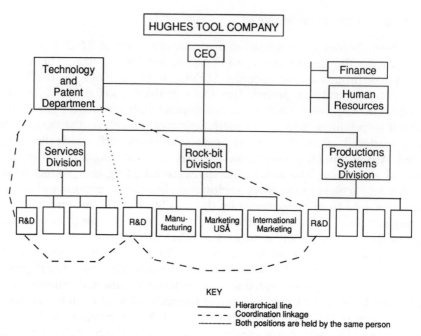

Figure 8.1   The position of R&D in the organization chart of Hughes Tool Company in 1986

Company, the world's leading manufacturer of oil drilling equipment, diversified into a variety of activities closely related to its original business. Figure 8.1 depicts the formal structure of Hughes Tool Company in 1986.

In the structure of Hughes Tool Company, the R&D function is decentralized; however, it is coordinated by the R&D department of the Rock Bit division, which has the greatest resources and technological potential, and by the Technology and Patent department at the corporate level, the same vice-president being responsible for these two units. Indeed, the patents owned by the firm allow it to implement a differentiation strategy and to legally protect itself from its competitors. The strategic importance of patents is such that it makes them an effective means of achieving integration for the entire corporation, together with the action of the Corporate Technical Advisory Council which coordinates the divisional R&D units. This council has no hierarchical authority but its purpose is to pool all the corporation's technologies and help the subsidiaries and smaller divisions in technological matters. The divisions can call upon the research laboratory of the Rock Bit division which, because of its importance, acts as the central laboratory; however, the services provided to them by this laboratory must be paid for.

DuPont de Nemours is another example of a corporation in which the R&D function is simultaneously decentralized and centralized: specific units are entrusted with the task of ensuring the coherence of the entire structure (see Figure 8.2). In this corporation, 80% of the R&D budget is allocated to the different divisions. The remaining 20% is distributed among the units conducting centralized R&D—the "engineering" unit (8%), and the central R&D unit (12%) which conducts fundamental research on emerging technologies. This latter function is defined as a "window on the world" with high scientific expertise. In order to ensure the convergence of the operational needs of the various divisions with the research projects conducted at the corporate level, the central R&D unit is partly financed through the research work it carries out for the divisions; the purpose of this system is to achieve the necessary integration. The equally necessary differentiation between long-term technological concerns and short-term operational issues is achieved through the partial autonomy of the central R&D unit which conducts a substantial amount of research on projects initiated internally. The executive board is responsible for part of the coordination of the R&D function: one of the vice-presidents who is a member of this board supervises the R&D activities of the entire company. This VP negotiates the R&D budgets of the different divisions and matches their requirements with the strategic orientations and resources of the entire organization. Moreover,

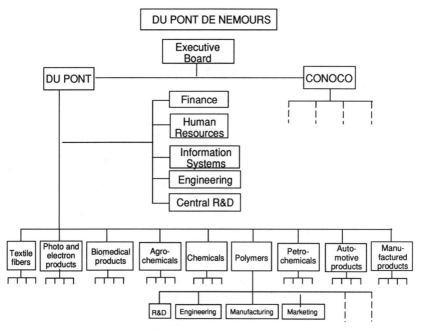

Figure 8.2 The position of R&D in the organization chart of DuPont de Nemours

the transfer of the technologies developed in the various divisions is carried out through "technology committees" in which the division managers discuss common issues; technological coordination is done in a more formal manner through monthly forums of divisional R&D managers. The vice-president responsible for technology sits on all the committees, whatever the agenda.

The examples outlined above show two mechanisms for coordinating R&D across divisions. At Hughes Tool Company, integration is carried out by the R&D unit of the main division of the organization (the same person being responsible for the R&D of the entire corporation as well as for that of this particular division). At DuPont de Nemours, there are specific units which are exclusively responsible for R&D coordination. These examples demonstrate that there is no single structure which "solves" all the problems of differentiation and integration. The challenge for each firm is to establish clear criteria which differentiate the R&D activities that need to be centralized from those that must be performed at the division or business level. The next step is to integrate the different activities through lateral, inter-division relationships. The simplest way of establishing such relationships is direct communication between divisional managers. However, more formal solutions are sometimes required: the appointment of coordinators, temporary work committees, interdisciplinary research teams, or integrators at the corporate level. Each involves different degrees of formality in inter-divisional coordination.

STRUCTURE, TECHNOLOGY AND STRATEGY

While the strategy formulated by the firm should ideally dictate the choice of structure, the existing structure also affects the strategy that is formed. The classic statement about the relationship between strategy and structure was made by A. Chandler[5]. According to Chandler, a firm must adjust its organization in accordance with the objectives it seeks to achieve. More precisely, each type of strategy or each stage of corporate development (a single product activity, a dominant product activity, multiple related product activity, unrelated diversification) is best achieved through a particular organization—structure follows strategy[6].

However, it has also been demonstrated that a given type of organization, for example a divisional organization, clearly influences the firm's strategy[8], especially in terms of technology. A particular distribution of the technological capabilities among the various divisions or between the central R&D departments and the divisional R&D units can prevent the firm from forming strategies that are not consistent with the divisional structure.

Aérospatiale, for example, is organized in four divisions: Aircraft,

Helicopters, Space and Missiles. The European space shuttle project Hermes, however, requires technological capabilities that are distributed across the firm's Space and Aircraft divisions. Indeed, Hermes can be considered either as an aircraft capable of flying into space, or as a spaceship capable of flying like an aircraft and landing. Aérospatiale, which was competing with Dassault for the prime contract on the program, should have capitalized on its dual capability in the quest for the contract; in fact, however, only the space division was committed to the project, and the company ended up having to share contract responsibilities with Dassault, another aircraft manufacturer. This can be attributed, at least in part, to inadequate integration of Aérospatiale's autonomous divisions. Organizational changes would be required to better exploit the technological synergy between the four divisions. The firm could face the same kind of problem in the future concerning the development of a vertical take-off and landing aircraft with tilting wings, whose design requires capabilities that are distributed across the Helicopters and Aircraft divisions.

Structure thus tends to confine technological know-how to particular businesses and divisions, with the unit being the exclusive user of the capability. Combining technologies in diversified organizations not only poses a problem of strategy, it also raises the issue of structure.

Internal Versus External Structures

The dispersion of skills which results from the partitioning of the organization into separate divisions makes it difficult to implement strategies based on technological synergy. Realizing synergies is difficult in divisional organizations whether such combinations occur internally (technology-cluster strategies) or externally (technology-based alliances). Additional structures must thus be developed to facilitate such strategies.

"Technology-cluster" Structures

While, in theory, each strategy has a corresponding structure, the identification of a specific structure for the technology-cluster strategy remains elusive. Analysts observe only that R&D and technology managers must assume an important position in the hierarchy in order for such a strategy to become a reality[9]. Yet, if technology clusters reflect a new kind of strategic behavior on the part of firms, it would seem unlikely that this strategic behavior is not accompanied by new, specific structures.

However, for firms displaying the technology-cluster strategy, corporate structure does not appear to differ from that of conventional multidivisional corporations. United Technologies, for example, was formed through successive acquisitions (Essex cables in 1974, Otis elevators in 1976, Carrier air conditioners in 1979, Mostek semiconductors in 1980 which it sold to Thomson in 1985, and a telecommunications activity which it bought from General Dynamics in 1982) around its original core businesses (Pratt & Whitney aircraft engines, Sikorsky helicopters, etc.). While remaining largely autonomous, these former companies have become the operational units of the corporation. United Technologies does have a large central laboratory and strives to exploit the technological synergies between the various divisions; however, its structure provides little insight into how this is done most effectively.

Relational Structures

Strategic alliances better lend themselves to the exploration of particular structures than do technology-cluster strategies[10]. Among the various types of technology-based alliances, the only one that has a specific structure is the joint production agreement, the other two types being, by definition, structure-less (see Chapter 7). We will distinguish two categories of joint production agreements in terms of their structures: simple coordination structures, and interfirm structures.

Coordination structures. In some collaborative agreements, no single partner has a dominating position and no autonomous structure is set up to jointly carry out the project. Thus, the Concorde program was conducted by a management committee including the top managers of Sud-Aviation, which later became Aérospatiale, and British Aircraft Corporation, which was later integrated into British Aerospace. The actual work, shared equally between the partners, required the establishment of coordination structures at all levels in order to ensure coordination between the work of the different teams, since no autonomous structure existed for the overall monitoring of the program.

While coordination by mutual adjustment avoids the cost associated with the creation of a specific structure for the program, it nonetheless implies considerable coordination costs; moreover, it does not eliminate the duplication of many tasks. Therefore, it was replaced in more recent programs by specific interfirm structures responsible for the implementation of such programs.

Interfirm structures. The main advantage offered by the establishment of a specific structure responsible for a program is that the overall interest of the program is stressed over the respective interests of the various partners. Interfirm structures, which have increased in number over the last fifteen years, can perform many functions and enjoy varying degrees of autonomy. On the one hand, they depend on the partners in that they are "joint subsidiaries." On the other hand, they replace the partners in the implementation of some of the tasks related to the joint program.

One of the most significant examples of such a structure is Airbus Industrie, which is controlled by the different partners in proportion to their respective equity participation and acts as prime contractor for the overall program (each partner becoming a sub-contractor); it is also responsible for the marketing of the aircraft. The managers and staff of Airbus Industrie, whether coming from one of the partner firms or recruited from the outside, do not retain their positions in their original firms. Role ambiguity is thus avoided. From a technological viewpoint, the very existence of an interfirm structure and its relative autonomy allows the joint venture to draw upon the most appropriate technologies that are available from the partners of the alliance. The statutes of Airbus Industrie stipulate explicitly that any technology developed by one of the participant firms can be used without cost by the other partners within the context of the program. In contrast, the system of coordination by mutual adjustment used in the Concorde program resulted in confrontation between the two partners, each wishing to impose its own technological solutions on the program.

Moreover, while the overall distribution of tasks is set by the initial agreement, specific assignments to the different partners can be made by the interfirm structure, according to the imperatives of the program and in some cases against the particular wishes of the participants. Thus, despite the opposition of the firms involved, Airbus Industrie was able to maintain specialization of roles for the firms over successive generations of aircraft. It thereby enhanced collective efficiency, to the detriment of the flexibility of the various participants.

Interfirm structures, which can be described as "buffer organizations" between partners, embody the collective interest, and often allow the elimination of stalemates which impede the functioning of joint production ventures. From a technological standpoint, such structures allow the exploitation of complementarities among the various partners, thereby giving impetus to the overall program.

STRUCTURES FOR INNOVATION

L. Steele, in his book *Managing Technology*[11], pointed out that if you examine the history of technology, you are forced to conclude that all technologies are fated to be replaced eventually. However, most attempts to replace them will fail and further investment in existing technology will usually produce better results. The real "paradox" of technology can thus be stated in the form of a question: How can the company simultaneously achieve efficiency in existing operations (incremental change) as well as effective repositioning and innovation for the future (radical change)? Differentiation of functions facilitates the maintenance of deep expertise and the generation of new knowledge but makes the fast and efficient transfer of technology or new

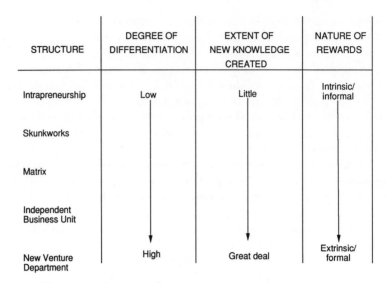

STRUCTURE	DEGREE OF DIFFERENTIATION	EXTENT OF NEW KNOWLEDGE CREATED	NATURE OF REWARDS
Intrapreneurship	Low	Little	Intrinsic/ informal
Skunkworks			
Matrix			
Independent Business Unit			
New Venture Department	High	Great deal	Extrinsic/ formal

Figure 8.3 The range of structural options

ideas difficult at best. Integration of technical capabilities, however, has the inadvertent effect of overcommitting the organization to the existing technical paradigm. Any attempt to walk this "technological tightrope" through a single organizational structure will be less than totally successful. Fortunately, there are several structural options which can be used in combination depending upon the particular needs of the firm[12]. As Figure 8.3 suggests, certain structures are better integrated with existing operations and are more effective at generating incremental, or continuous improvements. Other structures, however, foster maximal degrees of differentiation and are more effective at generating radical or more fundamental innovation. We briefly sketch the range of basic structural options below.

Intrapreneurship

Intrapreneurs are individuals within the firm who are empowered to implement their ideas through informal processes operating within the firm. The intrapreneur must act as the "champion" of his or her product and negotiate the financing and marketing of the latter within the company. This distinguishes the intrapreneur from a standard researcher, who is confined exclusively to technology development. Thus, intrapreneurship implies job differentiation such that technical people take on non-technical roles (see Figure 8.4).

Not all organizations can successfully integrate such people, half researchers and half marketers. According to the promoters of this

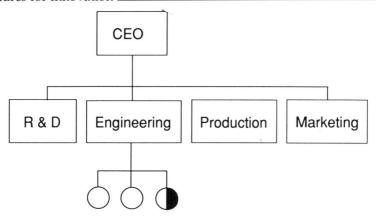

Figure 8.4 The intrapreneur

approach[13], creating an "intrapreneurial environment" requires an organization that avoids appointing experts to develop innovations and instead lets
them emerge through self-selection. Such a structure allows employees to
devote a part of their time and skills to work on innovative ideas. 3M, for
example, facilitates intrapreneurship by allowing employees to spend 10% of
their time on projects and initiatives of their own choosing. Thus, intrapreneurial organizations encourage a large number of experimental products
and not only tolerate but actively encourage "failure" and time "wasted."

Several large US corporations have used this type of approach to promote
technological innovation. For example, intrapreneurship is said to have produced General Electric's industrial plastics, several AT&T products, and
3M's "Post-it" notes[13]. The intrapreneurship approach requires exceptional
people who are not solely researchers and designers, but also managers and
negotiators. Such organizations share a number of features in common:
intrapreneurial organizations tend to foster a strong sense of purpose and
commitment around a particular technological focus. They also try to keep
the organization as flat as possible and take great pains to recognize people
for innovative behavior. There is also a strong element of personal challenge
and intrinsic reward associated with strongly intrapreneurial cultures: financial rewards are not at the heart of this form of organization[14].

Intrapreneurship thus represents a means of integrating technology with
operations. Replacing technologists with "intrapreneurs" ensures smoother
transfer from laboratory or bench to marketplace. However, it also deprives
the R&D function of highly specialized scientists and may hinder the development of longer-term or more fundamental innovation. Indeed, intrapreneurship is most effective at leveraging or improving upon an existing
core competence or technological potential.

Skunkworks

In some organizations, researchers covertly (or at least quietly) develop projects which are not "officially" approved, while continuing to use most of the R&D resources for budgeted projects. T. Kidder's excellent book *The Soul of a New Machine* contains a detailed and vivid account of such an underground project within Data General[15]. It describes how the group bootlegged people and resources and eventually outcompeted the "official" development project for a new minicomputer to compete against Digital's new line of VAX machines.

Other firms go beyond the passive acceptance of such underground work and purposefully establish so-called "skunkworks"[16]—small autonomous teams of researchers which are very flexible and do not have to report to the hierarchy—to work on the development of a new product or technology (see Figure 8.5). IBM's PC, for example, was created through a "skunkworks" structure. The corporation formed a team and located it away from the distractions of the existing organization. By using available technology, outsourcing major components as well as the design of the operating system, and relying upon open architecture for software compatibility, the skunkworks was able to develop a competitive response to Apple's new PC very quickly and effectively.

In order to maintain and enhance the firm's core capabilities, some companies create research positions outside the basic organizational structure; such positions must protect R&D teams from the pressures of the firm's formal systems and hierarchy. Thus, a firm may call upon researchers, for a

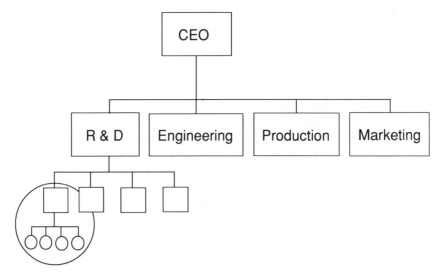

Figure 8.5 The skunkworks

given period of time, to develop a key technology. Once the technology has been developed, the team is dissolved and the central R&D unit is used for refinement and technological improvements. Such an approach is a way for firms to assume major technological challenges without jeopardizing the firm's financial situation.

Thus, the "skunkworks" structure constitutes, in effect, a special developmental unit of researchers and technical people, empowered to pursue a technology or design unencumbered by the usual demands of the corporation. In a sense, skunkworks are temporary countercultures. As such, rewards are primarily intrinsic. Indeed, the engineers at Data General described the reward of working on such teams as "playing pinball"—if you are successful, you get to play the game again. Skunkworks represent a greater level of differentiation than does the intrapreneurship model; they are usually kept isolated at a separate location. And since skunkworks are usually formed within a single function, it is often more difficult for the results to be integrated into the existing operation. The IBM PC is a good example of both the advantages and disadvantages of skunkworks. As noted above, the skunkworks approach enabled a small dedicated team to develop a competitive product quickly. However, by outsourcing major components and technologies, particularly microprocessors and operating system software, IBM effectively lost control of the product. By the mid-1980s, Intel and Microsoft, more than IBM, began to determine how PC technology progressed. An unruly mob of PC clone-makers slashed prices, setting up fierce competition which continues to this day. Only now is IBM recognizing that it must keep key software and hardware proprietary if it is to develop a sustained competitive advantage[17]. Such innovation, however, requires a concerted effort across the corporation and cannot be accomplished quickly through a skunkworks.

Matrix

The matrix structure, in effect, combines an organization structured by function with an organization by product or division (see Figure 8.6). In this structure, each person in the matrix reports to two separate "bosses"—a functional and product manager[18]. Thus, for example, the duty of an R&D matrix manager in a given product or division is both to take part in decisions concerning functional programs, budgets and strategies on the one hand, and to manage the specific technical activities for his or her particular product or division on the other.

In theory, this structure eliminates the dilemma of differentiation and integration. In the short run, however, such a structure may cause conflicts between the two axes of the matrix—the product divisions and the functions. Such conflicts, which are inherent in the matrix organization, can be

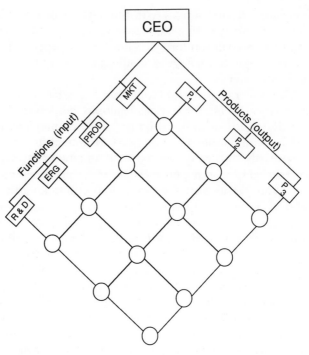

Figure 8.6 The matrix

aggravated by a clash of personalities and styles making for a difficult situation for the individuals responsible to both sides. In this sense, it is not a "structure" which can be implemented, but rather an "approach to management" which takes time to develop[19].

It is often difficult to achieve the proper balance between the two axes of the matrix. The ideal matrix maintains this balance of power by constantly shifting power from one axis to the other. However, such a balance between the two sides of the matrix does not necessarily suit all firms. For a number of reasons, the matrix can be—temporarily or permanently—"unbalanced" in favor of the product divisions (output side) or of the functions (input side). Indeed, as Figure 8.7 shows, when the technology associated with a product is new or changing rapidly, the matrix should be tilted in favor of the function[3]. Conversely, where the market is changing rapdily while the underlying technology is more stable, the matrix should favor the "output" or product side.

Since the matrix organization extends to the entire corporation, it represents a higher level of structural differentiation than does the skunkworks. However, since it is also multifunctional, it offers the opportunity for higher levels of integration. Matrix is conflict management. Depth of expertise must be balanced against near term application and the demands of the market. Since it is more formalized than either of the two previous structures, rewards also take on new meaning. The individual performance appraisal system associated with functional management must be balanced against the team-based needs of the division or product. Thus, both functional and product managers must have a say in rewards and incentives.

Matrix management is an effective means for managing complexity when the corporation has become too large to be managed on a purely functional basis. Indeed, it becomes essential where the competitive environment requires more than one focus or where rapid information processing is necessary[18]. Matrix facilitates rapid product development since the interests of the market are, by design, forced to confront those of underlying technology. In this sense, matrix management is effective at facilitating product diversification which exploits a strong technological potential—the "technology cluster" strategy. The matrix is less effective as a tool for creating radically new technologies, products, or businesses.

Independent Business Unit

As a means for pursuing a more fundamental departure from existing operations, some firms form totally separate business units to create and house new products or processes. While such units usually draw upon

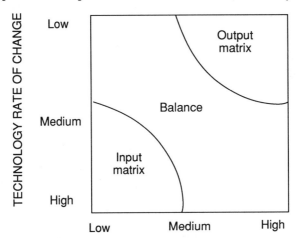

Figure 8.7 Balancing the matrix (Roussel, Saad and Erickson 1991. Reproduced with permission.)

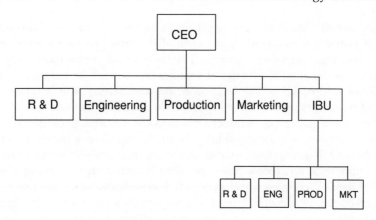

Figure 8.8   The Independent Business Unit (IBU)

technological resources at the corporate level, they are established with their own identity, strategy, structure, and formal systems (see Figure 8.8). For example, General Motor's "Saturn" Corporation was created in part to escape the entrenched bureaucratic systems, processes, and cultural norms within the parent company. Innovative labor-management practices as well as new product development and manufacturing processes were designed into Saturn from the beginning. While an expensive and time-consuming process, Saturn has indeed created a new model of management that stands in contrast to existing practices within GM[20].

However, one must question how quickly or easily these new behaviors and norms will be transferred to the rest of the company. While the high level of differentiation associated with this structure fosters new knowledge

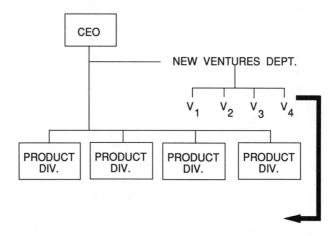

Figure 8.9   The New Ventures Department

generation, the transfer of such knowledge back to the parent organization becomes problematic. In the case of Saturn, for example, union workers were prohibited from returning to GM on the theory that nothing short of total commitment would carry the day. Managers were seen as the key sources of technology transfer. It was expected that key people would return to the parent company to diffuse the new philosophy throughout the existing product divisions. However, most are now unwilling to return to GM given the quality of their worklife within the new organization[21]. Indeed, some experts[22] suggest that using independent business units which are isolated from the operating hierarchy is potentially destructive. They hold that sustained technological innovation requires basic changes in the parent organizations themselves.

New Ventures Department

As a device to foster more fundamental innovation, the New Ventures Department offers the most diverse possibilities. It is both differentiated from the operating organization and may also focus upon developing or acquiring technologies not yet possessed by the organization. The NVD is usually located at the corporate level, separate from any of the existing product divisions or the central R&D lab (see Figure 8.9). Its purpose is to identify, sponsor, and commercialize new products; these opportunities may arise either internal or external to the firm. Many firms have experimented with new venture departments, including Exxon (Exxon Enterprises) and DuPont.

The NVD can use a number of different approaches: it can fund internal development projects, enter into joint ventures with other firms, make venture capital investments, spin-off product ideas, or license technology to outside parties. The choice of approach depends upon how closely related the innovations are to the existing products and markets of the firm[23]. Figure 5.6, for example, showed that when an innovation builds from existing technology and taps known markets (the "home base"), internal development is clearly the preferred development option. At the other extreme, where an innovation is based upon new technology and targets new or unfamiliar markets, licensing or commercial spin-off may be the best route. Between these two extremes are a range of innovation and structural alternatives, with internal options being preferred for more related innovations, and external options preferred for those that are more unrelated. Joint-venturing clearly makes the most sense where the firm possesses capability on one dimension (technology or market) but not the other.

Thus, the NVD can be seen as a structural option which can enhance and complement the other structures described above. In a sense, it provides the "technological scanning" feature for the corporation which enables it to stay fresh and keep taps into new and emerging technologies.

CONCLUSION

The above discussion makes clear four central questions regarding the connection between organizational structure and technology. First is the question of whether the technology function should be strongly differentiated or well integrated. Since both differentiation (for deep expertise) and integration (for ease of transfer) are desireable, this decision is never a simple or easy one. Second is whether diversified firms should centralize R&D resources at the corporate level or distribute the necessary capabilities across products and divisions. Since core competence and product-focused technical capability are both essential to success, the structural decision concerning this issue must seek to balance the demands for efficiency and effectiveness. Third, every firm must address the question of whether it will pursue technology internally (through R&D) or externally (through joint-ventures and alliances). In essence, this decision deals with the firm's orientation toward cooperation versus competition and turns on which technological capabilities are seen as essential to long-term success. Finally, the firm must decide how it will simultaneously improve its existing products as well as position itself in new technologies and products for the future (innovation). This translates into a decision between allocating resources and attention to traditional corporate or divisional R&D activities versus other structures aimed at fostering innovation, such as intrapreneurship, skunkworks, matrix, independent business units, and new venture departments.

Firms' responses to these four questions clearly interrelate. For example, decisions regarding centralizing or distributing technology will impact the ability to improve existing products versus generate innovation. But while decisions concerning organizational structure are important, solving the paradoxes posed by technology also requires strong internal processes and cultural values.

NOTES AND REFERENCES

1. P. Lawrence and J. Lorsch, *Organization and Environment*, Boston: Harvard Press, 1967.
2. A. Cadix, "Le Face-a-Face Recherche-Marketing", *Revue Francaise de Gestion*, January–February, 1980.
3. P. Roussel, K. Saad, and T. Erickson, *Third Generation R&D*, Boston: Harvard Business School Press, 1991.
4. "Why Kodak is Starting to Click Again," *Business Week*, February 23, 1987.
5. A. Chandler, *Strategy and Structure*, Cambridge, Mass.: MIT Press, 1962.
6. B. Scott, "The Industrial State: Old Myths and New Realities," *Harvard Business Review*, March–April, 1973.
7. J. Galbraith, *Designing Complex Organizations*, Reading: Addison-Wesley, 1973.

8. D. Hall and M. Saias, "Strategy Follows Structure," *Strategic Management Journal*, 1, 1980.
9. GEST, *Grappes Technologiques: Les Nouvelles Strategies d'Entreprise*, Paris: McGraw-Hill, 1986.
10. M. Hochmuth, *Organizing the Transnational*, Leyde: A.W. Sijthoff, 1974.
11. L. Steele, *Managing Technology*, New York: McGraw-Hill, 1989.
12. For further discussion, see J. Galbraith, "Designing the Innovating Organization," *Organizational Dynamics*, winter, 1982; M. Tushman and D. Nadler, "Organizing for Innovation," *California Management Review*, spring, 1986.
13. G. Pinchot, *Intrapreneuring*, New York, NY: Harper & Row, 1985.
14. J. Quinn, "Managing Innovation: Controlled Chaos," *Harvard Business Review*, May–June, 1985; J. Friar and M. Horowitch, "The Emergence of Technology Strategy," *Technology in Society*, **7**, 1985.
15. T. Kidder, *The Soul of a New Machine*, New York: Avon Books, 1981.
16. T. Peters and R. Waterman, *In Search of Excellence*, New York: Harper & Row, 1982.
17. D. Depke and R. Brandt, "PCs: What the Future Holds," *Business Week*, August 12, 1991.
18. S. Davis and P. Lawrence, *Matrix*, Reading: Addison-Wesley, 1977.
19. C. Bartlett and S. Ghoshal, "Matrix Management: Not a Structure, A Frame of Mind," *Harvard Business Review*, July–August, 1990.
20. M. Keller, *Rude Awakening*, New York: HarperPerennial, 1990.
21. Personal communication by the authors with several key Saturn personnel.
22. R. Burgelman and L. Sayles, *Inside Corporate Innovation. Strategy, Structure and Managerial Skills*, New York, NY: Free Press, 1986.
23. For further discussion, see H. Sykes, "Lessons from a New Ventures Program," *Harvard Business Review*, May–June, 1986; B. Burgelman, "Designs for Corporate Entrepreneurship in Established Firms," *California Management Review*, spring, 1984.

_____ Chapter 9

Technology and Process

Many technology-based companies appear quite similar in structure but perform quite differently in the marketplace. Indeed, firms while appearing similar in organizational or financial form demonstrate tremendous variation with respect to technology development, new product development, growth, and profitability. Clearly, neither a high level of R&D spending nor use of a particular organizational structure guarantee success. To explain these differences, we must dig below the surface, to the level of group and organizational processes. Innovative, fast-cycle companies demonstrate particular patterns of leadership, vision, communication, decision-making, and culture. In this chapter, we will first examine the processes associated with effective research and development. Since "research" is concerned with the creation of new knowledge whereas the purpose of "development" is to apply scientific or engineering knowledge, different processes appear to be required. With these distinctions in mind, the chapter then focuses directly upon the cross-functional processes required for rapid product development. It describes how fast-cycle companies move beyond the dominance of their functions and divisions to develop strong cross-functional linkages. Relationships among the various functions and areas of specialization are strongly interactive in innovative firms. Finally, the chapter touches upon three keys to new product innovation—leadership, teamwork, and simultaneity. Particularly important are top management vision, strong lateral or "program" management, well-developed teams, overlapping stages of development, and intensive communication.

MANAGING THE RESEARCH PROCESS

In some ways, it is unfortunate that research and development are virtually always interlinked, giving the impression that they are similar activities. The reality is that they are quite different activities. Research seeks to acquire new knowledge while development aims at a particular objective that is well-defined—usually a process or a product. The connecting link is "applied" research which seeks to develop specific pieces of knowledge to support the development or design of particular products or processes. Let us briefly focus upon the processes associated with effective basic and applied research.

Basic Research

T. Allen noted some time ago that engineers are not the same as scientists, and so the research process cannot be like the development process[1]. Engineers and scientists, despite surface similarities, are fundamentally different: their educational processes are different, they are socialized into different sub-cultures, and they often differ in personality and cognitive characteristics. Indeed, scientists usually possess the doctorate degree, value publication, and see the research process as an end in itself. They communicate with other scientists working at the frontiers of knowledge through informal visits, seminars, and conferences. Engineers (or "technologists"), on the other hand, usually stop their formal education at the bachelors or masters level, and value work on tangible products rather than publications. They tend to work closely with co-workers in their own organizations on mission-oriented products. As a result, they are less inclined to read or publish in the open academic literature[1].

Basic research can be defined as work that does not directly support any current development effort within the firm. Investment in basic research keeps the organization in touch with the network of scientists working at the leading edge in fields vital to the future prosperity of its business concerns; it helps develop competence in fields of potential technology that the company is convinced will have strategic importance in the long term. Basic research is thus a scientific reach into the unknown. It is not an activity which has an identifiable or immediate "return on investment." In most industries, basic research amounts to no more than 10% of the total investment in R&D and many firms choose either to conduct no basic research or to utilize university relationships (e.g. affiliate programs), participation in research consortia, or venture capital investments as their "lifeline" to this activity.

For those firms conducting their own basic research, several processes appear to contribute to effectiveness[2]. First, projects must be staffed with the highest quality scientists and best equipment possible. It is a waste of money to employ second-rate researchers. High-performing research projects evidence extensive intra-project communication, suggesting strong peer relationships among research team members. Every encouragement must be given to publish the work and there can be no confidentiality. Indeed, high-quality research is facilitated by strong connections to external parties, such as universities and professional societies. On the other hand, basic research projects tend to be relatively weakly connected to customers, suppliers, or personnel from the operating parts of the company. In short, effective basic research projects allow for extensive communication only with those areas that might provide technical input or critical evaluation. Such a free and unstructured process may be incompatible with other parts of the company, but if management tries to restrict or control the basic research process they will almost certainly destroy its potential value.

Applied Research

To be effective, basic research must be highly differentiated from the rest of the organization. However, as the previous chapter suggests, high levels of differentiation can spell trouble when it comes to integrating the unit's work with the rest of the organization. The case of Bell Laboratories is perhaps the best example of this problem. For decades, Bell Labs performed exceedingly well as a generator of basic scientific discovery. However, AT&T gained little strategic advantage from the Laboratory's work since other companies were able to capitalize on these discoveries as easily as the parent corporation. Thus, basic researchers cannot be left to work in a complete "vacuum," unaware of the potential applicability of their efforts. Indeed, at a minimum, basic researchers must be well-briefed as to the existing and future businesses of the company, and be alert to the possibility that a new discovery may be relevant to the company's commercial interests.

Beyond such informal connections, however, there are other processes that can be put in place to make the transition between fundamental research and product development smoother. Applied research represents such a potential link. Most corporate research is "applied" in that it focuses upon providing specific data required for the development of a product or process, the characteristics of which have been carefully specified. Applied research thus undertakes the discovery of new knowledge with the explicit goal of applying that knowledge to a useful purpose[3]. Thus, applied research is really "technology" development. In the automobile industry, for example, it is important to distinguish between *product* development projects (e.g. the new Mustang or Cadillac programs) and *technology* development projects (e.g. a new engine or powertrain). The latter involves extensive applied research and operates on a different time cycle from the former, which is more amenable to managerial intervention given its focus on the application of existing knowledge.

Given its focus, applied research must be strongly connected to the operating units of the company, particularly the marketing and manufacturing units. Cray Computer, for example, has selected as its goal the development of a supercomputer based upon gallium arsenide (rather than more conventional silicon) chips. This has necessitated extensive applied research to devise new ways of designing, fabricating, and manufacturing computer components using this material. Progress toward this goal involves elements of discovery, which entails significant risk. There is never certainty that applied research will produce a commercially viable outcome. Indeed, most applied research projects fail. However, failing to undertake such projects means that the company will never develop those products or processes which truly differentiate it from the competition. Thus, whereas basic research builds competency for the future, applied research is the essential driver of new technology for the firm.

MANAGING THE DEVELOPMENT PROCESS

While research is critical to the technological potential of the firm, "development" capability determines, in large measure, the current competitiveness of the firm. With the possible exception of new high-technology industries, technology development is quite different from product development. Technology may be necessary but is generally not sufficient for successful new product development. In fact, in many industries, the basis for competitive advantage is moving increasingly toward fast-cycle capability and high variety in product development. Figure 9.1, for example, arrays several products/industries according to the rate of change in product design (cycle time) and the number of models in existence (product variety). The sugar industry remains a basic commodity with low product variety and slow cycle time. Light bulbs, however, are an example of a product with high variety but slow cycle time. Memory chips (DRAMs) are the opposite—cycle times have quickened dramatically but product variety remains low. The fashion industry represents the extreme case, where both cycle time and variety are very high. However, a third dimension must also be taken into account: product complexity. The fashion industry represents a collection of relatively simple products. In contrast, most original equipment manufacturing firms produce complex products, but are also under increasing pressure to provide high variety as quickly as possible. The figure therefore shows autos, computers, and electronics moving toward the upper-right part of the diagram.

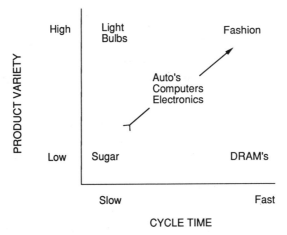

Figure 9.1 The importance of speed and flexibility to competitive success (Arthur D. Little 1990)

Thus, while deep expertise in basic science and well-managed applied research programs are important, so too is the ability to develop and commercialize products based upon that science and technology[4]. Successful new product development requires capabilities that extend well beyond the laboratory. In fact, it is now generally accepted that technology not only builds upon science but may also influence the nature of the scientific frontier[1]. Thus, the strategic management of technology requires capability both in terms of fundamental (revolutionary) innovation as well as more gradual (incremental) improvement around the product development cycle[5]. To be effective, a firm must not only be able to hit the "home run" but must also be able consistently to get the "base hits" necessary to win.

Defining the Product Development Cycle

Research on new product management suggests several phases or stages of new product development and introduction, including idea generation, screening and evaluation, business analysis, development, testing, and commercialization[6]. Within a manufacturing setting, where technological concerns become particularly salient, these stages can best be summarized as follows[7]:

- *Concept definition.* Information on future market needs, technical possibilities, and other conditions is merged into a new product concept. Opportunities are recognized and planners face the challenge of creating a concept that will attract future customers.
- *Product planning.* Planners translate the product concept into specifics for

detailed product design, including specifications, cost and investment targets, and technological choices.

- *Product engineering.* Full-scale commitment to engineering resources begins at this stage. The product concept must be translated into real parts and components to be built or sourced while satisfying business targets (cost and investment).
- *Process engineering.* Product designs are translated into process designs and ultimately into shop-floor production processes, including plant design, hardware and software design, and work design.
- *Product release.* After pilot testing, the process design information is converted into actual production factors—tools, equipment, and trained workers—that are deployed in volume production plants.

While this process is far from linear (indeed, there are many feedback loops and iterations which we will discuss later), it can usefully be portrayed linearly as a product cycle[8] (Figure 9.2). At some point in time, a market opportunity occurs, defined as moment T_O when a new technology or customer need becomes known. After some period of time, the opportunity is perceived by the firm and concept definition occurs (T_C). Product planning requires more time until point T_B, when the product development program actually begins. At this point cash flow goes negative (area A) as product and process engineering absorb significant time and resources. At point T_R the product is released to the market, at which time cash flow turns positive (area B). Break-even time, T_{BET}, is the time required for the positive area to equal the negative area. At some point down the road (depending upon the product life), the product becomes obsolete (T_E) and heads toward extinction. Somewhere in the positive cash flow area there is a point, T_S, when the first customers are satisfied. The *product development cycle* can therefore be defined as the time elapsed between T_O and T_S, the interval between the opportunity and the time when customers are first satisfied. The *product life cycle*, alternatively, can be defined as the time elapsed between T_R and T_E, the interval between product release and product extinction. The implication is clear: if the outer limit of cash flow is the extinction time of the

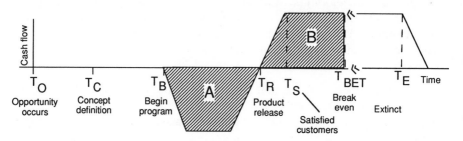

Figure 9.2 The product cycle (Adapted from Patterson 1990)

(which appears to be shrinking in many industries), the total amount of cash the product can generate can be increased only by reducing the product development cycle. This means compressing time in product conception, product planning, and engineering.

Advantages of Fast Cycle Capability

Evidence suggests that fast-cycle technology-based firms commercialize two times as many products and processes as do their competitors, incorporate twice as many technologies in their products, and bring their products to market in less than half the time of their competitors[9]. This translates into more customer-focused products which incorporate the latest technology. Figure 9.3 provides graphic evidence of this for the world automobile industry. For the period 1982–90, the Japanese producers increased their number of car and truck models from about 50 to 90 while also maintaining an average product age of about two years. The American producers, however, managed only to increase their product variety from about 40 to 50 models while the European producers actually decreased in variety. Furthermore, the rate of continuous improvement, as reflected by the product cycle, slowed dramatically for American and European producers. Indeed, during the 1980s, the average age of the American and European fleets increased

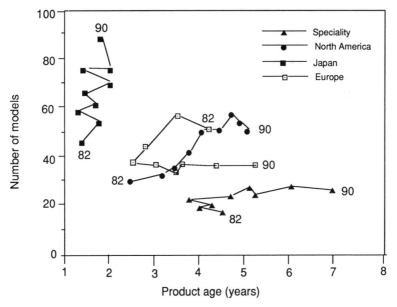

Figure 9.3 Product variety and age in the world auto industry (Womack, Jones and Roos 1990; Arthur D. Little 1990. Reproduced by permission of the International Motor Vehicle Program at the Massachusetts Institute of Technology.)

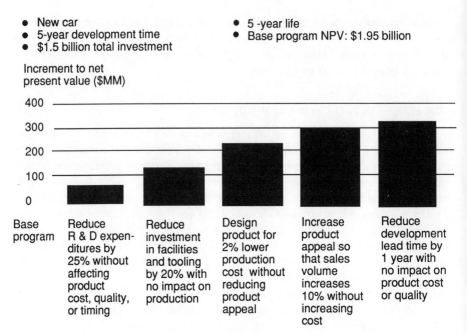

- New car
- 5-year development time
- $1.5 billion total investment
- 5 -year life
- Base program NPV: $1.95 billion

Increment to net
present value ($MM)

| | Base program | Reduce R & D expenditures by 25% without affecting product cost, quality, or timing | Reduce investment in facilities and tooling by 20% with no impact on production | Design product for 2% lower production cost without reducing product appeal | Increase product appeal so that sales volume increases 10% without increasing cost | Reduce development lead time by 1 year with no impact on product cost or quality |

Figure 9.4   Fast cycle time and the bottom line (Arthur D. Little 1990)

from about three to five years. The problem was even more severe for the specialty producers (e.g. BMW, Volvo, SAAB) where average product age ballooned to seven years. This means that the Japanese product cycle in the auto industry is now about four years compared with an American and European cycle of 10–14 years[10].

The performance implications of fast-cycle capability and high variety are staggering. Research by G. Stalk and T. Hout[11] indicates that fast-cycle companies not only grow three times faster than their competitors, but are also twice as profitable. The higher level of profitability stems from cost advantages attributable to speed, such as lower overheads, higher asset and labor productivity, and faster inventory turns. In fact, a financial model constructed by A.D. Little on the auto industry demonstrated that more rapid deployment of technology into products can yield immense financial rewards[12]. As Figure 9.4 shows, a 20% reduction of product development lead time increases the net present value of the new car program by almost $350 million compared with much smaller gains from similar reductions in R&D and facility investment or lower production costs. Even a 10% increase in sales volume without increasing cost produces only about $300 million extra in net present value. Indeed, for this model, the manufacturer would put almost $7 million in the bank for every week saved in product development lead time.

The Need for Cross-functional Cooperation

Studies suggest that in most organizations, less than 5% of the time between receipt of an order and shipment of a product is spent actually adding value[11]. There are many reasons for this astonishing lack of efficiency: functional experts have tight schedules resulting in delay, time is lost working between different locations, executives are very busy, making the approval process long and involved, and people cycle in and out of projects, resulting in start-up costs and loss of experience. Perhaps most significantly, specialists often work at cross purposes, cancelling out the contributions of those involved earlier in the process. All this suggests that there is tremendous room for improvement—time can be compressed dramatically, but only if organizational processes are drastically redesigned. Indeed, fast-cycle capability appears to require a fundamental change in management mindset or paradigm.

CROSS-FUNCTIONAL MANAGEMENT

Under the traditional model, individuals are held accountable for producing specific results through a formal hierarchy. Managers' jobs are geared primarily toward monitoring and control while functional units are seen as "competing" with one another for scarce resources. Conflicts arise through the functional units and are resolved by senior management. Managing for speed, however, requires that cross-functional teams (rather than individuals) be given shared responsibilities and held accountable primarily for team performance. Managers' jobs are geared mainly toward empowerment of individuals and facilitation of teams, while functional units are seen as cooperating with one another toward achievement of a common goal. Conflicts are resolved at the level where the best information and knowledge exists to address the problem. Several approaches to cross-functional management exist, each with its particular set of advantages and disadvantages. We discuss each below.

Types of Cross-functional Organizations

R. Hayes, S. Wheelwright, and K. Clark[13] described four distinct types of cross-functional organizations, with special emphasis upon product development. Figure 9.5 provides a graphic summary of each of these types. In the diagram, the rectangular boxes represent functional sub-units, and the horizontal relations represent various kinds of project or program coordination. Each functional organization (e.g. departments in Engineering, Manufacturing, and Marketing) is supervised by a functional manager (FM).

Personnel at the working level are shown as large circles; the smaller dots are "liaison" people (L) who represent the functional unit. A program or project manager (PM) coordinates efforts across functional units. The dotted ovals represent the areas in which the PM exercises strong influence. The area of influence may be limited to engineering or extend to production, marketing, or even the market itself.

The Functional Organization

The first model, in the upper left-hand corner of the figure, depicts the well-known "functional organization," commonly used where the traditional management paradigm is followed. Here people are grouped together by discipline under the direction of senior functional managers (FMs). Within each functional area, employees specialize in various aspects of the product or process under development. Coordination is achieved either through detailed specifications, agreed to by all parties, or by occasional meetings, orchestrated by functional managers, to resolve specific conflicts. The transfer of responsibility for different aspects of the effort is accomplished haphazardly and is sometimes referred to as "throwing it over the wall" to the next functional unit.

While the functional organization facilitates the development of deep, specialized expertise, it can also be slow and produce sub-optimal results from the product or customer point of view. Inadequate coordination among R&D, design, engineering, manufacturing, and marketing, for example, can produce disastrous consequences. An example from the automobile industry makes this point all too clearly. On one new car platform, the chassis had been completely redesigned by the product engineers. When this design was given to the manufacturing function to build, it was discovered that the new chassis would not submerge in the paint vats. One manufacturing engineer discovered that a series of holes could be drilled in the chassis without weakening the structure, allowing it to sink in the paint. The problem was solved. Unfortunately, upon final assembly, it was discovered that the car made a high-pitched noise whenever it exceeded 60 miles per hour. The marketing organization, charged with the responsibility of moving the vehicle to the customers, facetiously dubbed it the "whistling" car, and joked that if they had only been informed of this feature in advance, they could have incorporated it into their marketing campaign[14].

The Light-weight Product Manager

The second approach, referred to as the "light-weight product manager" model, takes a significant step toward solving the problems of coordination and sub-optimization associated with the traditional functional design.

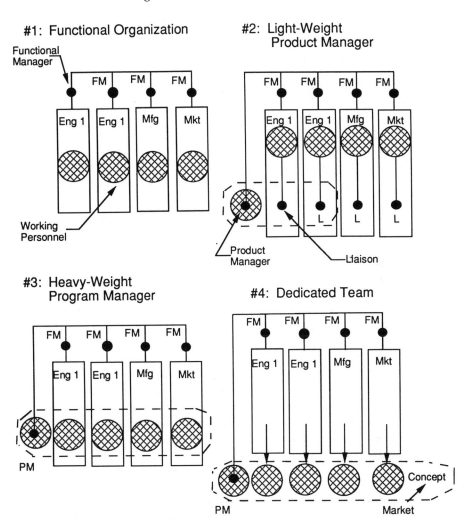

Figure 9.5 Types of cross-functional organizations (From Kim B. Clark and Takahiro Fujimoto, *Product Development Performance: Strategy, Organization, and Management in the World Auto Industry*. Boston: Harvard Business School Press, 1991. Reprinted by permission.)

Here, people still reside in the functions, but each functional organization selects people to represent it in a project or program team. These "liaisons" are expected to speak for and "deliver" their home functional organizations; that is, they should be able to commit their functions to performing specific tasks on a set time schedule. They work with a "light-weight" project manager who has responsibility for coordinating the activities of the different functions (although this coordination is often limited to the product and process engineering aspects of the program). The project manager is "light-weight" in two respects. First, the person is usually junior in status and therefore wields little influence in the organization. Second, while the project manager is responsible for coordinating project activity, the key people involved in the effort are "liaisons" who remain under the control of their respective functional managers: they are assigned to projects only on a part-time basis and continue to be evaluated and rewarded by their "home organizations." Thus, while the project manager may have some influence over *what* gets done, functional managers still exercise primary control over *who* is involved, *when* they get involved, and *how* they do their work.

The Heavy-weight Program Manager

The third cross-functional model, the "heavy-weight program manager," is represented in the lower-left portion of Figure 9.5. In contrast to "light-weight" managers, "heavy-weight" managers are senior-level people with extensive experience and visibility within the company. In some cases, they may be at the same level, or even outrank the functional managers. In short, they wield significant organizational "clout" enabling them to work as peers with key functional managers in the interest of the program effort. The heavy-weight manager usually has more direct control over the people working on the project since he or she supervises and evaluates their work on the team. Quite frequently, members of such program teams will have dual reporting relationships—they are evaluated both by the program and by their home function. However, career tracks are still defined by the functions, since project team members are not assigned on a full-time basis. Heavy-weight program managers thus serve as program "champions," exercising considerable influence over the selection, level of involvement, and supervision of program members. The program takes on more of the character of a "temporary" organization with the program manager assuming the primary leadership and coordination role. In addition to the engineering aspects, heavy-weight program managers are usually responsible for coordinating concept development, product planning, and manufacturing ramp-up as well. Figure 9.6 shows the "structure" of the program used to develop the Taurus/Sable by Ford Motor Company. Car Program Management (CPM) is at the center of the diagram, with the other key functional areas arrayed in a circular pattern around the outside. This chart sends two important signals. First, the "heavy-weight" program manager is at the "center" of the organization (i.e. coordinator) and not at the "top" (i.e. boss) as would be depicted in a traditional organizational chart. Second, the various functional specialities are all important and require conscious integration and coordination in order for the program effort to be successful.

Figure 9.6 Ford: team taurus

The heavy-weight model is roughly analogous to the "matrix" structure which we discussed in the last chapter. It constitutes a significant departure from the functional model of "one-man, one-boss" in favor of a "two-boss" or multiple command system. There are three key roles associated with this approach: top leadership, matrix management, and subordinate (two-boss) management[15]. As shown by Figure 9.7, top leadership is literally atop, or outside of, the matrix. Executives must oversee and guarantee the balance of power in the matrix, resolve conflicts, and set the overall direction and standards for the programs. In this sense, top leadership constitutes the ultimate "tie-breaker." In contrast, the "matrix" managers—functional and program managers—share subordinates in common with one another. Functional managers must balance the needs of their particular area of responsibility against the overall needs of the programs. Program managers, in contrast, have all the same responsibilities as a senior executive, but do not have the same clear authority. Thus, they are left with the job of influencing with limited formal authority. They must use their knowledge, relationships, clout, and skills to get people to do what is necessary for program or business success. Two-boss managers are those individuals based within specific functional organizations who are also involved in programs or

Figure 9.7 The matrix "diamond" (Davis and Lawrence 1977)

projects. Effective two-boss managers must be able to deal with ambiguity and help resolve the inevitable conflicts which will arise between program and functional management.

The Dedicated Team

The final form of cross-functional organization is the "dedicated team." Unlike any of the three previous models, individuals from the different functions are formally assigned or "dedicated" to a program on a full-time basis. Usually, such teams are also "co-located"—people work together at a separate location for the duration of the program or project. This stands in sharp contrast to the "program manager" model where work on a project literally moves from one function or location to another as it reaches different stages of development. The program manager is usually a "heavyweight" in the company and has full control over the resources—human, financial, and physical—needed to execute the effort. In addition to coordinating the functions in product development, the PMs of dedicated teams are often in charge of concept creation and maintain direct contact with customers. Given its centrality, the program management track becomes one of the most highly desirable career paths when this model is widely used in a company. And while team members require periodic return to home functional organizations to replenish and update themselves technically, functional managers are seen more as program facilitators and husbanders of special expertise.

The use of such "dedicated, co-located" teams has significant implications for the organization of work. In order to be dedicated to a program or project on a full-time basis, specialists will often have to broaden their area of expertise. For example, a door handle engineer who was able to work on five or more car programs on a part-time basis, may have to learn to design the entire door if he or she is to be dedicated to a single program. Consequently, it is possible to staff programs with many fewer people through the dedicated team model. Indeed, data from the work of K. Clark, B. Chew, and T. Fujimoto[16] on the world auto industry indicates that dedicated teams require only about half the number of people as the program manager approach and less than one-quarter the number of the traditional functional organization. Furthermore, the use of heavy-weight program managers and dedicated teams appears to shorten the product development cycle significantly, with gains being particularly important in the concept study, product planning and design stages of the development process.

KEYS TO NEW PRODUCT INNOVATION

Three key process issues emerge as central to new product innovation:

- *leadership*, particularly the importance of a clear program mission set by top management and persuasive leadership of a strong program manager;
- *teamwork*, especially the importance of well-developed teams with differentiated roles;
- *simultaneity*, the ability to overlap the stages of product development by solving problems concurrently rather than sequentially.

Leadership

Leadership is a multifaceted and multilevel phenomenon. In the context of product development and innovation, it is important to distinguish between at least two levels of leadership—executive (top management) and product-level (program management). Each is critical if the organization is to achieve both focus and flexibility in the development process.

Top Management Mission

In an effort to shorten the product development cycle, firms often focus upon the middle stages of the process: product and process engineering. At first glance, this makes sense, since the activities consume the bulk of the time and resources associated with product development. What goes on before the actual design and development work, however, has just as powerful an impact upon speed and effectiveness. Decisions made in the early stages of concept study and product planning establish the direction of

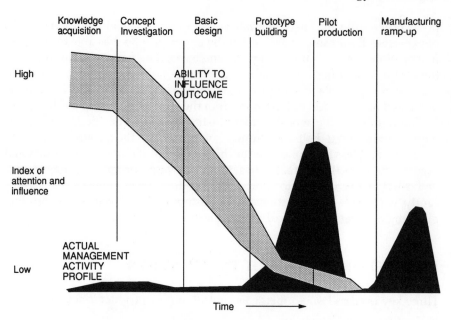

Figure 9.8 Top management attention and influence (Adapted from Gluck and Foster 1975)

the program and the parameters within which subsequent work will take place. Thus, the ability to influence a program declines rapidly as it moves along the product cycle. Yet top management often pays the least attention to those phases where their influence is the greatest (Figure 9.8). In fact, top managers often tend to get more involved when a project approaches market introduction, or if problems arise. It is not uncommon, for example, for top management to override the program manager about details, features, or "feel" of the product long after the basic concept has been established. This serves to undermine the credibility of the program manager and often sets the whole development effort back to an earlier stage.

Top managers in fast-cycle companies respect the position of the program manager and once the product has been conceived, they resist the temptation to intervene. They realize that much greater leverage can be gained by getting involved earlier in the process[17] and that their job is to act as a "coach" rather than a "controller"—to provide a clear mission and motivation to succeed, ensure that the players are well trained and prepared, and then let them play the game. Indeed, research by I. Nonaka suggests that top managers in fast-cycle companies kick off development efforts by signaling broad goals or general strategic directions. Senior managers also supply the needed technology, people, and money to sustain the effort. They rarely hand down a clear-cut new product concept or a specific work plan. This allows the program managers a wide measure of freedom and also establishes challenging goals[18].

In effect, top managers create "chaos" for program teams and then empower them to create the new information and knowledge needed to realize the goals. Canon, for example, in its bid to enter the photocopier business, realized it could never compete head on with Xerox in the high-end line; it lacked both the sales and service capabilities that would be crucial to success. Top management therefore challenged a new product team to create a "desk-top" copier at half the price and half the weight of the existing Xerox machines. The program team was thrown into a state of chaos by the seeming impossibility of this charge. Team members spent several long months working late into the night searching for a way to meet the program targets. All seemed hopeless until one evening a team member threw an empty beverage can across the room into the waste basket. At that moment it dawned on another member that by designing the previously bulky printer cartridge to be "disposable," a machine could be designed to meet both the cost and weight targets. Thus, challenging goals spurred innovation. Indeed, one team member summarized the role of top management as akin to "putting the team on the second floor of a burning building, removing the ladder, and telling them to jump"[19].

Program Management Clout

As we noted above, the most innovative firms tend to staff product development efforts with "heavy-weight" program managers. In Japan, these individuals, known as "shusha," carry great power and their jobs are among the most coveted in the company[10]. In contrast, slower, less innovative companies staff new product programs with relatively young and inexperienced managers and establish them only as "coordinators" working with "liaison" people from the functions. This is a frustrating role and many company executives view the job as a dead end.

In fast-cycle firms, the program manager usually has responsibility for the total program and reports directly to the CEO or the executive office rather than functional management or a product planning group[12]. Furthermore, the program team is empowered to make wide-ranging decisions involving financial as well as technical trade-offs. Outstanding program managers appear to combine two roles. First, they serve as "internal integrators" oriented toward achieving effective cross-functional and team coordination within the program. They resolve conflicts among teams and functional organizations thereby ensuring program continuity. Second, they serve as "external integrators" dedicated to integrating customer insight and market expectations into the development process[7]. In serving these two roles effective program managers are particularly adept at "going to bat" for the program with top management and using their influence and clout to ensure program integrity even in the face of changing competitive conditions or corporate priorities. They are, in short, "concept champions" who use their influence, clout, and power to realize a product with integrity and customer focus.

Teamwork

Effective cross-functional management requires a new mindset and approach to management. While many people are accustomed to working in groups with others from their immediate area, fewer individuals have experience in working on multifunctional teams. Indeed, one of the most difficult elements of rapid technology and new product developments is the lack of a good model for cross-functional teamwork. Most people do not know what such a team is or how it is supposed to function. Effective new product development requires a tightly knit group of diverse, yet committed individuals working toward a common goal. Thus, dedicated effort is required to integrate the multiple perspectives and differentiated roles of team members.

Well-developed Teams

We saw in the previous chapter how difficult it is to integrate highly differentiated functions. The same challenge is present here with respect to cross-functional teams: a group consisting of several technologists and engineers from different areas of specialization, a procurement specialist, a finance person, and a marketing representative may understandably find it difficult to work together.

A critical but often overlooked aspect of effective cross-functional teamwork is stability of team membership. Frequently, functional managers will change team assignments based upon work priorities in the functional organization. This involves the use of substitute team members sent to program meetings on a temporary or permanent basis. These changes have the effect of destroying the stability and continuity of the program team. As B. Tuckman[20] noted many years ago, teams develop through a series of stages. At the initial *forming* stage, members are feeling each other out, trying to gain insight into each other's attitudes and orientations. This is a particularly difficult stage with cross-functional teams since backgrounds are so diverse. Following the initial "forming" stage, groups usually then proceed to a *storming* stage where team members openly debate each other's point of view. This stage of group life can feel very uncomfortable; little productive work is accomplished and some members may leave the group at this stage. This is also the point at which substitute members may be sent, particularly if the initial team member complains to his functional manager that the team effort is a "waste of time." It is crucial, however, that members stay on board multifunctional teams through this stage. Once the conflicts have been resolved, the group reaches a *norming* stage of development where members, while different, begin to hammer out agreed upon work relationships and roles. Only after group norms have been cemented can cross-functional teams reach the final *performing* stage where real work is accomplished in an efficient manner. Thus, dedicated team effort is necessary if rapid technology development is ever to occur.

Initially, it may be necessary to designate team leaders. Ford Motor Company, for example, identifies both a "content" and a "process" leader for each of its teams working on car or truck programs. These individuals are responsible for structuring meeting agendas, facilitating team efforts, and feeding back minutes from meetings. Once teams have reached the "performing" stage, however, they become largely self-organizing. Designated team leaders become less necessary; leadership passes from one person to the next based upon which aspect of expertise is most needed at any particular point in time.

Well-developed teams yield important benefits in the product development process. Clark, Chew, and Fujimoto found, for example, that many US car programs fail to resolve critical trade-offs until very late in the project[16]. Team members show great reluctance to confront conflicts directly. In Japan, however, conflicts over resources and priorities occur at the beginning rather than at the end of the process (see Figure 9.9). In fact, in the fastest Japanese car development efforts, the number of people involved is highest

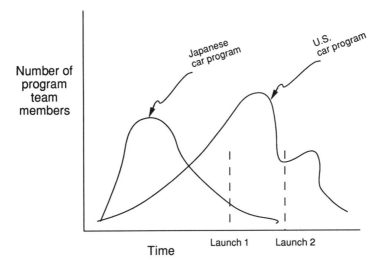

Figure 9.9 Dedicated teams and early conflict resolution

at the very outset. All relevant functional specialties are present and the program manager's job is to force the group to confront and resolve all the difficult trade-offs. In contrast, the slower US development efforts were characterized by growing numbers of people involved late in the process, including substantial numbers after product launch to fix unresolved problems[10]. Slower development efforts were also characterized by last-minute efforts to incorporate design changes and technological updates whereas faster programs froze the product definition early, minimizing "feature creep"; new features or technologies were saved for the next iteration of the project. Thus, poorly formed or unstable project teams cost dearly when it comes to the difficult job of resolving effectively the inevitable technical, market, and financial trade-offs in product development.

While "dedicated" teams appear to produce the best product results, team members must, periodically, return to a "functional" base to "recharge their batteries" and update on the state of the art. It is only through this mechanism that new products developed with dedicated teams continue to deploy the latest technology as quickly as possible. This raises interesting questions about measurement and reward systems. With the "functional" or "lightweight" program system, rewards are clearly administered through the functions, with obvious negative implications for speed and program effectiveness. With "dedicated teams," rewards are clearly administered through the programs, with team efforts being the overriding concern. The "heavyweight" program manager model, however, is more ambiguous. It sets up a matrix system with dual reporting relationships: employees are evaluated for both their *individual* contributions to the function and their *team* contributions to product development efforts. While manageable in theory, this dual reporting approach is exceedingly difficult to implement in practice. In companies where individual performance management systems pervade the culture and team-based performance assessments are overlayed, the former often dominates the latter. For example, efforts to encourage productive teamwork are effectively nullified when the individuals are later evaluated individually and "force ranked" for the purposes of allocating merit pay or determining promotional opportunities.

Differentiated Roles

As noted above, fast product innovation requires well-developed teams with shared objectives and norms. Team members must, however, perform many differentiated roles within the context of the team for it to operate effectively. Like all groups, cross-functional teams must have individuals who are both "task" and "maintenance" oriented[21]. Task functions, such as initiating, opinion giving, elaborating, summarizing, and evaluating, enable the team to solve the objective problem to which the group is committed.

Maintenance functions, such as harmonizing, compromising, relieving tension, and diagnosing, build and sustain group life[22]. Beyond these critical functional roles, however, are other, more specific roles related to both innovation and managing the boundaries of the team.

Innovation roles. Several efforts have been made to articulate the necessary roles to foster innovation[23,24]. In general, these roles can be summarized as follows:

- *Boundary spanning*—collecting and channeling information about important developments or changes in the environment, with a focus on either markets, technologies, or processes. This role is played by people who enjoy interpersonal contact and have a good sense of emerging trends. They read journals, attend conferences, and have extensive personal networks. Such individuals are critical to project team effectiveness since they serve to gather and make available up-to-date information.
- *Idea generating*—analyzing or synthesizing information from which an idea for a new or improved product, process or technical solution emerges. This role is generally played by people who are expert in a particular field and enjoy working as individual contributors. Creativity is the primary driver. While there is generally no lack of good ideas, project teams need to be able to tap such individuals for creative solutions. Their cause is often greatly aided by the efforts of boundary spanners.
- *Championing*—recognizing, proposing, pushing, and selling new ideas, approaches, or procedures for formal management approval. Individuals playing this role secure resources for creative individuals and tend to have strong application interest. They are business-oriented, energetic, and highly verbal. Good ideas often "die on the vine" owing to a lack of effective champions.
- *Sponsoring/orchestrating*—guiding and developing less experienced people in their critical roles. Individuals playing this role are often more senior, and serve as behind-the-scenes "coaches," offering critical support, protection, advocacy and sometimes funds. Program managers are the primary "sponsors" in most product development situations. They serve to buffer the teams from unnecessary organizational constraints.
- *Project managing*—planning, organizing and coordinating the diverse set of activities and people involved in moving a demonstrated idea into practice. The team leader or project leader is clearly the most direct reflection of this role in the product development context. Such individuals are sensitive to multiple parties' needs and know how to use systems and processes to get the job done.

With the possible exception of the "project manager" few of these innovation roles can be formally assigned or designated. Instead, they are informal functions or capabilities that individuals provide or possess. Innovation is greatly facilitated when all five roles are adequately played in a given organizational or team setting. Several assessment packages exist to help managers diagnose their organizations and identify gaps or problems with regard to the above innovation roles[23].

Managing boundaries. Beyond the task, maintenance, and innovation roles required for team effectiveness, there is also a set of important roles relating to external relations or boundary management between groups. Since most new product programs involve several teams, each performing a different aspect of the process, communication and coordination across teams is of critical importance to program success. Similarly, project or module teams must also be able to relate effectively with several functional or "home" organizations if needed expertise or support work is to be secured in a timely fashion. And while the program manager must be concerned with the coordination of individual project teams, so too must the members of each team if the whole effort is to proceed at the fastest and most efficient pace.

An example may help to clarify the issue. At the Ford Motor Company new car and truck programs are organized into three different types of teams. Program Steering Teams (PSTs), which include the program manager, serve to manage the entire program and oversee work of all other teams. Program Module Teams (PMTs) manage a group of related vehicle parts or subsystems such as doors, seats, suspension, powertrain, steering, etc. There may be as

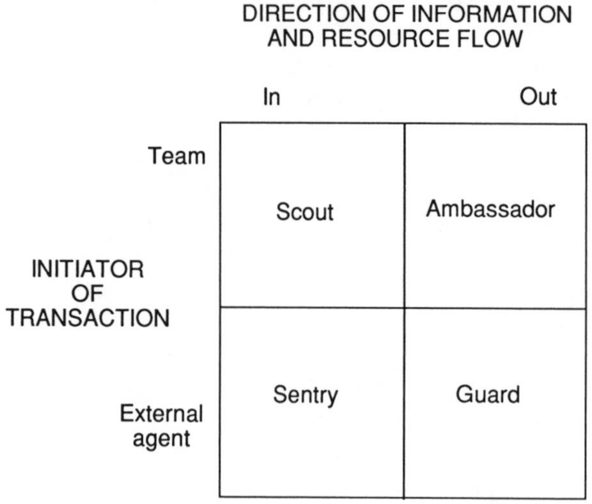

DIRECTION OF INFORMATION
AND RESOURCE FLOW

		In	Out
	Team	Scout	Ambassador
INITIATOR OF TRANSACTION			
	External agent	Sentry	Guard

Figure 9.10 External roles of new product teams (Reproduced from *Advances in Industrial and Labor Relations*, **4**, pp. 199–221, "Management Issues Facing New Product Teams in High-Technology Companies," by D. Ancona and D. Caldwell, 1987, with permission.)

many as 25 PMTs for any given car program. Finally, Program Activity Teams (PATs) look into specific problems or activities relating to a large number of modules such as a clay development team, an emission control team, or a launch team. There may be as many as 15 PATs for a given program. Thus, a new car program may consist of dozens of teams and hundreds of people all requiring coordination among each other and with the functional organizations upon which they depend for technical support.

For a given team, a range of external activities are therefore required making the "boundary spanning" role a complex set of activities indeed. D. Ancona and D. Caldwell[25] have defined a set of critical external roles or functions for new product teams (Figure 9.10). The roles depend upon whether the flow of people and information is into or out of the team and whether the transaction is initiated within or outside of the team. Four primary roles can thus be described:

- *Scout*—seeking out information or resources from other groups and attempting to bring them back into the group;
- *Ambassador*—transmitting information or outputs from the team to other teams or organizations;
- *Sentry*—responding to inputs, such as new information, from outsiders;
- *Guard*—processing outsiders' requests for information or outputs, such as progress reports or prototypes.

As with the innovation roles, all four external roles also appear to be critical to team effectiveness. The team leader may assume all boundary activities, but more likely, different individuals will assume particular roles. The Scout and Sentry roles both deal with information coming into the team and therefore influence team members' perception of the external environment. The Ambassador and Guard roles, alternatively, influence how other teams and organizations perceive the group itself. Both sets of roles are crucial to learning, information transfer, and coordination.

Simultaneity

Well-developed teams with differentiated roles aimed at a common vision are key to rapid product innovation. Speed is achieved, however, through the simultaneous accomplishment of what used to occur in sequence. Efforts to increase the level of simultaneity are reflected by the rise of such methods as "quality function deployment" (integrating marketing and design) and "concurrent engineering" (integrating product and process engineering). All such methods share the desire to integrate more effectively "upstream" activities with "downstream" activities, and in the process, shorten the development cycle. Two capabilities are critically important to achieving simultaneity: (1) collapsing the stages of development and (2) fostering "multilearning" among program participants through intensive communication.

Overlapping Stages

Rapid technological development is greatly facilitated by the ability to work simultaneously on different aspects of product development rather than having to address each in a purely sequential manner (see Figure 9.11)[26]. Under the sequential approach, a project passes through the many stages— conception, planning, product engineering, process engineering, launch—in a step-by-step fashion, moving from one phase to the next only after all requirements of the preceding phase are completed. This "relay-race" approach controls risk but tends to be slow and is extremely vulnerable to delays, bottlenecks, or changes at any step of the way. In essence, the product is "thrown over the wall" from one step to the next, one function to the next and one individual to the next, with little opportunity for integration or creative problem solving. "Upstream" activities, such as product planning and design, are effectively segmented from "downstream" activities such as process engineering and manufacturing. And just as in a relay race, if one "contestant" drops the batton, it spells disaster for the entire team.

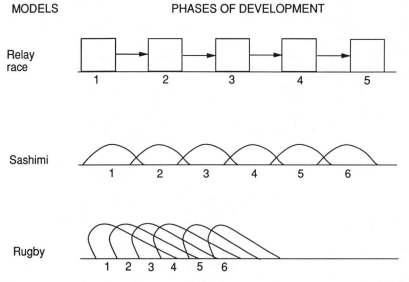

Figure 9.11 Three modes of stage overlapping (Takeuchi and Nonaka 1986. Reprinted by permission of *Harvard Business Review*; from "The New New Product Development Game" by H. Takenchi and I. Nonaka, January–February 1986. Copyright © 1986 by the President and Fellows of Harvard College; all rights reserved.)

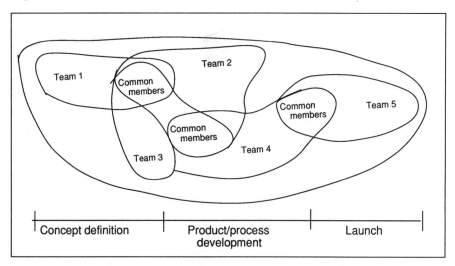

Figure 9.12 The rugby team (Reproduced from William E. Souder, *Managing New Product Innovations*, 1987, with permission.)

As alternatives to the relay race approach, H. Takeuchi and I. Nonaka[19] observed two competing modes of transferring work in product development—Sashimi and rugby. The Sashimi mode compresses overall cycle time by partially overlapping the stages of the process (Sashimi is a Japanese dish consisting of raw fish arranged on a plate, one slice overlapping the other). Unlike the "relay race" mode, there are no discrete transfer points where one party hands off their finished portion of the project and another picks it up. Rather, the transfer points entail the gradual transmission of information and people. For example, product engineers collaborate temporarily with process engineers rather than simply "handing off" finished designs or blueprints. This approach requires more extensive interaction than the relay race mode but stops short of full-scale collaboration throughout the development process.

Under the "rugby" mode, however, there are no identifiable hand-off points at all. Core program team members stay intact from beginning to end and are responsible for integrity of the total product. As in the game of rugby, all the players "run the full length of the field, passing the ball continuously." And while each team member has an area of specialization, each is also a "generalist" capable of adapting to the situation at hand. This means that as the product development process moves from early conceptual work to full-scale production, there is great overlap of both teams and team members (Figure 9.12). The development process takes on a more organic and less mechanistic flavor. The rugby approach is thus a radical departure from the "relay race" mode from both a managerial and organizational point of view.

Research indicates that the rugby mode of overlapping stages is substantially faster than either of the other two modes. In the world automobile industry, for example, Japanese manufacturers, which typically use dedicated teams, heavy-weight program managers and rugby processes, have an average product development cycle time of 43 months, compared with 62 and 63 months respectively, for American and European producers, who are still dominated by light-weight project managers and relay race processes[7]. This advantage is particularly evident in the concept definition and product planning stages where conflicts are confronted and resolved early and efficiently.

M. Cusumano and K. Nobeoka[27] have also shown the importance of rugby processes in interproject relationships: both development time and replacement rate of new product programs appear to be enhanced by the transfer of information and technology *across* programs. In the automobile industry, the slowest companies were characterized by little communication across programs. Existing models were replaced after a period of time by engineers working on that particular program. Speed was enhanced when companies transferred knowledge gained from one completed program to another that was just getting underway (sequential transfer). However, the fastest companies demonstrated an ability to transfer information and design ideas across different programs while they were at various stages of completion (concurrent transfer).

Multilearning

As noted above, overlapping the stages of product development is crucial to fast-cycle innovation. However, to achieve such overlap, deep interaction and communication is required between specialists who traditionally have remained separated by function. Simultaneity thus requires that functional specialists identify not only with their immediate area of expertise, but also with the end product and the total development process. Being both a specialist and a generalist requires "multilearning"[28].

For program teams, each member must contribute specific skills and play particular roles; each must also become conversant with other members' capabilities and roles. Such multilearning enables each individual to enter the territory or specialty of the others. By providing information, criticism, or feedback, a given team member may be able to identify or solve a problem which the team's specialist may have missed. Without "redundant" information held by team members about each other, however, it would be impossible for such synergy to occur. The appropriate level of redundancy or multilearning in project teams can be calibrated using the following simple test: can every team member represent the team's purpose and status to outsiders without the latter being able to tell the member's particular area of functional specialization?

Communication is critical to multilearning. Clark and Fujimoto have noted that rapid product innovation depends not only upon overlapping stages of development (which most organizations now do to some extent) but also upon "intensive" (as opposed to "batch") communication among team members[7]. Batch communication is akin to "throwing the design over the wall"—it is unilateral, one-shot, and usually entails little personal contact. Intensive communication, however, involves frequent face-to-face contact and sharing of preliminary, as opposed to final, information. Rugby-style management can be achieved only when communication between upstream (e.g. design) and downstream (e.g. manufacturing) activities is rich, frequent, and two-way. Corporate efforts to overlap the stages without the fostering of intensive communication networks yields little of the potential advantage of simultaneity. In fact, it may serve to frustrate or even alienate employees who already feel burdened with new job responsibilities due to downsizing or competitive pressures.

In fact, Clark and Fujimoto found, in their study of the world automobile industry, that the most important difference between Japanese, versus

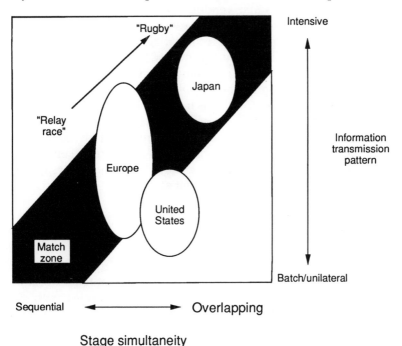

Figure 9.13 Stage overlapping and multilearning (From Kim B. Clark and Takahiro Fujimoto, *Product Development Performance: Strategy, Organization, and Management in the World Auto Industry*. Boston: Harvard Business School Press, 1991. Reprinted by permission.)

American or European auto firms, had to do with the level of intensive, informal communication and mutual adjustment among functional specialists—their level of "multilearning." Figure 9.14 shows that the fast-cycle Japanese producers have been able to combine stage overlapping with intensive communication to produce world-class product development American or European auto firms, had to do with the level of intensive, informal communication and mutual adjustment among functional specialists—their level of "multilearning." Figure 9.14 shows that the fast-cycle Japanese producers have been able to combine stage overlapping with intensive communication to produce world-class product development performance. The US and European competitors lag behind on both dimensions and the American producers, in particular, appear to be forcing stage overlapping without developing the necessary level of multilearning or intensive communication. This imbalance appears to account for much of the difference in product development performance observed between the different firms.

The importance of multilearning also appears to extend beyond the company proper to suppliers and vendors. Fast-cycle firms involve suppliers much earlier in the development process and also depend upon them to contribute significant amounts of technical and engineering skill. Japanese suppliers in the automobile industry, for example, do four times more engineering work for a typical car program than do US suppliers[7]. This mutual dependence between suppliers and manufacturers turns upon close coordination and communication. Contact is frequent, sharing of personnel is common, and information flows are dense. Fast-cycle companies grant suppliers long-term guarantees but demand significant responsibility in return. Long-term relationships and supplier specialization frees internal engineering resources to focus upon new technology and components design, thereby leveraging the firm's technological potential.

CONCLUSIONS

Organizational processes are crucial to the strategic management of technology. This chapter makes clear, however, that the processes required for effective research differ dramatically from those associated with effective product development. Periodic innovation driven by breakthroughs in science and technology are not adequate for sustained competitive advantage. The firm must also acquire fast-cycle capability in product development and process improvement. Effective product development requires cross-functional management and deep communication between previously segmented functions within the organization. To facilitate the necessary level of cross-functionality, top management must demonstrate their commitment by setting clear, challenging goals for product development but then empowering program management teams with the capability and authority to "call the shots" from there. The selection of program managers is a key factor for success and should be done carefully. It is clearly in the company's interest to groom a cadre of "heavy-weight" program managers capable of leading effectively the ambiguous process of product development. Ultimately, product development performance depends upon well-developed cross-functional teams rather than the existing functional units. Indeed, for fast-cycle capability, pyramids are the "buggy-whips" of organizations. It is only through intensive cross-functional communication that simultaneous development can occur, thereby compressing product development cycle time. Often, moving from an organization dominated by the sequential transfer of work between the functional units to a cross-functional organization using "rugby" processes is a difficult transition entailing significant resistance. Changes in the firms identity and culture may be required. It is to this issue that we turn in the next chapter.

NOTES AND REFERENCES

1. T. Allen, *Managing the Flow of Technology*, Cambridge: MIT Press, 1977.
2. M. Tushman, "Managing Communications Networks in R&D Laboratories," *Sloan Management Review*, winter, 1979.
3. P. Roussel, K. Saad, and T. Erickson, *Third Generation R&D*, Boston: Harvard Business School Press, 1991.
4. For a further discussion of this issue, see R. Gomory, "From the Ladder of Science to the Product Development Cycle," *Harvard Business Review*, November–December, 1989; T. Nevens, G. Summe, and B. Uttal, "Commercializing Technology: What the Best Companies Do," *Harvard Business Review*, May–June, 1990.
5. For an in-depth discussion of the concepts behind continuous improvement, see M. Imai, *Kaizen*, New York: Random House, 1986.
6. Booz, Allen and Hamilton, *New Products Management for the 1980s*, New York: Booz, Allen and Hamilton, 1982.
7. For an in-depth discussion of these issues, the reader is referred to K. Clark and T. Fujimoto, *Product Development Performance*, Boston: Harvard Business School Press, 1991.
8. M. Patterson, "Accelerating Innovation: A Dip in the Meme Pool," *National Productivity Review*, autumn, 1990.
9. T. Nevens, G. Summe and B. Uttal, "Commercializing Technology: What the Best Companies Do," *Harvard Business Review*, May–June, 1990.
10. For a detailed discussion, see J. Womack, D. Jones, and D. Roos, *The Machine that Changed the World*, New York: Rawson Associates, 1990.
11. G. Stalk and T. Hout, *Competing Against Time*, New York: Free Press, 1990.
12. Arthur D. Little, *Managing Rapid Technological Development*, Boston: A. D. Little, 1990.

13. R. Hayes, S. Wheelwright, and K. Clark, *Dynamic Manufacturing*, New York: Free Press, 1988.
14. D. Denison, S. Hart, J. Kahn, "A Model of Cross-Functional Teamwork," Ann Arbor: University of Michigan, working paper.
15. For further discussion, see S. Davis and P. Lawrence, *Matrix*, Reading: Addison-Wesley, 1977.
16. K. Clark, B. Chew, and T. Fujimoto, "Product Development in the World Auto Industry", *Brookings Papers on Economic Activity*, **3**, 1987.
17. F. Gluck and R. Foster, "Managing Technological Change: A Box of Cigars for Brad," *Harvard Business Review*, September–October, 1975.
18. I. Nonaka, "Creating Organizational Order Out of Chaos: Self Renewal in Japanese Firms," *California Management Review*, spring, 1988.
19. H. Takeuchi and I. Nonaka, "The New New Product Development Game," *Harvard Business Review*, January–February, 1986.
20. B. Tuckman, "Developmental Sequence in Small Groups," *Psychological Bulletin*, 63, 1965.
21. R. Bales, "Task Roles and Social Roles in Problem-Solving Groups," in E. Maccoby, T. Newcomb, E. Hartley (Eds.), *Social Psychology*, New York: Holt, Rinehart and Winston, 1958.
22. For details, see E. Schein, *Process Consultation: Its Role in Organizational Development*, Reading: Addison-Wesley, 1988.
23. For example, E. Roberts and A. Fusfeld, "Staffing the Innovative Technology-Based Organization", *Sloan Management Review*, spring, 1981.
24. M. Maidique, "Entrepreneurs, Champions, and Technological Innovation", *Sloan Management Review*, winter, 1980.
25. D. Ancona and D. Caldwell, "Management Issues Facing New Product Teams in High-Technology Companies," *Advances in Industrial and Labor Relations*, **4**, 1987.
26. Here the reader is referred to several excellent references on simultaneous development of new products such as W. Souder, *Managing New Product Innovations*, Lexington: Heath, 1987, Chapter 13; see also notes 7 and 19.
27. M. Cusumano and K. Nobeoka, "Product Development Strategy, Management, and Performance: Findings from the Automobile Industry," paper presented at the Academy of Management Annual Meeting, Miami, August, 1991.
28. For a detailed discussion of these concepts, the reader is referred to I. Nonaka, "Redundant, Overlapping Organization: A Japanese Approach to Managing the Innovation Process," *California Management Review*, spring, 1990.

Chapter 10

Technology and Culture

Beyond the formulation of sophisticated technology-based strategies and the design of suitable organizational structures and processes, success or failure depends upon an additional dimension of business policy. This "hidden face" of strategy, difficult to analyze and formalize in a rigorous manner, has been variously termed as "philosophy," "shared values," "organizational culture" or "corporate identity"[1]. Corporate culture and identity are essential components of business policy and have a profound influence on firm strategy, structure and decision-making processes. In more specific terms, corporate culture and identity seem to determine to a large extent the way that enterprises think about technological factors and integrate them into their strategy. The importance of technology to the firm is also a key element in its culture and identity. We will begin, therefore, by defining the concepts of corporate culture and identity. Next, we will outline the specific features of the culture and identity of enterprises which succeed in using technology as a major element in their strategy. Finally, we will analyze how a technologically-oriented culture influences simultaneously the strategy content and process of the enterprise.

CORPORATE CULTURE AND IDENTITY

BASF, in a recent advertising campaign, claimed to be energized by the "spirit of innovation." Similarly, Saint-Gobain contends that "our tradition is innovation"; they go on to declare: "For thirty years, we have been the leaders because of our advanced technology. Innovation means winning"[2]. "We were the first and we are the future," declares McDonnell–Douglas in its advertisement which refers both to the old DC-3—"the first plane to enable airlines to make a profit by carrying passengers only"—and to the new MD-91X—"new technology that pays off in profits"[3]. Aérospatiale announces, "Airbus and Ariane give heart to our technology," referring to its research in artificial hearts. This research, though derived from the company's technology, belongs to a field far removed from Aérospatiale's primary activity. Finally, the German firm Bosch gives a long list of its technical innovations under the slogan "From tricycles to satellites: a hundred years of progress"[4].

We could continue listing examples of companies which regularly refer to technology in their advertising and annual reports. Beyond its immediate value in marketing (creating a positive image in the eyes of constituents), references to the technological competence of the firm are also frequently directed at the firm itself, rather than its customers or constituents. Indeed, a company's message concerning technology is often targeted primarily at employees. For example, United Technologies' recent advertising campaign stressing the importance of "sharing what we know" and "reaching for a single goal" was a message undoubtedly designed to foster technological synergy across its diverse and historically unrelated businesses (aerospace, elevators, air conditioners, and telecommunications). Without question, technology is a key factor which helps direct a firm's activity and has a decisive impact on competitive strength. However, at the same time, the image that the employees have of their company's technology, the rhetoric related to it, and the way in which technological considerations affect interpersonal relations, are all part of the corporate culture and the corporate identity. Since technology is often both a strategic factor and an essential symbol for employees, it is one of the fundamental components in the definition of the mission and purpose of a company. Before analyzing in detail these issues, it may be useful to specify what we mean by corporate culture and identity and to clarify the main concepts behind these terms.

Definitions

Corporate "culture" and "identity" refer to the underlying values, beliefs, and principles that serve as a foundation for an organization's management system as well as the set of management practices and behaviors that both exemplify and reinforce those basic principles[5]. Because of its particular culture and identity, each enterprise is unique, different from others. They give employees a sense of purpose and belonging to the company, and rally them around a common mission[6]. Thus, culture and identity are intimately intertwined: shared values form the basis for consensus and integration which encourages the motivation and commitment of meaningful membership. These same shared values also define the institutional purpose that gives individuals meaning and direction[7].

G. Hofstede and his colleagues[8] have demonstrated, however, that people's core assumptions and values have more to do with nationality, age, and education than membership in an organization per se. Indeed, values appear to be acquired in early youth, mainly in the family, neighborhood, and school. If company member's values depend primarily upon the above factors, then the way values enter the enterprise is via the hiring process. Employee's subsequent socialization is a matter of learning about and adopting specific *practices* and *behaviors*. Thus, shared perceptions of daily practices and norms are at the core of corporate culture and identity. These consist largely of the observable artifacts associated with daily life in the organization (e.g. rhetoric, myths, rites and rituals)[9].

We can therefore say that corporate culture and identity are built around collective organizational "imagery" which is revealed to the external observer through symbols. Organizational images are shared by all members, in varying degrees, depending on the strength of the culture. The symbols produced by the organization define the main characteristics of the corporate culture and identity and reveal acceptable behavior and thought patterns. The employees manifest their sense of belonging and their attachment to the values of the enterprise by conforming to these patterns. Symbols include all the physical manifestations of corporate culture and identity, such as the company's official rhetoric, the myths related to its past history, and its rites, rituals and taboos. We can thus analyze the role played by technology in shaping the corporate culture and identity of enterprises by examining both organizational symbol and organizational imagery.

TECHNOLOGY AND SYMBOL

When technology represents a major competitive advantage for a company, symbolic references to technology are often ubiquitous in the myths concerning the company's history, in its existing rites and rituals, and in its official rhetoric.

Technology and the Official Rhetoric

The official rhetoric of companies is expressed through their institutional and commercial advertising. The advertisements and the slogans that we cited earlier highlighted the company's technology, testifying to the fact that, for some, technology is one of the main themes of the official rhetoric. When BASF boasts about its technology, it may be primarily to boost its sales. When Saint-Gobain enunciates its contribution to technological progress, its aim is possibly to inspire the confidence of potential investors and to smooth the path of privatization which was then taking place for the formerly state-owned enterprise. In contrast, the advertising messages of United Technologies, Aérospatiale, and McDonnell–Douglas concerning their technological excellence probably have little real commercial impact. Their messages seem to be primarily targeted at motivating and mobilizing employees. We can describe this process as the "mirror effect"[10], where the company projects on the public a technological image of itself, which is reflected back to the company by the employees through their day-to-day dealings with the outside world. Thus, the place of technology in the organizational imagery is consolidated.

When Aérospatiale, a state-owned enterprise, enunciates its role as the creator of the Concorde we can ask ourselves whether the implicit message is that the organization and its top managers prize technological achievement over commercial success[11]. Conversely, when McDonnell–Douglas emphasizes the profits made by its technology, it probably seeks to stress the fact that technology is not an end in itself. And as noted above, United Technologies' emphasis upon "sharing what we know" is clearly aimed at fostering a sense of "synergy" or relatedness across its previously fiercely independent business units.

The messages that advertising transmits are the most accessible to the outside observer. However, advertising is not the sole means of communicating the official rhetoric of the company. Internal communication channels, statements of top managers, names, and logos all serve to convey coded messages concerning the enterprise, what it believes itself to be, and what it wishes to become. Jean-Luc Lagardère, CEO of the Matra group, for example, declared in a general meeting: "By producing quality materials which sell in highly competitive international markets, Matra has developed the most rigorous management and production systems. In a way, it is an industrial model . . ." This statement indicates that for Matra's top managers and the majority of its staff, the success of the group depends less on its technology than on the judicious use that is made of this technology; what at Matra is described as the "company spirit."

In the middle 1970s, United Aircraft changed its name to United Technologies. The new name symbolized a change of strategy; i.e. a shift from only aerospace activities to applications in a wide range of different industries. Johnson & Johnson's move from consumer products like Band-Aids and baby shampoo to far more sophisticated medical technologies, through acquisition of firms like Technicare, was mirrored in the construction of the new high-tech company headquarters. This was another way of institutionalizing the strategic shift and the new emphasis given to advanced technologies[12].

In enterprises where the official rhetoric focuses on technological excellence, it aims not only to project the company's image to the outside world, but also to emphasize the essential priorities to the entire workforce. Ford

Motor Company, for example, has been running advertisements for several years which state that "at Ford, quality is Job 1." This type of rhetoric reflects an "ideology," defined by Baechler[13] as "rhetoric linked to collective action." Such ideological rhetoric:

- evokes what is central to the company;
- is produced by an identifiable actor, usually top management;
- conforms to a number of basic rules: the assertion of principles, the schematization of reality, and the de-emphasis of problems that could jeopardize attachment to the rhetoric.

The fact that technology is often the basis of ideological rhetoric indicates that it can mobilize an entire enterprise. Technology helps the organization deal with the uncertainties regarding the future and justifies the sacrifices and the efforts made by all employees for the company. Aside from being a recurrent theme in the official rhetoric of many companies, technology is also prominent in the myths relating to company history.

The Mythical Dimension of Technology

Technology is often associated with "heroes"—the "great men" from the organizational past. Thus, technology acquires a mythical dimension in the oral and written histories of companies whose development was based on technological advantage. At DuPont de Nemours, the creation of nylon has, for obvious reasons, been invested with the quality of myth; it serves to highlight the importance of technology in the company's past strategy and, for present research teams, remains an "ideal" to be emulated. At Hughes Tool, technology is closely bound together with founder Howard Hughes Sr. The mythical value of technology is indicated by the permanent exhibition in the lobby of the headquarters, showing all the technical innovations developed by the company since its inception.

An example of a more recent myth is that of the "two Steves"—Steve Wozniak, the technological genius, and Steve Jobs, the visionary manager, who together created Apple Computer. This myth, which has spread widely, still remains alive within the company, despite the departure of the two heroes. Similarly, Cray Research, the world leader in supercomputers, still depends heavily upon founder Seymour Cray for its identity despite the fact that he left the company several years ago and has recently begun a competing firm. Despite his departure, an enduring myth remains: each year, so the story goes, Seymour Cray builds a new sailboat and then burns it at the end of the summer, demonstrating that what worked in the past will not work in the future. Indeed, success in supercomputers depends upon the continual re-invention of the product. Thus, myth conveys collective ideals and offers protection against the real and imaginary dangers of the environment. Technology serves a mythical function especially because it links the past to the future. Past successes, based upon technology, project into the future, thereby ensuring the continuity of the company. Thus, as part of the official rhetoric, and embued with a mythical quality, technology provides a focus for behavior—through rites and rituals—which integrates it into the daily activities within the organization.

Technology in Rites and Rituals

The importance given to technology in the company's activities is revealed by the presence of celebrations, rites and rituals centered on this theme. As noted above, the lobby at Hughes Tool headquarters in Houston displays an imposing "memorial to inventors" which commemorates all the employees responsible for an invention patented by the company, listed according to the number of patents they were awarded. This list of names engraved on a copper plate is headed by that of Howard Hughes Sr., the founder, and by far the most prolific inventor of the firm.

Each year, United Technologies awards four trophies to employees or teams for outstanding achievements in engineering or science. For example, the "George Mead Medal Award" is granted to an employee or a team in recognition of a major scientific or technological contribution to the company's activities. The award is intended for achievements by an individual or a small group, not for large jobs accomplished through sheer weight of resources or organization. The emphasis is placed on the "inventor," his initiative and his genius, as opposed to large and anonymous research units. The first prize consists of a gold medal and $10000 in cash; second prize is a silver medal and $5000 in cash. The "Board of Directors Trophy" rewards an outstanding engineering achievement leading to a major contract or tender bid which is important to the future of United Technologies. The "Rentschler Memorial" is presented annually to the operating unit of United Technologies judged to have made the most significant contribution to technical knowledge on behalf of another unit. Finally, the "Homer Citation" is awarded to operating units "whose performance has best demonstrated the importance of cooperation and team spirit for the greater good of the corporation"[14].

Awards of this type can be found in many companies, and can be defined as commemorative rites and rituals reinforcing the corporate identity. They testify to the importance of technology and of certain behaviors linked to technology in the company's value system. These rites rally the employees together in a common quest for technology. In order to succeed in the enterprise and to be recognized, an employee must adhere to the norms implicit in these awards. To do so, the employee must demonstrate that he or she understands them and displays commitment to them. Those who best observe the organizational norms are rewarded by having their name inscribed on the "memorial to inventors" at Hughes Tool, or by being granted medals at United Technologies.

Thus, the ritual granting of awards not only recognizes those who follow in the tradition, but also serves to proclaim the importance of behavioral norms and expectations to all employees of the company. These norms are deciphered by analyzing the major themes behind the rites and rituals. Of particular importance in technology-based firms are norms relating to teamwork and consensus.

Teamwork

The quality of collaboration within research teams and of cooperation across different teams, operating units and divisions, are important factors for success in companies where technology represents a competitive advantage. It is not surprising, therefore, that norms meant to encourage teamwork and collaboration between research units are reinforced through rites and rituals.

Two of the four trophies awarded by United Technologies are intended precisely to recognize technological collaboration. In many R&D departments and indeed in many technology-based companies, the absence or the de-emphasis of formal heirarchical structure serve both to demonstrate and to promote team spirit. The French computer group Bull sponsors a yacht team called "L'Esprit d'Equipe" (team spirit). Top managers are the first to admit that the yacht is sponsored for the purpose of setting norms about teamwork rather than for external image. The emphasis on technology usually goes hand in hand with an organization where power stems from superior technical competence, rather than from age or seniority. Thus, at Dassault, it was possible for a 40-year-old engineer to become the technical director, a position second only to that of CEO.

Consensus

Consensus across different departments is another important norm in technology-based companies, and forms the focus of many ritualized practices. As we saw in the last chapter, consensus facilitates the necessary integration of research, production, and marketing. The need for such integration gives rise to rites which are a means of emphasizing its importance in the minds and behaviors of employees. For example, at United Technologies, Texas Instruments, and DuPont de Nemours, the divisional managers participate in the orientation and evaluation of those within the main research departments. In some cases, these meetings are also attended by leading scientists, who are invited to give advice and provide support.

Apart from their practical objectives—coordinating the work of the research laboratories with the operating needs of the different divisions—these meetings serve an important symbolic function. They aim at obtaining the commitment of the entire enterprise around a technological orientation, and, by implication, the future direction of the company's activities.

In a leading pharmaceutical firm, the working relations between researchers and sales managers are fostered by a system of periodic meetings and organized contacts. The sales managers are required to inform the researchers of market needs, and their opinion carries weight in decisions concerning long-term projects and development activities. The other departments also have their say when research projects are presented. Executives from all departments participate in the discussions, together with researchers from other laboratories of the firm. Once again, these integration mechanisms, aside from their immediate objective, can be interpreted as rituals forming part of the corporate identity aimed at reinforcing the internal consensus essential to a technology-based strategy. Indeed, executives in the company, well aware of the symbolic value, talk of these meetings as "High Mass," which they attend with reverence.

Finally, we must also consider taboos, which often stem from technological failures. At Dassault, employees are reluctant to talk about the Mirage V (a vertical takeoff and landing aircraft) and the Mirage G (a swing-wing fighter aircraft) which, owing to technical problems, were never commercialized. Even technical successes which turn out to be commercial failures are transformed into taboos. The Mercure, a commercial jet similar to the Boeing 737, rarely figures in the brochures and annual reports of Dassault since only eleven units have been sold. Similarly, it was not until ten years after Concorde's first flight that Aérospatiale started claiming it as an extraordinary technical achievement. Only 14 Concorde aircraft have been sold and this supersonic transport is considered to be one of the greatest commercial failures in the history of aviation.

The analysis of technological symbols is of interest only if it allows us to better grasp and manage the underlying organizational imagery of the company. Organizational imagery is the very backbone of corporate culture and identity. It is through this imagery that culture influences strategy.

TECHNOLOGY AND ORGANIZATIONAL IMAGERY

In technology-based firms, organizational imagery revolves around technology. The image that employees have of their company is that of technological excellence and a capacity for innovation; the image of the model employee is one who has technical competence, is technology-minded, is well-trained and specializes in a suitable field; and the image of the distribution of power within the enterprise is one where the research departments, the laboratories and the technical units have the leading role. We now consider each of these aspects in turn.

Technology and the Image of the Enterprise

Employees have an image of their firm which differentiates it fundamentally from others and makes it a unique and special place. These individual representations are sufficiently homogeneous to enable us to talk of a collective image. The organizational image presents a number of dominant traits which together form a kind of common filter. The filter influences the reactions, attitudes and behaviors of the employees in an important way; it serves as a set of criteria allowing them to interpret information, events, and decisions, and judge how well these conform to the image that they have of the company.

In situations where technology is the main source of competitive advantage, we often see that the internal image of the enterprise tends to be focused on technology. In such cases, employees and top managers use certain terms to describe their company: "modern," "dynamic," "innovative," or "turned to the future." At Ford Motor Company, for example, the publically advertised goal is "to build the highest quality cars and trucks in the world." The image of belonging to industry's "elite," due to strong technological competence, provides great imagery for employees.

Technology thus helps to shape the image that the employees have of the company, and helps to project the enterprise into the future. This simultaneously gives rise to apprehension and generates hope among employees. A technology-oriented internal image can thus be extremely compelling for employees. It can mobilize the organization to achieve objectives which reinforce this image. Given the power of organizational imagery, strategic change, for example, the shift from a differentiation strategy to a cost leadership strategy, can be very difficult and risky. In addition to strategic difficulties resulting from the redeployment of the firm's resources, there are psychological problems stemming from the refusal of employees to accept changes which they feel are not compatible with the image that they have of the firm. For example, Aérospatiale, quite successful in the complex, high-technology applications which characterize the aerospace industry, failed miserably in its bid to enter the kitchen appliance market. Strategies which threaten to alter employees' organizational image or to render it "commonplace" often meet with strong internal resistance.

Technology and the Image of the Employee

The image of the enterprise is linked to the image of the model employee; i.e. a shared perception of the qualities that the company looks for in its members. This image of the model employee is often revealed by observations about the kind of person who makes a career in the company, or the specific qualities that the company expects in its people.

In technology-based companies, technical competence is often the most important quality for an employee. This would be expected for technical personnel, but seems more surprising as a criterion for accounting, finance, sales and management positions. However, even for these positions, technical competence, or at least technical literacy, and sometimes technical experience, are considered indispensable. In such companies, technical considerations are important in all activities of the enterprise. At Dassault, for example, even sales managers are engineers, because it is said that they should be able to discuss technical matters with customers as well as with the technical units of the firm. Similar background and interests among functional managers facilitates the necessary integration of the different tasks of the enterprise.

Surprisingly, the importance given to individual technical competence in the organizational imagery does not necessarily help the enterprise keep abreast of technological developments. In fact, if the status of individuals in the enterprise depends on their technological capability, technological change can be perceived, unconsciously, as a threat. As we saw in Chapter 4, this reaction explains why large corporations fail to keep up with important technological advances[15]. The engineers at General Electric, RCA and Sylvania, for example, specializing in vacuum tubes, "refused" to accept the emergence of transistors, and later of integrated circuits, because these new technologies made their competence obsolete, thus compromising their status and their position as model employees in the organizational imagery. Here we see the third aspect of organizational imagery at work—the power distribution within the enterprise, which also shapes the attitudes and behaviors of employees with respect to technology.

Technology and Power

In all organizations, employees hold an image of the distribution of power. The importance given to technology in the strategy of the firm is almost always reflected in the position that the technical units and the technical managers occupy in the organization. At Dassault, for example, the general technical department is clearly the most important department in the company. Indeed, aside from Marcel Dassault, the founder and major shareholder, the main figure in the company has always been the general technical manager.

In Japanese high-technology companies, technical managers are placed high in the organizational hierarchy, and top management committees include a large number of people with technical backgrounds. The situation is very different in large American corporations which, for the last twenty years, have crafted their strategies using business portfolio methods and growth through acquisition. A Japanese expert claims that American managers are technologically illiterate, and points out that only one-third of the managers occupying the three highest positions in the twenty largest American companies have scientific or technical degrees, compared with two-thirds in the twenty-four top Japanese companies[16]. A prominent American consultant shares the same view and has remarked that, because of the lack of emphasis given to technology by American managers, the scientific director carries little weight and often has an administrative rather than a strategic role in the firm[17].

Thus, the emphasis placed upon technology is directly related to the position of the technical managers in the organization. For example, in 1984, in the thirty largest French enterprises, sixteen CEOs had a scientific and technical background and fourteen among them were graduates of the prestigious Ecole Polytechnique[17]. We can thus ask ourselves whether the shift towards technology in the strategy of some companies is not at least partly due to the concentration of technical managers in powerful positions, in lieu of executives having sales, financial or managerial backgrounds.

No one would deny the need to consider technology—a long neglected factor—in the formulation of strategy. It is only natural, therefore, that this new emphasis has become, to some degree, fashionable. The new focus on technology legitimates and reinforces the power of the engineers and scientists in relation to other functionally trained managers. The importance now being given to technology also provides engineers and scientists with a means of regaining their role in the strategy-making process, after having been ousted from power in the 1960s and 1970s by managers from the marketing and finance functions. Thus, technology-oriented strategies, such as the "technology-cluster" strategy, allow engineers to regain their place at the head of large enterprises.

PROFESSIONAL CULTURE AND IDENTITY

A firm's "business" defines both the nature of the work performed and the social identity. The business(es) of the firm define the areas in which the company operates and seeks to build competitive advantage. It is through the business (or businesses) that the firm defines itself and emphasizes its contribution to the economic and social environment to which it belongs. This symbolic aspect makes a company's business a major component of its corporate identity.

A company's "business" is characterized by certain know-how and competence. Being a doctor, architect or engineer implies possessing specific skills, usually acquired through training and certified by a degree. In the same way, when an enterprise describes its business as aerospace, automobiles, chemicals or advertising, it claims to have certain skills. If technology has an important place, both in real and symbolic terms, in the company's activities, its business can best be defined on the basis of those technological skills.

When the business of the company is defined almost exclusively in terms of its technology, with little emphasis being given to the fields in which these technologies are applied, the corporate identity is compatible with a technology-based strategy, such as the "technology-cluster" approach. In symbolic terms, the company's business originates in its technological potential, which can thus be exploited through diverse products, in widely different fields. The technological potential of the company cannot be separated from the competence of its members, or at least from those who possess technical know-how. There is thus a continuity between the competence of the employees, the technologies used by the enterprise, and the definition of the business (or businesses) of the firm. The individual has a strong sense of belonging to the organization when the above elements are compatible with each other. If this is not the case, the feeling of belonging to the company becomes secondary to the feeling of belonging to a profession, which is primarily defined by the technologies used.

Thus, if the organizational imagery of the company takes a back seat to the technologies used, the corporate identity sometimes becomes secondary to the "professional" identity of employees. The individuals at the center of the technological processes have a feeling of belonging, not so much to an organization, but rather to a more abstract technological environment which can be pursued through a number of organizations. They display high levels of commitment to their "field" and its professional/ethical standards; corporate identity, as expressed through the firm's management practices, remains secondary[18]. This explains the high rate of turnover in some industries, for example, computer firms in the Silicon Valley. As an exception to this phenomenon, Tandem Corporation is often cited as an example of a company having a very strong internal culture and a turnover rate that is three times lower than that of the industry average. Its strong corporate identity, however, seems to be based upon elements other than technology[19].

Several studies have explored the idea of "industry" culture; i.e. the culture of entire industries[20]. Corporate culture is thus only one aspect in a broad range of cultural units including: the culture of the subsidiary, the division, or the work group on the one hand, and the culture of the nation, the region, or the industry on the other[21]. In certain industries the culture shared by a profession is particularly strong. Thus, for individuals, the feeling of belonging to a profession is at least as important as the feeling of belonging to a specific organization. Universities provide one of the best examples of this phenomenon. Indeed, professors generally feel much greater affinity toward their colleagues working on similar problems at other universities than they do their fellow faculty members at a given institution.

In fact, in certain industries, technology is probably becoming the core of a professional identity[22]. Just as trade unions gave rise to lateral identities, such as those of the steelworkers, printers or autoworkers, we can surmise that today, a new identity is being formed, focused on technology, which transcends the limits of the firm, and may serve to undermine corporate identity. The sense of belonging to a "high technology" industry, for example, creates a feeling of solidarity in the face of an uncertain future. The resulting rhetoric goes beyond the limits of any one firm, or even beyond those of the industry. In a harsh, competitive world, what matters is to remain in the race and continue to belong to a high-technology industry. Today, "high technology" seems to be a source of security for an entire professional sub-culture, by conferring on it a feeling of strength and durability, and allowing it to overcome its anxieties about the future. Thus, as technology and the "knowledge" worker grow in importance in the coming years, managers will be challenged to discover new ways to win the loyalty of key employees to the firm.

CONCLUSION

Technology is often an essential factor in the success or failure of the firm, and forms the focus of the vital relations which the enterprise maintains with the external environment. The technological competence of the firm is the sum of the technological competencies of its members. Technology is at the center of the definition of the business of the enterprise, occupying an important place in the organizational imagery and giving rise to important symbols. Thus, technology is frequently at the very core of corporate culture and identity. Far from being an extraneous variable imposed on the enterprise, culture is one of the essential components of business policy and must be understood and actively managed by senior leadership. Through official rhetoric (e.g. advertising, logos, name changes), the nurturing of myths and heroes, and the use of rites and rituals, top management can have an important influence over the shared practices and norms of organizational members. Imagery about the enterprise, the ideal employee and the importance of technology in the power structure of the company also help cement a set of shared values and practices around technology which serve to complement and enrich the strategy, structure, and processes employed by the firm.

NOTES AND REFERENCES

1. T. Peters and R. Waterman, *In Search of Excellence*, New York: Harper and Row, 1982; T. Deal and A. Kennedy, *Corporate Cultures*, Reading: Addison-Wesley, 1982; E. Schein, *Organizational Culture and Leadership*, San Francisco: Jossey-Bass, 1987; P. Frost et al., *Organizational Culture*, Newbury Park: Sage, 1985; J. Larcon and R. Reitter, *Structures de Pouvoir et Identité de l'Entreprise*, Paris: Nathan, 1979.
2. See, among others, *Le Nouvel Observateur*, no 1147, 31 October–6 November 1986, p. 5 and 6.
3. See *Business Week*, June 23, 1986, p. 15.
4. See *Le Monde*, November 18, 1986, p. 45.
5. D. Denison, *Corporate Culture and Organizational Effectiveness*, New York: Wiley, 1990.
6. J. Dutton and J. Dukerich, "Keeping an Eye on the Mirror: The Role of Image and Identity in Organizational Adaptation," *Academy of Management Journal*, **34**, 1991.
7. For expanded discussion on these themes, the reader is referred to: T. Deal and A. Kennedy, *Corporate Cultures*, Reading: Addison-Wesley, 1982; S. Davis, *Managing Corporate Culture*, Cambridge: Ballinger, 1984; D. Graves, *Corporate Culture, Diagnosis and Change*, London: Francis Pinter, 1986; B. Uttal, "The Corporate Culture Vultures," *Fortune*, October 17, 1983; D. Denison, *Corporate Culture and Organizational Effectiveness*, New York: Wiley, 1990.
8. G. Hofstede, "Motivation, Leadership, and Organization: Do American Theories Apply Abroad," *Organizational Dynamics*, summer 1980; G. Hofstede, B. Neuijen, D. Ohayv, and G. Sanders, "Measuring Organizational Cultures: Qualitative and Quantitative Study Across Twenty Cases," *Administrative Science Quarterly*, June, 1990.
9. E. Schein, "Coming to a New Awareness of Organizational Culture," *Sloan Management Review*, winter 1984; R. Reitter and B. Ramanantsoa, *Pouvoir et Politique: Au-Delà de la Culture d'Enterprise*, Paris: McGraw-Hill, 1985, p. 3.
10. B. Ramanantsoa and C. Hoffstetter, "La Maîtrise de l'Identité par le Processus de Focalisation: une Nouvelle Donnée Stratégique?" *Direction et Gestion*, July–August, 1981.
11. *Newsweek*, October 13, 1986, pp. 6–7.
12. "Changing a Corporate Culture: Can Johnson and Johnson Go from Band-aids to High-tech?" *Business Week*, May 14, 1984.
13. J. Baechler, *Qu'est-ce que l'Idéologie?* Paris: Galimard, 1976.
14. United Technologies Corporation internal document.
15. R. Foster, *Innovation: The Attacker's Advantage*, New York: Summit books, 1986, pp. 139–147.
16. Y. Tsuruhi, *High Technology*, April, 1984.
17. R. Foster, quoted in *Sciences et Techniques*, special issue, "Rapport sur l'État de la Technique," March 1985, pp. 16–17.
18. S. Resnick-West and M. Von Glinow, "Beyond the Clash: Managing High Technology Professionals," in M. Von Glinow and S. Mohrman, *Managing Complexity in High Technology Organizations*, Oxford: Oxford University Press, 1990; M. Badawy, "One More Time: How Do You Motivate Your Engineers," *IEEE Transactions on Engineering Management*, EM-25, 1978.
19. T. Deal and A. Kennedy, *Corporate Cultures*, Reading: Addison-Wesley, 1982; G. Hofstede, "Motivation, Leadership, and Organization: Do American Theories Apply Abroad," *Organizational Dynamics*, summer 1980.

20. E. Rogers and J. Larsen, *Silicon Valley Fever*, New York: Basic Books, 1984; B. Ramanantsoa, "Integrating Technology in Strategic Analysis: A Question of Organizational Structure or Corporate Identity?" *International Conference on Strategic Management Proceedings*, ESSEC, June 1986.
21. G. Lodge and E. Vogel, *Ideology and National Competitiveness*, Boston: Harvard Business School Press, 1987; M. Porter, *The Competitive Advantage of Nations*, New York: Free Press, 1990; M. Thevenet, "La Culture d'entreprise en Neuf Questions," *Revue Francaise de Gestion*, special issue on corporate culture, September–October, 1984.
22. E. Rogers and J. Larsen, *Silicon Valley Fever*, New York: Basic Books, 1984; D. Segrestin, *Le Phénomène Corporatiste*, Paris: Fayard, 1985.

Index